Charles A. Beard: An Appraisal

Charles A. Beard

AN APPRAISAL BY ERIC F. GOLDMAN

HAROLD J. LASKI · HOWARD K. BEALE

WALTON HAMILTON · GEORGE SOULE

MERLE CURTI · GEORGE R. LEIGHTON

RICHARD HOFSTADTER · MAX LERNER

LUTHER GULICK · GEORGE S. COUNTS

ARTHUR W. MACMAHON

HOWARD K. BEALE, *editor*

OCTAGON BOOKS

A DIVISION OF FARRAR, STRAUS AND GIROUX

New York   1976

Reprinted 1976
by special arrangement with Georgia Robison Beale and Harry B. Rosenberg
as Trustees under the Will of Howard K. Beale

OCTAGON BOOKS
A DIVISION OF FARRAR, STRAUS & GIROUX, INC.
19 Union Square West
New York, N. Y. 10003

Library of Congress Cataloging in Publication Data

Beale, Howard Kennedy, 1899-1959, ed.
    Charles A. Beard: an appraisal.

    Reprint of the ed. published by University of Kentucky Press,
    Lexington.

    "Bibliography of Beard's writings by Jack Frooman and Edmund
    David Cronon": p.
    Includes bibliographical references.
    1. Beard, Charles Austin, 1874-1948.
[E175.5.B37   1976]   973'.07'2024   [B]   76-25945
ISBN 0-374-90493-6

Manufactured by Braun-Brumfield, Inc.
Ann Arbor, Michigan
Printed in the United States of America

Introduction

THIS VOLUME grew co-operatively out of the desire of friends and admirers of Charles A. Beard to do him honor while he was still alive and under serious attack for his latest writings. Among the planners of the volume and the contributors to it, those who disagreed with the point of view of his last two books were more numerous than those who shared Beard's intellectual position. Participation in the volume by no means implies agreement with all of Beard's opinions or the absence of emphatic criticism of some of them. Uncritical eulogy would not have been a tribute worthy of Beard. Beard himself would not have wanted it. The contributors to this volume are rather people of various "frames of reference" who would differ with each other and with Charles Beard on many scholarly and public questions. Some of them are highly critical of his foreign policy views. Others have differed with him on other matters. None of them has agreed with him at every point. Charles Beard did not pick his friends among "yes men." He reveled in heated discussion, so long as it stayed high above personalities and other pettiness. Each contributor was asked to deal with his particular subject critically. If differences in interpretation exist, it is because the editor wished each author left free to do his own interpreting. What has bound the planners and contributors of the volume together has been a respect for Charles Beard the scholar, a sense of obligation to Beard the provoker of thought, an admiration for Beard the devoted public man, in some instances a sense of having been profoundly influenced by Beard or his writings, and in the case of all of us who knew him personally an abiding affection for a great human being. These feelings led the contributors to undertake essays that in some cases were arduous tasks performed by busy men who had no time to do them. Several of the essays are veritable labors of love that could not have been commanded for even handsome fees.

In 1939 or 1940 two volumes of essays were projected as orthodox *Festschriften,* one in history edited by Louis Hacker and one in political science edited by Arthur Macmahon. Since Beard had not taught long enough to produce the usual flock of Ph.D.'s and since his teaching was never confined to the classroom in any case, the lists of contributors were chosen not from among "students" in the usual sense, but from people thought to have been "influenced" by him. Then World War II came. Some men who had loved Beard came to dislike him bitterly. The contributors became involved in wartime activities. The participants lost interest. Wartime shortages made impossible the publication of a *Festschrift.* Hence both projects died. Whenever a group of us who loved and admired Beard gathered together someone was certain to protest that we really should "do something to express our regard for Uncle Charley." Out of one such session in the winter of 1945-1946 grew a determination to do something more than talk. Two of us drew up suggested lists of contributors and subjects. Then various interested people were invited to luncheon at the Princeton Club in New York. Some of those invited expressed such dislike of what Beard stood for that they would have nothing to do with a project to honor him. Others like Merle Curti and Fola La Follette too far away to come expressed interest and encouragement. Thomas C. Cochran, Eric Goldman, Matthew Josephson, and Roger Shugg helped plan the volume. At the Princeton Club luncheon it was decided that the book should not be an ordinary *Festschrift,* a vehicle for the publication of otherwise unpublishable essays of Beard's students or friends, but should be Beard-centered. Beard himself was important enough to be the subject of all the essays. A list was drawn up of subjects and contributors that should be included. Each participant in the planning was to obtain certain commitments of others. Soon it was discovered that a co-operative editorship did not work. Ultimately the present editor was persuaded to undertake the obtaining of commitments for essays and to edit the volume.

The plan was to obtain one of the top people in each field in which Beard was important to write about Beard's influence in that field. First we discovered that it was impossible to determine or measure "influence," and that concept was abandoned. Then it was discovered that the people best suited to do the essays were extraordinarily busy people. A surprising percentage of those on that original list, in spite of lack of time, finally came into the venture out of devotion to Beard. Others who would once have wanted to be included are missing. Some of them, once friends and admirers of Beard, had come to hate what he stood for. Others who still cherished the old affection were too completely out of sympathy with him to say kind things and did not want to say harsh ones. The original plan of presenting the work to Beard for his seventy-third and then his seventy-fourth birthday was prevented by repeated delays and then by Beard's death. During the delay in publication, three of the essays originally written for this volume were published elsewhere and are now being republished here. What began as a testimonial to a man vitally alive and in the thick of controversy has ended as a memorial.

The editor and those who with him planned this book are aware that collecting a whole volume of essays dealing with Charles Beard made certain overlapping inevitable. Repetitive matter and use of the same incidents by two or more authors have been eliminated where possible. That some overlapping remains everyone is aware. No one essay on a particular field could have been complete, none could have done justice to

Beard in that field or satisfied the author of the essay, if all duplication had been ironed out. The alternative was an ordinary *Festschrift* on subjects unconnected with Beard or with each other, or a biography by one of us. We believe that the advantages of this group effort outweigh the disadvantages. We hope that the total effect of the Beard-centered essays by men who are leaders in Beard's several fields of activity or men whose association with Beard gives them competence to speak about his personal qualities will present a composite picture valuable in itself as at the same time it gives all of us the opportunity we seek to honor Beard.

For generous permission to quote from the writings of Beard and of others about Beard, the authors of the essays and the editor wish to make grateful acknowledgment (1) to the following publishers: The Cambridge University Press, the Columbia University Press, Dial Press, Farrar, Straus, and Young, Ginn and Company, Harper and Brothers, the Houghton Mifflin Company, the Johns Hopkins Press, the Marshall Jones Company, Alfred A. Knopf, Longmans, Green and Company, the Macmillan Company, the McKinley Publishing Company, the New American Library, the Oxford University Press, Rinehart and Company, the Ronald Press, the Rutgers University Press, Charles Scribner's Sons, the University of Chicago Press, the Vanguard Press, the Viking Press, the Yale University Press; (2) to the following periodicals: the *American Historical Review*, the *American Quarterly*, the *American Political Science Review*, the *Columbia University Quarterly*, *Harper's Magazine*, *Harvard Graduates Magazine*, the *Nation*, the *New Republic*, the *Political Science Quarterly*, the *Saturday Review*, *Scribner's Magazine*, *Social Education*, *Social Frontier*, *Social Studies*, *Yale Law Journal*, the *Yale Review*; and (3) to the following organizations: the Governmental Research Association, the Institute of Public Administration (formerly the New York Bureau of Municipal Research), the National Education Association, the Social Science Research Council.

Many people besides the authors of essays have contributed much to this volume. George Leighton is grateful to George H. E. Smith, collaborator with Beard on *The Idea of American Interest, The Open Door at Home,* and *The Old Deal and the New,* for suggestions concerning the Leighton essay. Merle Curti expresses appreciation to Herbert Gutman and John N. Stalker, research assistants at the University of Wisconsin, for help in collecting materials for his essay and for constructive suggestions, and the editor is similarly grateful to them for critical reading of several essays. The editor is deeply indebted to Merle Curti of the University of Wisconsin, to William T. Hutchinson of the University of Chicago, to George S. Counts of Teachers College, Columbia University, to Fola La Follette of Arlington, Virginia, and to the late Algie M. Simons of New Martinsville, West Virginia, for criticism of his own and parts of other manuscripts, to Thomas LeDuc of Oberlin College for assistance in gathering the bibliography, and to Livia Appel, editor of the University of Wisconsin Historical Society, for critical reading of his own essay and for suggestion and assistance in technical problems of editing. The editor is further grateful to Jane Wolfe Sossomon, secretary of the Department of History at the University of North Carolina, and to Marjorie Blaisdell Smith, his secretary at the University of Wisconsin, for tireless and painstaking typing of manuscripts and of the correspondence that the project involved. To Genevieve Winchester, reference librarian at the University of Wisconsin, and Georgia Faison, reference librarian at the University of North Carolina, the editor owes much for tireless and intelligent help. David Mearns, Willard Webb, and members of the staff of the Library of Congress have been helpful in securing information otherwise unobtainable. The publishers of Beard's works have been most co-operative in supplying figures concerning the number of copies printed or sold and in contributing titles, particularly of book reviews, for the bibliography. The editor is indebted to his research assistant at the

University of Wisconsin, James D. Smith, for a meticulous checking of facts, quotations, and citations in all the manuscripts and for numerous helpful suggestions and criticisms. Finally, he is indebted to another research assistant, Alfred D. Sumberg, and to his friends E. David Cronon of Yale University, J. Merton England of the University of Kentucky, and Robert A. Lively of the University of Wisconsin for careful proofreading.

HOWARD K. BEALE, *editor*

Madison, Wisconsin
November 1, 1952.

Foreword

MANY YEARS ago I read *The Rise of American Civilization,* written by Dr. Beard and his wife. The experience was exhilarating. Here the early history of our country became a moving and fascinating story, as easy to read as a fine novel. Instead of repeating popular myths about early Americans, Dr. Beard brought them down to earth and made them walk and act like men, giving new greatness to their achievements. He showed how our institutions grew out of the ideals and everyday experiences of the people, thus providing stronger support for our national faith in liberty and justice for all. That passionate faith was a constant theme in all the books and articles Dr. Beard wrote.

This book is about Dr. Beard—his writings and his active life. Twelve persons, friends and admirers of Dr. Beard, have contributed essays on phases of his beliefs and his career. These twelve writers have unusual qualifications for discussing the recurring problems of government and society. The result is a most interesting book which I hope others may read and enjoy as much as I have.

JUSTICE HUGO L. BLACK

Washington, D. C.
January 15, 1954

Contents

ERIC F. GOLDMAN

Charles A. Beard: An Impression

THE FIRST TIME I met Charles Beard he was sitting in his
Johns Hopkins office, the door thrown open invitingly, a spring
sun breaking over the gray head. I paused diffidently. I might
have an appointment, scrupulously arranged, but this was the
1930's, and in the 1930's almost any college student with a
pretense at intellectualism had his special awe for Charles A.
Beard.

"Come on in," Mr. Beard said. "I'm just checking over
some prices my man up in Connecticut paid for cows." The
ruddy face crinkled into a frown. "You know the prices are
getting outrageous."

*Cows? Charles Beard, my intellectual hero, fussing over the
price of cows?* I was flabbergasted. All during the interview,
while I stumbled through an explanation of the article I was
seeking advice about, my mind was a jumble of impressions.
There was more of the same hardheadedness, blunt and cor-
rosive. There was, running through the toughest sentences, a
kindliness, a laughing, warming kindliness, that carried me over
every awkwardness. There was the atmosphere he created, the

feeling that he and I were working together toward the greatest of goals, researching and thinking and writing in order to prod America toward the realization of its exciting ideals. And permeating any of his remarks there was something intangible, something quite beyond quick formulation. Over the years that followed, I had the privilege of knowing Mr. Beard better, but nothing ever really changed the first impression. There was only one Charles Beard: a crisscross of hardheadedness, kindliness, patriotism—and the element that lay beyond.

Beard's hardheadedness is obvious enough to anyone who reads his books, but it took on broader meaning as you listened to him talk about his life. "My father," he used to point out, "was named William Henry Harrison Beard, and you will understand better some of the differences in the approach of Frederick Jackson Turner and myself if I add that his father was named Andrew Jackson Turner." The Beard family, the first citizens of the region around Spiceland, Indiana, took unembarrassed pride in their fertile acres and their extensive business holdings. They were Republicans straight out of the property-conscious Federalist-Whig tradition, and Charles was their true son.

"People ask me," Mr. Beard once remarked, "why I emphasize economic questions so much. They should have been present in the family parlor, when my father and his friends gathered to discuss public affairs." Throughout his life, whether the youthful conformist or the later iconoclast, Beard bluntly called a property drive a property drive; he was leary of men who disdained workaday analyses; he delighted in plain Anglo-Saxon words that stripped the ruffles from abstractions. At the height of the liberal enthusiasm of the 1930's, he would often emphasize that he had never been a complete progressive in the days of Teddy Roosevelt or Wilson, and that he had his doubts about the New Deal. He was suspicious of their "fuzzy" Jeffersonianism, their "confusion of ideals with reality," their "unrealistic trustbusting." And the zest of personal business competition could bring a special glint to Mr. Beard's china-

blue eyes. Once he spent a good deal of time successfully re-
trieving the value of some family stocks, and he told the story
with the relish of a robber baron. If Beard had come to maturity in a different age, he might well have been a successful
businessman, a happily successful one.

Instead he came to maturity in the 1890's, when a rapidly
industrializing and urbanizing America was conducting itself
with a crassness that grated on the nerves of thousands far less
humane than Charles Beard. As field trips for a course at
DePauw University, he made his first visits up to Chicago and
was shocked by the spectacle of raw industrialism. The well-
fed, well-dressed young man rode horse cars on which the
drivers labored fourteen hours a day, unprotected from blazing
heat or biting cold, for $1.65. He read about the pauper in-
sane, who were found chained in basement cells with both feet
frozen. He visited the stockyards, in which workers had little
protection from steaming vats, and the City Hall, where votes
were sold with a smirking shrug. He noted how the newspapers, the churches, almost all respectable Chicago, could line
up against workers when they struck for a fifty-five-hour week
or $2-a-day wages. Soon he was an avid participant in the dis-
cussions at Hull House, listening to Populists arguing with
socialists and Clarence Darrow arguing with both, trying this
or that heresy for himself, daily moving further from the certi-
tudes of Spiceland.

After his graduation from DePauw, at the turn of the century, Beard spent almost four years in Europe, and this period
capped his dissidence. On visits to Germany, he came into
first-hand contact with a country where the government's anxiety to undermine socialism was bringing about a striking series
of state-sponsored reforms. To a generation that has lived
through the Nazis and learned the continuity between Bis-
marck and Hitler, it may seem fantastic that Junker Germany
could have served as a stimulus to liberal thinking, yet in the
case of dozens of American scholars that is precisely what happened. Beard left Germany amused at the pretensions of Ger-

man professors, fuming at Prussian soldiers who forced him into the gutter rather than share the sidewalk, and more convinced than ever that America was lagging far behind in social legislation.

Most of Beard's period abroad was spent in England, where he was swirled along on a dozen streams of dissidence. Deeply affected by Ruskinism (for years afterward he carried a copy of *Unto This Last* in his pocket), he helped set up the working man's Ruskin Hall at Oxford; he beered and argued and worked with trade unionists, Tory reformers, suffragettes, single-taxers, and socialists. Lecturing before labor audiences throughout the Midlands and the North, dashing off a belligerent pamphlet, *The Industrial Revolution,* hobnobbing at Labour Party councils, the young American became so prominent in the Labour coterie that Ramsay MacDonald had an eye on him for the Labour Government, which they all thought was around the corner. By the early 1900's, Beard was back in the United States, finishing his Ph.D. dissertation, joining the little band of rebels on the Columbia faculty, hurrying into a half-century of outraged protest.

It was always there, this quick sense of outrage, this abounding kindliness. There was nothing maudlin about Beard; he valued sentiment too much to be sentimental. His manner was hardly that of uplift; it was forthright, rugged, acrid. He did not suffer fools gladly. The mind was too pile-driving, the knowledge too massive, and there was more than joking in his remark that he was glad of his deafness because one unseen flick of a button gave blissful escape from many of the sessions he had to sit through. Charles Beard simply hated to see human beings hurt, especially by troubles not of their own making.

I remember one particular occasion when Mr. Beard, then under grinding pressures of time, gave more than an hour to what was supposed to be a ten-minute interview with one of the most irritating specimens of that peculiarly difficult genus, the college sophomore. The boy, only a scholarship removed from the dankest slums, was flagrantly rude and impossibly egotistical. When the session was finally over, I burst out: "Why in the world did you let that awful performance drag on?"

The answer was simple—and definitive. "That boy," said Mr. Beard, "is carrying somebody else's cross."

So the hardheadedness was harnessed to the demands of humaneness, and what a team they made. So much of American reformism, particularly in intellectual circles, had smacked of academe, of crinoline and mezzotint, of bloodless abstractions. For many of us, growing up in an angry quest for reality, Charles Beard was a fresh wind out of the heart of things as they were. You could read your Hemingway and your Beard in one evening and feel that you were in the same world.

It was this quality, I think, which especially made *An Economic Interpretation of the Constitution* and *The Rise of American Civilization* such Bibles to thousands of us in the 1930's. There were bread lines outside, and smug men, hurrying by them, said that something or another in the Constitution blocked making moves against poverty. *An Economic Interpretation* hammered the Constitution down into the arena of material interests and broke open a way to make sure that democratic constitutionalism included jobs and bread. There were exciting issues in the air, a whole reinterpretation of democratic aspirations into NRA's and TVA's and fair labor laws, and so many of the histories droned on about state rights and the slavery issue and the naval engagements of the Spanish-American War. *The Rise of American Civilization* tumbled everything, battles, treaties, even Sherman's march through Georgia, into a dogged war of ordinary Americans against buccaneers who would strip them of their heritage of opportunity. Beard's books, we were sure, were so tough just because they were so idealistic.

Whatever the impression he left on young men of the 1930's, in Beard's own make-up, it seems to me, the hardheadedness and the humaneness were brought into fusion by his patriotism.

I realize this is a jarring conjunction of words; the patriot, in the Era of Joseph McCarthy, is hardly associated with any variety of humaneness. But it was the good fortune of Beard, and of so many of his generation, that they could speak of love of their country without embarrassment, and it was their glory that they identified American nationalism with incessant pursuit of a better-fed, better-housed, better-educated, and—above all—a genuinely and richly emancipated American people.

Mr. Beard lived and worked in an image of what he delighted to call—and who ever pronounced the words quite as he did?—"The American Republic." He could talk of any phase of the national life in a way that gave a lyrical quality to his usually hard-driving language; when he said "The President of the United States," one could almost hear the ruffle of drums in the background. To him, hardheadedness and humaneness were twin ingredients of a proud Americanism—the practicality that was building a mighty production machine and the traditions that could transform the miracle of production into the even greater miracle of production generously used.

In time Mr. Beard's deep-seated patriotism was to help lead him down a road of foreign policy where many of us could not follow, but in the 1930's, it was part of his tremendous personal impact. He could call up, even in the most blasé liberal, a reveling in sheer Americanness. The rugged body, the great head with the sharply outlined features, the magnificent wrath and the simple compassion, the wit lashing out against any pretension—all of this made Charles Beard on the lecture platform a rousing symbol of what American liberalism wanted to be. Once I took a friend, a decidedly aesthetish liberal, to a Beard lecture, and when the hour ended, the friend was unwontedly silent. Then he blurted out: "Damn it, I know better than all these silly symbols. But right now, that man looks to me like the American eagle."

The American eagle, yes, but an eagle with a quite different feather in his bristling plumage. You were aware of it when Mr. Beard fidgeted at some oracular discourse. You sensed it even more when he took up the conversation on a philosophical theme and the powerful mind would go on probing, carefully, endlessly probing.   Perhaps most of all it was plain in his puckishness, his sudden laughing away of his own tendency to dogmatize, the joshing of anyone else who dogmatized and particularly anyone else who dogmatized from the writings of Charles A. Beard.

I never quite knew how to lay hold of this quality until one evening Mr. Beard caught it himself.   He was visiting a close friend, and after dinner the talk took a deeply personal turn. Somewhere in the middle of things, Mr. Beard leaned back on the sofa, his eyes misty.   "When I come to the end," he said, "my mind will still be beating its wings against the bars of thought's prison."   That was it—the quality that always lay just beyond the hardheadedness, the kindliness, the patriotism— the man's restive quest, somehow, sometime, to wring a bit more truth and good from the jumbles of the world and the frailties of himself.

Here was no simple man, and to all of us fortunate enough to have known him, he gave no limited gifts.   Listening to Charles Beard the tough-minded, warm-hearted patriot touched the whole study of public affairs with excitement.   Glimpsing the Charles Beard far off on the lonely edges of knowledge, defiantly assailing those bars of thought's prison, was stirring in a way quite beyond excitement.   For then, unforgettably, you knew the meaning of greatness.

HAROLD J. LASKI

Charles Beard: An English View

FROM THE ANGLE of a European observer, Charles Beard's work
is among the most distinguished of American contributions to
the social sciences. It is impressive for the breadth of its insight as well as for its depth. It is rich in large-scale generalisa-
tion. It has always displayed the great merit of Beard's refusal
to submit to the narrow passion for specialism that has been
one of the worst results of the conquest by the academic scholar
of areas rarely seen in their real nature by men who live in the
cloistered calm of a university life. Beard, with the co-operation of his distinguished wife, has shown remarkably that it is
possible to make history and politics deeply interesting to the
ordinary reader without departing from the exacting demands
of critical scholarship. His work, moreover, has been humanist
in temper. He has been conscious that the historians and the
political theorists are themselves affected by the climate of
opinion that operates in their own day, and upon themselves.
He has, therefore, refused to see the past, or to analyse contemporary institutions with the specious air of impartiality that
is usually an artifice by which unstated premises are concealed

from sight. Consequently, too, he has stressed the interrelation between man and his institutional inheritance and has thus
avoided leaving a system of government looking like a pallid
combination of bloodless forms, as if it had a life quite separable
from the judge or politician or voter that gives it flesh and
colour and energy.

There was a time when Charles Beard seemed, even to
Americans of outstanding distinction, to be a dangerous iconoclast seeking to destroy the gods of the American Valhalla.
That period has now passed; and it is becoming easier to recognise the influence that gave its special shape to his work. If
one puts aside the useful, but still minor, writings of his post-
graduate period, books like his study of the justice of the peace
in mediaeval England,[1] or his one-time most useful summary
of *The Industrial Revolution,* it is clear enough that Beard's
work was born of the Progressive movement of the first quarter
of the twentieth century. It is clear, too, that this Progressive
movement, in the midst of which Beard wrote, was an outcome,
at once more conscious and more intellectually mature, of the
Populism that, in the eighties and nineties, learned well enough
the depths of its frustration without being able seriously to
discover either the sources or the remedies of the evils it sought
to fight. Beard is one of those who found his vocation in the
effort to arrest the emergence of a plutocratic America, self-
confident, determined, even arrogant, that was seeking to sub-
due the promise of American life to the service of a narrow
oligarchy. Beard early quarrelled with the value judgements
of a ruling group to whom Cleveland and McKinley were ad-
mirable Presidents, Mark Hanna the ideal broker between
business and politics, and Bryan and Eugene Debs dangerous
demagogues who threatened the security of the great economic
empires that oligarchy was bringing to completion. To understand the significance of Beard's contribution, it is important
to remember that he gave out the results of his researches into
the origins of the American Constitution and the victory of
Jefferson and its aftermath a decade and more before J. Frank-

lin Jameson published his epoch-making lectures on the social implications of the American Revolution[2] or Parrington wrote the remarkable work[3] on American literature that, despite some almost sophomoric judgements as it reached the contemporary scene, set the feet of the critics on new and creative adventures. Pupils or friends of Beard, like Arthur M. Schlesinger[4] and Clarence W. Alvord,[5] were mapping out new roads in historiography, which were to render obsolete the kind of analysis that, only a little earlier, had made James Ford Rhodes[6] seem to the conventional academic of the time an eminent historian. It was significant that Beard in the department of politics at Columbia was the younger contemporary in the academic world of William James and John Dewey in philosophy, of Thorstein Veblen in political economy, and of Arthur F. Bentley in political science. It was important that, only a year after Beard had published his first major work (just as Woodrow Wilson had entered the White House), Herbert Croly had been able successfully to launch the *New Republic* (1914). Holmes was on the Supreme Court, Brandeis within three years of his appointment to it. The basis of a new and realistic jurisprudence was being laid. While Beard was launching his economic interpretation, a new generation of law professors in the major American universities was modernising the study of law in a perspective that was not entirely welcome to the leaders of that classic generation for whom Christopher C. Langdell and James B. Ames had virtually completed the appropriate technique of American legal education.

We can see now—what was less obvious at the time—that when Beard's first outstanding work was published, we had already crossed the road that led into a new time. If Woodrow Wilson looked backward, rather than forward, for his central inspiration, even so, it was obvious that with him something new was entering the White House. In Great Britain, from 1906, the greatest reform government since 1832 was in office; and though, in 1913, the shadow of conflict, both domestic and foreign, brooded over its operations, no one could fail to

remark that it held office by virtue of the votes of a Labour
Party. This Labour Party was not only increasingly uncom-
fortable at its quasi-alliance with the Liberals, but increasingly
unwilling to accept the prophecy of President Lowell, of Harvard, that its destiny was to be no more than that of a permanent, but subordinate, wing of the party led by its skilful Whig
Prime Minister, Herbert H. Asquith. In France, not only had
the Dreyfus case brought, among its spectacular results, the
separation of church and state, but Normaliens were beginning
to reconstruct, as with Jean Jaurès and Celestin Bouglé, the
traditional approach to politics and sociology, and Maxime
Leroy was beginning, with Léon Duguit, to put the classic
French jurisprudence on the defensive. Germany, in spite of
the fairly consistent socialist gains in the Reichstag, seemed
still impenetrably the Junker–Big Business state; yet, even
here, Eugen Ehrlich and Hermann Kantorowicz in law and
Rudolf Hilferding in economics were revealing, like Josef
Redlich and Karl Renner in Austria, that new winds of doctrine were beginning to blow. And, though few outside his
own ranks were aware of it, Lenin and his followers in Tsarist
Russia had become growingly confident that the abortive Revolution of 1905 was only the rehearsal for a greater drama for
the leadership of which they must prepare themselves. There
were the echoes of challenge to the old order both in India and
in China. Indeed, all over the world, scholars were beginning
to find a new significance in social studies, which, as the reception of Beard's first great book was to show, made men uneasily
aware that a debate had been reopened that they had been content to regard as happily closed. For the next generation the
social sciences were as much the major battleground of conflicting philosophers as had been theology a century before.

Beard's *An Economic Interpretation of the Constitution of
the United States* (1913) and its sequel, the *Economic Origins
of Jeffersonian Democracy* (1915), were, from the standpoint
of research, books that laid the foundation of a new and cre-

ative approach to the subjects with which they dealt. But even more important than the brilliant use of the material that went into their making was the value of the solid foundation they offered to the criticism of those who sought to see American history in realistic terms. Apart from the maintenance of order, Beard pointed out, "the making of the rules which determine the property relations of members of society" is always the central objective of government. A ruling class, therefore, "whose rights are thus to be determined must perforce obtain from the government such rules as are consonant with the larger interests necessary to the continuance of their economic processes, or they must themselves control the organs of government."[7] Beard showed that the Constitution of 1787 owed its character to those who, with money or public securities in their hands, as manufacturers and traders, or as the shipping interest, were gravely threatened by the chaotic insecurity that developed under the Articles of Confederation. He argued that the men of Philadelphia produced "an economic document based upon the concept that the fundamental private rights of property are anterior to government, and morally beyond the reach of popular majorities."[8] He showed that Jeffersonian democracy was not the outcome of a reasoned debate for and against certain abstract principles of freedom, but "a conflict . . . chiefly between the capitalistic and agrarian classes." "Jeffersonian democracy simply meant the possession of the federal government by the agrarian masses led by an aristocracy of slave-owning planters, and the theoretical repudiation of the right to use the Government for the benefit of any capitalistic groups, fiscal, banking or manufacturing."[9]

These two remarkable works are, as it were, the prelude to the great *Rise of American Civilization,* in which Charles Beard, with his wife, wrote what is certainly one of the half dozen most effective general narratives of a people's history that any nation possesses—a narrative the more valuable in that it was not merely abreast of modern scholarship, but contained, as in its treatment, for example, of the Civil War, new concep-

tions and ideas as valuable in their suggestiveness to the special-
ist as to the general reader.[10] What is significant in this historical work is Beard's power to penetrate behind the ration-
alisations by which men seek to defend their interests, and to
make plain the inner essence of the purpose they sought to
serve. It is quite unjust to regard this analysis as "materialistic" or to insist that it is intended as a neosocialist attack on
American institutions, still less to argue that it seeks to dethrone
the great heroes and the great legends of American history. Its
value lies, first, in its realism, and, second, in its power to show
that behind the mask the great statesman, the great judge, the
great business pioneer, is forced to wear in public, there operate the same impulses as in the men and women he influences.
More than that. It rescues American history for scientific exploration. It permits us to see how men have to co-operate with
their environment in order to master it; it enables us to recognise what it is in their character and experience that makes
them willing to effect this co-operation or to refuse to seize their
moment when it arrives. The American Constitution, as
Charles Beard has analysed it, may be stripped of the false gilt
with which men like James M. Beck, in the field of legal rhetoric, or Calvin Coolidge in the political, sought to disguise it.
Yet, under Beard's handling, it had the merit of becoming an
actual constitution the dynamics of which, at least, emerge in-
telligible. Beard's history may have little of Bancroft's incur-
able romanticism in its pages. But Bancroft, after all, had about
the same relation to creative historiography as the Lamartine
who wrote the *Histoire des Girondins.* Just as the description
of the Constitution vouchsafed us by James M. Beck may
make us understand the fantastic torrent of eloquence Roscoe
Conkling poured out in *San Mateo County* v. *Southern Pacific
Railroad,* or Joseph Choate in the *Income Tax Cases,* so what
Beck leaves unexplained, Beard makes us understand. Beard
reveals what Chief Justice Marshall was really doing in *Mar-
bury* v. *Madison;* he vividly portrays the currents and cross currents in the national life of America that led that able and

stout-hearted Republican, Mr. Justice Miller, to write with so deep an emotion about the forces and men against whom he moved out to battle.

The value of Beard's method is the important fact that we see how the play was written as well as what was involved in putting it upon the stage. So, also, with his work in the field of government. It is less an attempt to grapple with the fundamental problems of political philosophy than it is an effort, first, to show how American institutions really work, and, second, so to criticise their working that an indication is given of ways of suitable change. *American Government and Politics*—still, it may be suggested, the best descriptive account of American government and politics in operation—and the *American Leviathan* (written in conjunction with his son, William Beard), with *The Republic,* that interesting combination of major insight with minor, though significant, blindness, together represent an impressive attempt to explain the dynamic of American institutions. Their quality comes from two things: (1) They are written by a man who has tried to see from within the interrelation between men and institutions. (2) They are also the outcome of a mind that is almost restlessly seeking the ways and means whereby government can aid the ordinary man to overcome his servitude to his past and break the fetters of tradition without repeating the tragedy, sordid as well as magnificent, of violent civil war.

For it is important to emphasise that, although Beard, as his well-known pamphlet *The Economic Basis of Politics* makes clear, has always given primacy to the economic factor as that which shapes our social life, still he has never drawn conclusions of a Marxist, or, in any decisive way, even a socialist character. He has never seen in the class war the central instrument of advance to freedom. He has never admitted the necessity of catastrophic change. He has deeply disliked the arrogant certainty of those who are convinced that, with the key of dialectical materialism, the doors of the future can be unlocked in the confidence that we know what lies beyond them. He has

never even been a good party man in the sense of being willing
to accept the directives of Republican or Democrat or Socialist
as more than a rather better choice than the alternative of a
given moment in time. Profoundly democratic in temper,
strongly progressive in ideas, in the field of political action,
Beard has for the most part sought temporary alliances only.
There is, indeed, an important sense in which he has been
sceptical of those who give their permanent allegiance to a general corpus of doctrine. Political doctrine must, in its day to
day application, be left to the stewardship of men to whom
politics mean whatever definition of issues will bring them a
majority of votes, and with it, office and power, on election day.
Politicians Beard distrusted. He has preferred to give his
energy, outside of writing and teaching, to the effort to make
the institutions by which we live more fully known, their results more precisely capable of measurement, our power to
improve them, as a consequence, more ample. He has sought
to make the case for change one sufficiently capable of proof
that we argue, not about concepts of a tight and logical system
of politics, but of experiences so examined that a repetition of
the examination only gives new emphasis to the original results.
No one who knows of the time and thought that Beard has giv-
en to bodies like the New York Bureau of Municipal Research
can fail to see how much of his outlook has been shaped by
breaking up general principles into a series of separable problems, and inquiring, without the search for a general metaphysic, how each of them can be answered.

Charles Beard has always been a man of progressive ideas.
We in Britain are not likely to forget that, just a half century
ago, he was one of the founders of Ruskin Hall, Oxford, a resi-
dential institution, which has had a vital part in shaping the
character of the British Labour Party generally, and of many
of its members, especially since 1915, who have entered the
House of Commons. Though not one of its editors, he was
for many years one of the outstanding influences upon the
New Republic in the period when Herbert Croly, its founder,

was also its chief editor. He helped to start the New School of Social Research in New York; and one English visitor to his lectures there can testify that, particularly in a moderate-sized seminar, he was a teacher whose power to communicate ideas, and to evoke them, if equalled, was not surpassed even by Frederick Jackson Turner. He was always open-minded, always a little sceptical. Upon occasion he was liable to passionate devotion to impossible ideas. Invariably he was stimulating. Yet he was patient with everyone and everything except the facile rhetorician and the student who thought that the wisest social policy for the United States was a return to laissez faire.

Beard was always a planner and an experimentalist. He started from two principles: First, that since decisions must be made, they had better be made by a responsible body, and therefore, in important matters, by government rather than by private persons; second, that history gives us no warrant for the belief that an unfettered market economy is the necessary alternative to centralised authoritarianism. Beard saw, almost from the outset of his career as an historian, that government must control business men, or business men would control government. In the light of his investigations into the early history of the American Constitution, moreover, he saw the importance of realising that the concentration of great economic power implies the development of an economic sovereignty that may easily determine the nature of the sovereignty implicit in the state-power. Given, therefore, the continental character of the American economy, he felt that only the federal government would have at its disposal the authority to tackle the great corporations. He was never seduced into the belief that the Sherman Act could ever be a decisive weapon, or that there was reason to assume that the states in the American Union could, within their own area, reshape the devices of the eighteenth century into adequate means for grappling with the problems of the twentieth. He does not seem even to have been tempted to Mr. Justice Brandeis' ardent belief that the large unit must, inherently, be inefficient. And, though he knew that disinterested men, Mr. Justice Holmes, for instance, or Senator George W. Norris, could sit on the Supreme Court or in the Senate, he never sought to persuade himself that, profound emergency apart, the drive of a political system was ever likely to transcend the general property relations upon which it was built. He agreed that the men who made the Constitution intended the Supreme Court to control both state and federal legislation through judicial review. Whatever they created, they did not intend to found a social democracy. They assumed that the state-power would be primarily exerted to protect the *status quo* in property relations against being overturned by the vote of the masses.

Yet Beard is insistent that, whatever the limitations placed upon the government of the United States by the framers of the Constitution, they did not commit it to pursue a policy of laissez faire. "I am sure as fate," he has written, "that they intended to set up a government endowed with broad national powers and that they expected their posterity to use those powers in dealing with questions, crises, and disturbances arising from generation to generation."[11] The expectation that a power will be used depends, however, upon the institutional elbow-room to use it. Beard is clear that, in contemporary America, this elbow-room does not exist. "Our federal political machinery," he has written, "devised for a simple agricultural society, is not competent to resolve efficiently the issues forced upon government by the needs of our great industrial nation." He regards this antiquated machinery as making for delay, deadlock, and "utter irresponsibility." But he regards much of the evil as "self-imposed by politicians, sometimes for the very purpose of escaping responsibility and preventing the introduction of efficiency." He is anxious that the "talents of the country" should be concentrated once more on "the design of adapting our Government to the needs of our society."[12]

None the less the reader of Beard's work, whether historical or political, will find that he is in no sense "radical" in his outlook. He rejects laissez faire, and accepts the need to plan; he cannot, however, be said to have any general body of principles upon which the planning is to be conducted. He recognises the need for large-scale reform in the structure of government. But, despite a considerable admiration for parliamentary government, he does not think its implications fitted to the psychological traditions that history has shaped in the American scene. He thinks that the Constitution was essentially geared to eighteenth century ideas of liberty and equality. It was made for a small agricultural society, only beginning to realise the full significance of the market economy. Yet, while he is anxious to turn the mind of America to profounder thought, in the grand manner of the *Federalist,* about the basic principles of politics, still, his anxiety is less for a rewriting of the Constitution itself, than for forcing the politicians in Congress and the state legislatures to reassess the obstacles they have themselves placed in the way of fulfilling the opportunities given to the United States by its founders. The Constitution, he believes, contains powers large enough to embrace every general issue that might be raised by the shifting aspects of the national welfare. He has great faith in the possibilities of administrative reform. If he is irritated by the obvious deficiencies of the American party system, he is nevertheless impressed by its capacity, sooner or later, to reorganise itself around the issues in politics that need to be solved. He thinks, indeed, that the very fact that the American party is a loose affiliation of sectional interests increases its chances of settling fundamental problems. He believes that the capacity for give and take that characterises American parties makes representative government easily the best form of government for a political community like the United States.

Beard is a collectivist, but not a socialist; or, at any rate, he is not a socialist to whom the tradition of Marxism has been appreciably important. If, indeed, he is to be called a socialist at all, it is mainly because he so strongly repudiates the natural rights philosophy that, in important phases of American history, has seemed to attach to the claims of property something eternal and unprescriptible. Unlike judges who have constantly sought to safeguard property, and legislatures, chosen to represent the changing needs of the American people, who have regarded property rights with humble reverence, Beard has never placed property above human interests. He has always regarded rights as the creatures of positive law, as soon as they are discussed in a political context. There are, maybe, claims whose moral character ought to win for them the effective status of political recognition. But then, in his view, if they have this character, they ought to win for themselves, through the opportunities afforded by the processes of democracy, transfer from the moral to the political plane.

Yet, on one side of his outlook, it is not unfair to note in Beard the traces of a frontier inheritance. He lays great store upon the central civil freedoms—the right to speak one's mind without penalty, the right to freedom of worship, the right to freedom of association, the right to live in an American society where the courts of justice give the citizen an assurance as absolute as any assurance can be in human affairs, that the political dissident, or the man who, in some given situation, belongs to an unpopular minority, can be certain of a fair trial, or of an unprejudiced hearing by a superior court if he is driven to appeal against an unfair trial. Normally, there is a certain looseness about Beard's style, as if he distrusts a search for the exact word as a form of preciousness. His style reveals the comfortable ease of a man who speaks spontaneously the thoughts that are in him and is not too nice about the need to clothe them in any elegant precision. Yet, it is hardly erroneous to catch a sterner note, a willed tautness of phrase, when he speaks of the Bill of Rights, of the Alien and Sedition Laws, of cases like those of Frank Mooney and Sacco and Vanzetti, of Negroes brought unjustly within the sight of execution, of religious fanatics turned into political victims by the angry clamour of a critical time. In general, for example, Beard has high regard for the late Mr. Justice Holmes; it is notable, however, that when he discusses the "clear and present danger" test used by Mr. Justice Holmes in interpreting the Espionage Act cases in the first World War, he is careful to point out how wide, in fact, is the loophole it affords to the persecutor. He writes in a different spirit when he discusses the famous dissent in the Abrams case, and he writes of the decision of Mr. Justice Black in *Chambers et al.* v. *Florida* (1940) that it "will ring with power as long as liberty and justice are cherished in our country."[13] Obviously, in the realm of civil liberties, Beard has feelings that go far deeper than the easy tolerance that, in other realms, makes him accept the famous comparison by Marcus Aurelius of the people to "little children, quarrelling, crying, and then straight away laughing."

Broadly speaking, it is fair to regard Charles Beard as a pragmatist, whose leanings both intellectual and emotional were, by nature and the impact of the historic scene, inclined to the Left in most matters of social constitution. He was not a crusader for the dogmatists of the Left, but he was ready to be a crusader against the dogmatists of the Right. That was because he knew that life means change, and that change means the power of continuous adaptation. The dogmatist of the Right is a threat to the operation of this power because he insists on blinding himself to the dynamic of social processes. The dogmatist of the Left may be wrong; but at least he knows the need for change, and by compelling his opponents to discussion, he makes the probability high that the necessity of change will, if slowly, and sometimes painfully, in the end be admitted. Beard felt this the more acutely because he was aware, above all after 1914, that our civilisation was in a crisis and that nothing could do it greater harm than ignorant resistance to change, on the one hand, and ignorant demand for it, on the other.

He was sure that the old securities were gone. Nothing was to be looked for from the historic religions. And men only deceived themselves if they thought that scientific method could be applied to human affairs. There was, he thought, a sectar-

ianism in the social sciences as fatal to their attainment of a
genuinely scientific control over human affairs as was the mul-
tiplicity of Christian denominations fatal to the triumph of the
Christian spirit.   Mankind was not destined to any genuine
prevision of its own future; science provided instruments of
partial analysis, but the light of science reached only a little
way. "The scientific method has been defeated," he wrote,
"and must be defeated in the effort to reach the supreme goal—
the reduction of large areas of human affairs to isolated groupings subject to unequivocal law; and were it to reach its impossible goal, victory would be defeat for mankind, that is,
imprisonment in a doom actually foreknown."[14] That was not
an expression, on Beard's part, either of anti-intellectualism
or of pessimism.   It stated his sense that social organisation
is too complex for man to know all the evidence necessary to
scientific prediction.   The most that he would urge was the
importance of holding fast by the democratic faith, and applying its valuations to the decisions we are ceaselessly compelled
to make on evidence that makes all social action in large part
an act of faith.   We can never know the total consequence of
the choice we make; that does not, and ought not, to deter us
from the obligation to choose.   If, moreover, we act by making the most we can of the imperfect science we have, and set
it in the framework of democratic values, at least we live by
a faith that gives us manhood by giving us freedom.   If this is
but a partial security, it is yet the most we are entitled to claim.

He did not think his a blind faith, even if it lived under the
compulsion of Pascal's mandate: *chercher en gemissant.* He
saw no reason to believe that history would repeat itself; he
did not anticipate for America the fate of Rome. "Our Republic," he wrote, "with authority and liberty constantly readjusted
under constitutional principles, will long endure; forever, I
hope." He did not deny that he might be wrong. Still, he
thought this "calculation" was supported by all the findings
of critical scholarship, and was "formulated with reference to
the highest degree of probability that seems warranted by these

facts."[15] Analogies with other societies he rejected. He was uninterested in efforts to explain historical development by analogies drawn from biology or physics. They merely falsified history, and made even partial prediction useless because they were "delusive rhetoric."[16]

No one, he thought, can say when a nation is old. After nine hundred years as a united nation, England "is still full of vitality and promise."[17] China was young when it was a thousand years old. Beard thought there was no evidence in the facts of a relentless march towards some inevitable goal. No doubt there was a certain body of given fact in the world, and this set limits to human effort. But where the boundaries were marked we could not know because they depended so largely on the exercise of the opportunities given us by creative intelligence. The objective world outside us was altered by the effort of the human mind. In spite of calamities like war and dictatorship, the social heritage of civilisation would always remain unimpaired enough to admit of restoration and progress. There was a tenacity in civilised living that would survive the worst onslaughts of barbarism.[18]

Beard wrote those words in what, to an American, must have been the most heart-breaking period of the second World War. He wrote them conscious of the fact that there was no shortcut to Utopia, whether through the middle-class self-confidence in "free enterprise" or through the communist faith that violent revolution would permit a swift leap from the realm of necessity into the realm of freedom. Within sight of his seventy-fifth year, he saw before him the chance through great effort to use our moral and intellectual powers to build the heritage of civilisation more amply and more richly. He was, indeed, convinced that the "unresting spirit of Americans" would make any defeat unreal. No one who knew Charles Beard will fail to recognise in this outlook the central spirit of his personality. The vigour and alertness of his mind, his zest for action, his eagerness to continue the search to know, were all of them informed by the unshakeable faith that the effort was worth

while. He was humble about the outcome of his personal
striving; he did not doubt the ultimate importance of the
collective striving. "This combination of faith and knowledge . . . [was] the workable truth of the business before *us*."[19]

He lived his whole life in that spirit; he infused all with
whom he came into contact with the sense of its determination
and its beauty. To say this of a man is, after all, to have
formulated his claim to be a great citizen as well as a great
scholar. It is the proof that he was touched by the Socratic
fire. He never stopped seeking to understand; and, with Beard,
knowledge and action were an inseparable unity.

MAX LERNER

Charles Beard's Political Theory

A GREAT HISTORIAN has to be a good deal more than a historian.[1] Charles Beard had, of course, a proper contempt for the fences set up between the social studies to keep away the rival bands of poachers; yet for me and for many others he was as much a political thinker using historical techniques as he was a historian using political insights. One of the founders of the realistic school in American political study, he was most of his life one of its recognized leaders. In constitutional law as well as constitutional history, in American government as well as in the history of American civilization, his was a name to conjure with. He had a feel for the practical problems of politics, from city planning to federal administration, and he had a finger in not a few congressional bills and investigations. He was interested in historical thinkers like Condorcet and Buckle, but even more he was interested in Aristotle, Machiavelli, Madison, and the justices of the United States Supreme Court. The two basic concepts that absorbed him most were those of *power* and *civilization;* and if the second attracted him because of its dynamic unfolding of the whole life of a people, the first gave him—as it has given so many other political thinkers—the sense of the hard bedrock of reality.

His greatest work was *The Rise of American Civilization* and his best art form was history, but he used it less as a narrative than as a time frame within which to present a continuing social analysis. I suspect that he turned to history for his major effort, after several primarily political studies, because history offered the most fertile chance for a great synthesis that was glaringly lacking in American intellectual life. I have fancied him using the delicious burlesque lines that Thomas Love Peacock gives to a marauding chief:

> The mountain sheep are sweeter,
> But the valley sheep are fatter;
> We therefore deemed it meeter
> To carry off the latter.

While Beard carried off the fatter sheep of historical writing, I do not let myself forget that he found the mountain sheep of political theory sweeter.

The story of his early academic years is the story of the preparation of a political thinker who had been trained in historical evidence and theory and was exploring the dynamics of politics. As in every education of an original thinker Beard had first to unlearn a good deal he had been taught. At Oxford he had studied under F. York Powell, and through him he had been exposed to the methods of the Big Panjandrum of English constitutionalism, Bishop Stubbs, whose three-volume *Constitutional History of England* and whose nineteen Introductions to the nineteen volumes of the portentous Rolls Series of medieval chronicles clung like an incubus to every student of history and politics in England. The three pillars of the Stubbs edifice were: scrupulous sifting of the documentary evidence; the belief in the Teutonic origin of democratic institutions; and emphasis on the local unit of government as well as history. Unlike many American academic pilgrims who returned at the end of the century from their hegira to European universities,

Beard revolted against the Teutonic theory. "For more than a generation," Beard later wrote in 1913, "the Teutonic theory of our institutions deeply influenced historical research in the United States; but it was exhausted in the study of local government rather than of great epochs."[2] This was a shrewd judgment, but Beard might have added that his own Ph.D. thesis, *The Office of Justice of the Peace in England* (1904), had been part of this emphasis on the local unit. After that came his books on municipal government and reform, on the short ballot, on the initiative and referendum, and on the doctrine of judicial review.

All of them were fresh, vigorous, and searching in their handling of materials. Yet they might have been written by any one of a number of bright young scholars in political science at that time. What happened to turn Beard from the writer of these books into what he had become by 1913 when he published *An Economic Interpretation*—a young lion, roaring in the classroom, as in his book, against formalism, stuffiness, timidity, and reaction? What was it that turned Beard into a smasher of the icons of political thinking in his generation?

Some of the things that were happening outside of Beard, in the intellectual atmosphere around him, may give a clue to what was happening inside his mind. The first decade of the century saw a great ferment in American social thought. There were the legal realism of Holmes's dissents on the Supreme Court, the militancy of Brandeis's work as a crusading attorney and social reformer, the rise of sociological jurisprudence under Pound and others; there were Dewey's pragmatism in philosophy, James Harvey Robinson's emphasis on the history of the West as the history of idea systems rooted in great epochs of social change; there were Veblen's brilliant demolition of classical economics, and the beginnings of an institutional theory; there was a vague but unmistakable whiff of Marxism in the air, which reached even the academies in the work of Simons and of Gustavus Myers on economic and social forces in American history; there were still Bryanist-Populist stirrings; there

were clamorous demands for a new program of social legislation
to balance the irresponsible power of the Big Money; labor was
struggling for a place in the sun; there was a bitter contest over
the power of judicial review of legislation by what Professor
Burgess had proudly called "the aristocracy of the robe," and
over the way the Supreme Court majorities were using this
power in order to entrench an aristocracy of money.

Beard was no academic *laudator temporis acti;* he was fiercely
of his time. The ferment I have described worked mightily in
his mind, and mingled with the yeast of his own temperament
and background. His Indiana origins marked him from the
Midwest; his early conditionings were those of rural means, a
small town, a small college. He was unimpressed by the magni-
tudes around him, and by the glitter of eastern cities and
businessmen and their intellectual apologists. He came from a
region and class (to apply his own environmental approach)
which felt that the original democratic promise of America had
not been fulfilled, and that the heady claims of the idealist view
of America did not always have much substantive meaning for
the disinherited. He was restive at any attempt to clap blinders
on him, passionate against the injustices he saw, contemptuous
of whatever was shoddy or phony or inflated in its pretensions.

One can often get best at what a man becomes by studying
what he rebels against. The consummate symbol of everything
Beard was fighting in political science was his teacher of American constitutional law, Professor John W. Burgess, whose great
work was his two-volume *Political Science and Comparative
Constitutional Law* (1890). Beard later did a longish analysis
of Burgess's thinking, as part of the history of American social
thought that forms the gist of *The American Spirit* (1942).[3]
Trained in Germany, Burgess ruled for years over the empire
of political science and constitutional law at Columbia, and his
doctrines had shaped the thinking of most of the political science teachers of Beard's generation. In his theory of representative government he leaned heavily toward Montesquieu's state-

ment that it had originated "in the forests of Germany." In his theory of the state he was a Hegelian idealist, scornful of any economic interpretation. In his teaching of economic policy he accepted laissez faire completely and inveighed against governmental interference with individualism. In his teaching of constitutional law he was a champion of the mechanical jurisprudence of the conservative Supreme Court justices. In his outlook on nationalism and internationalism he pleaded for the civilizing mission of the Teutonic nations in extending their power and culture over the backward races.

It is possible to see the body of Beard's political thinking, as it came to maturity over later years, in terms of a five-pronged attack upon the sort of thinking Burgess and his school represented. First, instead of making the state Godlike, in Hegelian fashion, Beard deflated it, and deflated also the lofty myths of the idealist school, which saw the state as somehow working out its abstract destiny in the vacuum of the "laws of freedom" in history. His revolt against the formalism of this thinking led him to a realistic study of the actual origins and actual operations of governments. His revolt against the moral hypocrisy of this thinking led him to emphasize the factors of hard-bitten economic and class interest, both in the actions of the owning classes and in the movements of popular revolt. This furnishes a clue to his studies in economic interpretation.

Second, Beard revolted against the mechanical theory of law and politics. Just before his death he wrote, in a mellow and reminiscent mood, about his early experiences as a student and teacher of American constitutional law. "At the opening of this century, when I began the systematic study of constitutional law at Columbia University . . . a justice of the Supreme Court, in the theory of the classroom, seemed to be a kind of master mechanic. Indeed, as I heard the budding lawyers and judges talk, I was often reminded of a machine once used in the Bank of England to test the coins deposited day by day. When a coin was gently placed on its delicately balanced receptacle, the machine trembled for a second or two and then dropped the coin,

right or left, into the proper chest as sound or spurious according to its monetary merits. To me, fresh from seminars on historical methods, the weighing, measuring, and logistical method
of 'learning' constitutional law seemed in 1902 a strange way
of searching for the meaning and upshot of cases." No one
went to the briefs, or to the personality and political opinions
of the justices, or to the social struggles behind the case that
could give the legal arguments and rationalizations some concrete meaning. The discussion of an income-tax case like *Pol-
lock* v. *Farmers Loan and Trust Co.* was carried on "as if it had
been an adventure in deductions drawn from a major premise
grounded in the ineluctable nature of things."[4] What applied
to law applied also to politics. The Burgess school saw man as
abstracted from all interests except the political. Beard preferred to see the whole man, to study not only the formal pro-
nouncements of a statesman or a judge, but his opinions and
interests as a whole.

Third, Beard revolted against the laissez faire mumbo jumbo,
which made a fetish of individualism and forbade any state interference with business enterprise. He saw the doctrine of
economic individualism for what it was—an effort to clothe the
property interests of a plutocracy with the sanctity of a taboo.
He refused to be seduced by the moral loftiness of the individualist ideal into ignoring the consequences of the resulting
economic anarchism. Some of his most vigorous writing—in the
pamphlet, *The Myth of Rugged Individualism* (1932) , and in
the opening two chapters (on the Hoover era) in *America in
Midpassage* (1939) , "The Golden Glow" and "Dissolutions"—
is on the futility of trying to run an economy simply by faith
in the businessmen whom Beard called "Lords of Creation."
Beard was not frightened, as Burgess and his school were, by the
threat of "socialistic legislation." He believed that the state had
a direct interest in the general welfare and should act when
necessary to protect that interest. It is curious to note that
Burgess, while idolizing the state as against the individual, believed in practice in a weak state and a powerful elite of in-

dividuals; while Beard, who had a healthy skepticism about the state as an abstraction, believed in using it for the people, and while he scorned the *doctrine* of individualism he believed in practice in creating the conditions under which individuals would not be crushed by economic chaos. His interest in public administration flowed directly from his thinking about the regulative and control functions of the government.

Fourth, Beard revolted against any racist notions of the mission of a people or nation. His attack on "the Teutonic theory of our institutions," in the first chapter of his *An Economic Interpretation of the Constitution,* was meant even more for Burgess than for Stubbs. Some twenty years later, in an essay on "The Teutonic Origins of Representative Government," he went at the whole theory with a devastating thoroughness. He could not accept the idea that representative government or democracy was due to the "genius" of any race; nor could he accept the idea of Burgess that the Teutonic peoples, endowed with this political "genius," had therefore the mission of civilizing the rest of the world.[5] "The civilized state," wrote Burgess, "should, of course, exercise patience and forbearance toward the barbaric populations . . . but it should not be troubled in its conscience about the morality of this policy when it becomes manifestly necessary."[6] Beard had no patience with racism, whether it was this polite form, or the ruthless form of the Nazis. He was equally impatient with it when it was directed, as he thought, against the Japanese in World War II.

Fifth, Beard reacted against the imperialism that he found in Burgess, which was rampant in American thought at the turn of the century. He was extremely skeptical, in fact, of any kind of internationalist interventionism, and was inclined to regard the high-sounding slogans of American intervention as only window dressing for more sinister purposes. Himself no chauvinist, he came to believe in a system of economic nationalism, or what he called "continentalism." His studies in Jeffersonian thought and policy, which he pursued early in his career, entrenched him in this.

It must be clear from this that while Beard did not develop his mature system of political thought for some years, all the threads of it were present in his early years as a teacher. They emerged from his rebellions against the arid, mechanical, and reactionary political thinking that he found in academic circles; and they were reinforced by the new stirrings of political and legal and economic thought in the world outside the academies.

The clearest single statement of his approach to political science may be found in the Columbia lecture on *Politics,* which he gave as adjunct professor of politics in 1908. Quietly but unmistakably Beard delivered the manifesto of what might have been called the "new political science." He told his listeners that politics was not a narrow study, that the notion of "man as a political animal acting upon political, as distinguished from more vital and powerful motives, is the most unsubstantial of all abstractions."[7] He committed himself against the deductive theories of the state, and spoke highly of the Historical School, and especially of Maitland's work. He thought that the best way to study institutions was to study their evolution. He applied this especially to property. The question for political study, he said, was not whether "private property as such be abolished, for the nature of man demonstrates that it cannot be," but what forms property should take and to what public uses it should be put.[8] He wanted a science of politics that would move away from moral judgments. He detected in the literature of politics a healthy trend away from natural rights theories, from theories of Providential guidance of the destinies of men and nations, and from theories of the racial character and mission of peoples. He detected also an emphasis on the diffusion of power among the masses. He called for greater realism in the study of the functioning of democracy: an effort to study the sources of democratic ideas, as Henry Jones Ford and Frank J. Goodnow had already begun to do, in their relation to the conditions of eighteenth century society; a recognition of the unreality of the doctrine of divided powers in the complex world of the twentieth century; a realistic study of party government, especially through the kind of historical studies that would try to analyze precisely the makeup of parties and describe them realistically in their social and economic setting.[9] He saw that under modern conditions the exclusive stress on individual liberty no longer could be justified, that laissez faire was being challenged, that there was a continued increase in the functions of government, and that a new industrial democracy was in the making.

This was new and challenging doctrine. Yet had Beard kept to such generalizations, he might have been feared but he would not have been made—as he was to be—the prime target of the conservative attack. It was when he launched upon specific studies of the hot problems of the day that he got into trouble. The hottest problem of all, because it reached most deeply to the protection of corporate interests against legislative assaults, was the problem of the Constitution as the guardian of private property, and the Supreme Court as in turn the guardian of the Constitution. Beard sailed into the stormy waters in his little book on *The Supreme Court and the Constitution* (1912). He did not, however, take the tack of challenging the Court's right to the power of judicial review. In fact, after a skillful survey of the historical conflicts over the Court's exercise of that power, and a scrupulous use of sources as he had been taught to make under York Powell, he concluded that the framers of the Constitution and the statesmen and judges of the Republic's first generation *did* intend the Court to have it. Nevertheless, the overtones of the book made it clear that Beard reserved the right to his own judgment on how particular Court majorities exercised their power of judicial review. In dealing with the debates in the Constitutional Convention and the ratifying conventions, and among both the supporters and opponents of the Constitution, he gave his readers a foretaste of the realistic method he was to follow in his book on the framing of the Constitution.

The storm that was raised by *An Economic Interpretation of the Constitution of the United States* (1913) has been many times described. By the very boldness of his title Beard had

served notice that he was nailing a thesis on the doors of the
academies. "The theory of economic determinism," he wrote,
"has not been tried out in American history, and until it is
tried out, it cannot be found wanting."[10] Twenty years earlier,
in his famous paper on the frontier, read at a meeting of the
American Historical Association, Turner had tried out another
theory—and the members of the historical profession had found
it far from wanting. There can be little doubt that Beard was
trying to do for his generation of historians what Turner had
done for his. The big difference, of course, was that while
Turner's theory had outraged some of the professional vested
ideas in history, it had not been dangerous to the contemporary
business vested interests. In fact, as Beard was later to point out
in a discussion of Turner's doctrine, "although Turner did not
invent the phrase 'rugged individualism', he did in effect . . .
identify it with the frontier spirit. . . . Turner set many historians to thinking that individualism had been the driving
force in American civilization. Wittingly or not he fortified the
teaching of Sumner in economics and sociology and of Burgess
in political science."[11]

This sheds a good deal of light on Beard's own intent in his
book on the Constitution. He was still carrying on his assault
on the false gods of Burgess and Sumner—the gods of individualist capitalism. He was testing out a theory which, if it
proved tenable, would undo much of Turner's influence in
bolstering capitalist individualism, and would show that the
real dynamism of American history was the conflict of group
and class interests—a conflict so profound that it operated even
in the sacred area of the framing and ratification of the Constitution itself, and in the minds of the most sainted and revered
men of American history.

It must be clear from this that Beard's book differed from
Turner's thesis in another respect also. Turner had developed
an approach to American history—in fact, one that was so closely
restricted to the particular conditions of American life that it
has itself become one of the sacred writings in the thesis of the

uniqueness of the American experience. Beard's book, although outwardly addressed to historians, was actually an essay in the general theory of politics. It was a study in the dynamics not only of American history but of political conduct as such; the inference was that the founding fathers acted not as Americans or as capitalists but as human beings. It was thus primarily a study in political motivation, in the drive behind great political events and great epochs, in the dynamics of class interest.

The tempest it stirred was thus tempestuous on a number of counts: Beard's book hit at the tradition of individualism in American thinking and therefore in American economic policy; it undermined the belief in the uniqueness of the American experience; it stripped the veil of piety from the study of the motives of political conduct, even in the case of the great heroes of American history; it brought the theory of group interests and of class conflict into the center of the study of American politics; it dealt a blow to the conservative Supreme Court majorities and their apologists, for if it was true that even the founding fathers were human beings governed by their sense of economic interest, it was a fortiori even truer of the Supreme Court justices who passed on the validity of federal and state legislation that sought to control Big Property. Thus it dealt a blow to the strongest panoply in which property in Beard's day clothed itself—the inviolate panoply of Constitutional "due process of law." At the same time it gave the *coup de grâce* to the mechanical jurisprudence of the time, the rebellion against which (as I have suggested) was one of Beard's own strongest motivations. Thus Beard's book had even more importance in the field of public law and the study of politics than it had in the study of American history.

I think it is pretty clear that Beard meant it to be thus. The doctrine on which he based the central thesis of his book was, as is well known, that of James Madison, and the *locus classicus* of that doctrine was in Number 10 of the *Federalist Papers*. After quoting in his first chapter a long excerpt from Madison's essay—on "the division of society into different interests and parties" and on the proposition that "the most common and durable source of factions has been the various and unequal distribution of property" between "those who hold and those who are without property . . . those who are creditors and those who are debtors . . . a landed interest, a manufacturing interest, a mercantile interest, a moneyed interest"—Beard comments: "Here we have a masterly statement of the theory of economic determinism in politics." He adds that Madison is an adequate disproof of the position of "those who are inclined to repudiate the hypothesis of economic determinism as a European importation."[12] Thus, while the material Beard was to use to document his thesis came necessarily from historical archives, and the episode he dealt with was an episode from American history, the study was essentially an adventure in political analysis.

Beard's next two important books tried to make explicit some of the implications of his approach for politics. The *Economic Origins of Jeffersonian Democracy* (1915) was an effort to apply Madison's thesis to the origins of American party government and to show how not only the party antagonisms of the Federalists and Republicans but also the basic economic and political thinking of their spokesmen—Hamilton and Adams on the one hand, and Taylor and Jefferson on the other—grew out of the divergent property interests of the economic groups who composed the parties. This book left its mark on all later writing on party politics. It was more sprawling and less tidily put together than the one on the Constitution, but in some ways it was the meatiest and richest that Beard wrote. Students of politics can still quarry in it for evocative leads. For Beard himself it was important because it rooted his own political thinking in Jeffersonianism. He was never to cast himself loose from Jefferson, whether in his agrarian sympathies, his attitude toward capitalism, his conception of a gracious life, his cultural values, or his outlook upon Europe's entanglements and their relation to American foreign policy.

It would be a mistake to interpret Beard's political theory as Marxist, and he himself repeatedly warned against such a misconception. To be sure, Marxism was in the air all around him; like everyone else who lived and thought in the last quarter of the nineteenth century and the first half of the twentieth, Beard could not escape the shadow of Marx. But the direct influence of Marxism upon him was minimal. Even in the days when he was trying to apply the materialist interpretation of history, there was never any hint that he cared about the dialectical process that was so dear to the Marxists. He believed that class interest and economic motives explained a good deal, but he would have been horrified about committing himself to a class-struggle view of politics. He was horrified by the Communist state and its values, and he never showed much interest even in a commitment to democratic socialism. The fact was that he was no systematic political thinker himself and that systems like the Marxian filled him with dismay.

Had he sought a social theory in which to root his own thinking, he could have found it in Thorstein Veblen's work. Veblen, in some ways as original as Marx, in many ways more subtle and credible, had dug deep to the anthropological, economic, and psychological roots of modern institutions. As early as 1904, a decade before Beard's books on the Constitution and on Jeffersonianism, Veblen's chapter on "Business Principles in Law and Politics" in his *Theory of Business Enterprise* had anticipated most of Beard's conclusions. But Beard feared other people's systems, whether they were European or American. He preferred to build on the *aperçus* in the essays or random statements of a Madison, a Hamilton, a Marshall, a Webster. That left him unfettered to apply his interpretive lead to the specific conditions of a historical period. As he had put it in his 1908 lecture on *Politics:* one of the things the historian could do for politics was "to discover inductively the precise composition of parties or their relation to surrounding social and economic phenomena."[13] To make his detailed studies of his theories of the dynamics of politics, Beard had thus to become a historian:

It was the only way he could study the relation of whatever his problem was to the "surrounding social and economic phenomena." For the most part he left it to others to extract the implications. He had a horror of what might be called "grand political theory." He never formulated a theory of the state. Randolph Bourne, for example, using as his point of departure the Beard studies, ventured on such a "grand" theory, in his "Unfinished Fragment on the State" (1918) ;[14] but it was more than half a failure, and Beard—given his conditionings and his strong empirical bent—was wise to forego this sort of adventure, which the young radicals of his time, inspired by his work, undertook.

The political thinkers in the American tradition who interested him most, aside from Jefferson, were Madison and John Taylor of Caroline in the early period, and in his own day Brooks Adams, Justice Louis D. Brandeis, and Justice Hugo L. Black. What ties these men together is a hard-bitten, unfooled quality they had in common, rather than any ideological uniformity. Madison saw the property divergences behind the party system; Taylor saw the hollowness of "the aristocracy of paper and profit"; Brooks Adams, for whose *Law of Civilization and Decay* Beard wrote an introductory essay in his last years, saw that the rise and fall of civilizations followed not upon ideological or moral factors but upon the shifting of the trade routes of empire in history; Brandeis and Black were judicial radicals who talked about economic realities rather than juristic categories. This was what Beard went for, wherever he found it.

The closest he ever came to making explicit his own political theory of class interest was in his little book of Amherst lectures, *The Economic Basis of Politics,* delivered in 1916, but not published until 1922, with additional material in later editions. Where in his *Economic Interpretation of the Constitution* Beard had tried to prove too much by tracing the direct economic impulsions of particular men, he shifted in his Amherst lectures to a broader and somewhat vaguer theory of the economic interests of classes, industrial groups, and occupational groups, and their impact on politics. He stuck to his contention that it is the conflict of economic interests that underlies and conditions the political process, and is therefore the shaping force in politics as in history. Beard refused to see this conflict —as the Marxists saw the class struggle—as beginning after primitive communism and ending with the construction of a utopian communist society. He rejected utopianism, whether in the golden age of the conjectural past or the golden age of the conjectural future. He saw the conflict of groups and classes as inherent in history and in political society, and therefore never ending. He refused to believe that man "may so control the distribution of wealth as to establish an ideal form of society and prevent the eternal struggle of classes that has shaken so many nations to their foundations."[15] In all this his thinking was essentially valid and has not been shaken by events.

But the political thinker who refused to accept the dogmas of Marxism was also skeptical of some of the dogmas of democracy, at least in his earlier days. In tracing the growth of Western political theory under the pressure of changes in class position and class interest, Beard made it clear that he considered the Industrial Revolution of James Watt more important than the equalitarian revolution of Rousseau.[16] He tended always to see political ideas as the rationalization of a class bid for power. Thus he saw Rousseau as a "passionate propagandist" who "set forth the moral and philosophic justification for the revolt of the third estate," and found his system of the "general will" as embodied in the mathematical majority "so unreal, so ill-adapted to the world of industry and trade, commerce and agriculture, that . . . we can hardly imagine how it could become the philosophy of any people."[17] While Beard was aware of the extent to which America borrowed the equalitarian idea from Europe—from Locke even more than from Rousseau—his emphasis was less on democratic theory than on the new economic base that the theory found in American social conditions. Americans had done away with the landed owners of Europe, they had no aristocracy or clergy with any power, and they had no European type of proletariat. Besides, the wide distribution of land "brought about in fact a considerable economic equality to correspond to the theory of political equality."[18] Beard saw with clarity that the theory of political equality did not have easy going even under the social conditions of America, that the owning groups feared the spread of Rousseauist Jacobinism in America, that they would have liked to stratify citizenship and introduce the estates system by writing into the Constitution a personal property qualification for voters, had not they known they could not get away with it. They relied instead upon the system of checks and balances "to secure the rights of property—particularly personal property—against the assaults of the farmers and the proletariat." And Beard acidly added: "Much ingenuity has been spent by American lawyers in elaborating the theoretical fictions of Montesquieu. The real significance of the separation of powers and its relation to the balance of class interests in society was appreciated by eighteenth century writers, but if more modern statesmen have understood them they have seldom been frank in setting forth their views."[19]

Thus Beard made his basic position clear on the study of economic interests and political ideas. It was one that depreciated political power as compared with economic power; regarded political contrivances (like the system of checks and balances and the division of powers) as the shadow and not the reality, as the mask that hid the face and the glove that clothed the hand of class interest; saw ideas and idea systems as having no initiating force of their own, but mainly as reflections of class drives. Beard was later to retreat from this position, and a book like *The Republic* (1943) came close to being a defense of a system of political and economic pluralism, and of checks and balances, as the only possible basis of a free society. The Beard of the earlier phase, however, was more summary and abrupt. He was fond of quoting Maitland's remarkable insight that "the whole [of] constitutional law seems at times to be but an appendix to the law of real property."[20] One may guess that there were moments when Beard saw himself as an American Maitland who had engineered the tour de force of showing American constitutional law as a sort of appendix not to land tenure but to personal property and security holding. Maitland, said Beard, "was entirely emancipated from bondage to systematists."[21] Beard's career was similarly a campaign to emancipate American political science from the systematists. He fought the arid pedantry of systems, whether Marxist or any other. He fought the dreary platitudes of the mechanical thinkers of the checks-and-balances school. He fought also the rhetoricians of the democratic idea, whether they were Rousseauists, idealists, or Wilsonian "world-imagists" who sought to extend a moral imperialism over the world. Finally he fought all the thinkers, liberal and conservative alike, who preferred to gloss over the underlying realities of class and group interest. "Have the economic groups once recognized by statesmen and political philosophers disappeared?" he asked. "The answer is emphatic. It is to be found in the census returns, which, as certainly as the domesday book of William the Conqueror, record the perdurance of group and class interest despite the rhetoric of political equality."[22]

When Beard came to write the several volumes of *The Rise of American Civilization,* he stuck to the emphasis on changing economic realities. As a historian, he was a political thinker applying his basic approach to the successive social situations in the time frame of American life. Yet in the crucible of the actual conditions of American history, Beard modified the fierceness of his early position. He was no longer concerned to prove a theory of economic determinism, but only to show that the economic factors were the most important in the whole complex of forces that shape a political society. When he came to write a new preface in 1935 to *An Economic Interpretation of the Constitution,* he whittled down his intent by saying that the economic factors had been "so long disregarded" that he had tried "to redress the balance." During the whole latter part of his life, he belonged most clearly with what may be called the "multiple causation" school of political and social theory.

To most students of government Beard is best known for his descriptions and interpretive writing on American government in action under contemporary conditions. The successive editions of his textbook *American Government and Politics* influenced a whole generation of teachers and students. *The American Leviathan: The Republic in the Machine Age* (1930), written with William Beard, was without much doubt the best statement of his thinking in this area, and has not been surpassed since for its realism, its balance, and its perceptions. What Beard did for the study of American government was to help shift the emphasis from the structure of government to its dynamics, from the mechanisms and procedures of government to its daily impact on the lives of the people, from government-in-books to government-in-action, from the pietist to the behaviorist. His books were especially fruitful in the discussion of the economic and human factors in the working of the judicial power, in the new dimensions of the Presidential office, in the realistic factors involved in the party system, and in the immense new importance of public administration and the administrative process.

Beard had in his early Columbia years come under the influence of Goodnow, one of the pioneers in the study of administration. In the municipal field he had worked with what he called the "ABC" trinity—Allen, Bruere, and Cleveland. He had spent some time in Tokyo helping to reorganize municipal administration. Sometimes, as in his Princeton address on *Philosophy, Science and Art of Public Administration* (1939), he tended defensively to overestimate the scientific precision of public administration. But there were few students who did as much as he to underscore the role of technicians in the government services, especially in the Departments of Agriculture and the Interior, and the character of administration as a form of technology. When, in 1928, he edited a symposium called *Whither Mankind?* he struck an affirmative note in his introductory essay. He sturdily stood up for the civilization of the machine age, flinging out the challenge that "the imagination of an Einstein, a Bohr, or a Millikan, may well transcend that of a Milton or a Vergil." As for the charge of materialism leveled at our age, he asked whether "the prevention of disease by sanitation [is] more materialistic than doing it by touching saints' bones? Is feeding the multitude by mass production more materialistic than feeding it by a miracle?"[23] Two years later, in 1930, he returned to the attack in another symposium, *Toward Civilization*. Written on the eve of the depression, his last chapter is a plea for rational planning of the economy and the application of engineering techniques not only to industry but to society. He points out that Plato was a utopian planner, and Aristotle a planner who advocated critical rational intelligence; that the laissez faire philosophy of nineteenth century England was a temporary break in the sweep of civilization; and that the Greek philosophers had more sense about government than Cobden and Bright. He traces the progression of planning from the city to the national unit, prophesies that it is only in its beginning on the national plane, and ends with a somewhat grandiloquent flourish: "Imagination, informed by the known laws of nature, but unbound and free to experiment and dare, combined with the spirit of rationality, lives and flowers in the engineering age and will swing new planets into the ken of those who watch the heavens for signs of the future."[24]

This is Beard the rational radical and the scientific humanist. It is the Beard who ended the second volume of *The Rise of American Civilization* with the now classic sentence, "If so, it is the dawn, not the dusk, of the gods,"[25] perhaps unconsciously paraphrasing Franklin's little speech about "the rising, not the setting, sun" at the conclusion of the Constitutional Convention. If Beard was too optimistic at the time on the eve of the Great Depression, it was largely because he failed to distinguish between the rational forces of technology and the irrational forces of unplanned business enterprise. The intensity of Beard's recoil from the spectacle of what business had done with the resources and technology of American life may be measured in an article of his in the *Forum* of July, 1931, on "A 'Five-Year Plan' for America." He sketches the outlines of a program that includes a National Economic Council, the repeal of the anti-trust laws, a declaration making all major industries into public utilities, a Board of Strategy and Planning to do the basic work of forecasting and of allocation, and a series of "syndicates" for the government of industry. This is rather breathtaking, given the moderation of Beard's views on economic policy in later years, and his fears that the drastic increase in governmental power would lead to totalitarianism. But it is indicative of how far in the radical direction he was willing to go under the stress of great events which, as he saw them, required drastic action.

This is not the place to analyze in any detailed way Beard's views on economic and foreign policy. I want here to note only that as a political theorist Beard was caught in a difficult dilemma. He was willing to accept most of the New Deal program; yet in his later years he began to have doubts not only about the interference with the judicial power represented by President Roosevelt's ill-fated "court-packing" plan, but also about the trend of centralized power as he saw it in the successive Roosevelt terms. His skeptical mind saw through the rhetoric of "national honor" and "national interest," as those phrases were generally used: His book on *The Idea of National Interest* (1934) pulled few punches; at the same time he found himself, in the companion volume, *The Open Door at Home* (1934), advocating what amounted to a policy of economic nationalism. He did not quite face up to the logical corollary of such a program, which would have meant socialism and a managed economy. Yet I do not intend my emphasis here to be wholly critical. Whatever the roots and the validity of Beard's isolationism—or as he called it "continentalism"— he had the courage of his convictions; and there was an inner logic that tied these views of his in with his earlier writings on idea systems as the rhetoric of class interest.

Beard was not a systematist. He published no theory of the state, and even in *The Republic,* he had little that was fresh to add to the analysis of the basic nature of democracy. His strength lay in his capacity to deflate the pompous and to shift the discussion always to the concrete material of economic life. He was largely a theorist of power in its varied and bewildering forms—the party machine, the Presidency, the pressure group, the corporation, the press, the engines of propaganda and diplomacy, the wheelings and maneuverings of power politics in the international field. He belonged, with Machiavelli, to the tough-minded rather than the idealist school of political thought. In his urgency to get at the bedrock of economic power, he tended to underestimate the political factors, just as he almost always underestimated the innate force of ideas and the role of leadership. But his influence on American political thinking was both astringent and invigorating. He squeezed a lot of the water out of it, and a lot of the inflated sawdust stuffing. His basic motivation was that of a satirist who is determined to strip away the phony and pretentious, and to unmask the realities, however unlovely they may prove. His whole career sheds a decisive light on the organic relation between history and political science when politics is analyzed— as Beard analyzed it—in terms of dynamism, and when history is written—as Beard wrote—in terms of the realities of power.

LUTHER GULICK

Beard and Municipal Reform

MUNICIPAL REFORM in America is an oft repeated process of
falling upstairs. Reform starts in waves of exposure, investigations, and journalism. It climbs to the level of political
activity, newly organized citizen parties, surveys, governmental
research, and creative ideas. The highest point of its ascent
is reached in charter reform, forward looking programs, civic
organization, new officials, and the rise of professionalism in
the city service. Then in a decade or so reform falters and
falls back as the public interest of the good citizen turns to
newer concerns. At that point, often by default, forever active
special interests and self-seeking political groups again take
over the management of municipal affairs. In due course these
selfish interests finally overreach themselves, and the process
repeats itself, but each time at a somewhat higher level of
administrative accomplishment. Thus the municipalities are
advancing. Each time they go forward two, or four, or six
steps, and with each fall they slip back one or two paces, but in
the end the progress in unmistakable.

The most constructive generation of municipal reform in American history thus far has been the period from Lincoln Steffens' *The Shame of the Cities* to Judge Seabury's exposures, the end of the Walker regime, and the rise of reform under LaGuardia. During this period there were not only the disclosures that destroyed many an urban political dictatorship, but the founding of the governmental research movement in New York in 1906, the blossoming out of the National Municipal League with its conventions and model laws, and the establishment of the Training School for Public Service. The same period saw the invention of the short ballot and city manager government, the inauguration of the home rule crusade with a hundred good city charters, the importation of proportional representation, the development of voting machines, and a most striking set of improvements in the techniques of municipal administration. The administrative reforms included budget systems, standard accounts and reports, central purchasing, personnel administration, city planning and zoning, and the professionalization of health, police, fire, engineering, teaching, welfare, and many other municipal services.

In all of this, most publicists, many reformers, and even some historians have missed the central distinction between action based on knowledge and action based on human desires, human beliefs, and human interests. The first we are reducing to technology; the second is still the major realm of politics. The first rests on science; the second on human nature, man's aspirations, and individual and social drives. Human nature is not changing perceptibly, but human knowledge is going forward by leaps and bounds. So, too, in municipal reform: Over the generations we have a right to look for great permanent advances in technology, from which there is no backsliding, even though we may find little advance and frequent recession in the intertwined structure and behavior of politics.

Following the steps of Frank J. Goodnow, Charles A. Beard saw this distinction and threw his major energies in municipal reform into the advancement of the technology of politics and the technology of governmental administration. This led him to become an active member and long-time officer of the National Municipal League, and to join the New York Bureau of Municipal Research, of whose Training School for Public Service he was director from 1917 to 1922. During this period he was largely responsible for the development of the Training School and for the introduction of many Columbia University graduate students into the laboratory approach to political science and administration.

During these years also, Beard was the critic who forced Frederick A. Cleveland and his associates then at work in the Bureau of Municipal Research to refine their own thinking and to put their ideas into terms that could be understood by others. He was also the director of a number of major state and municipal surveys, such as the project of 1919 in Newark and the study that led to reorganization of Delaware in 1918. Beard's unique contribution in these charters of reform was to demand real scholarship in place of easy and superficial generalizations, to demonstrate the need for broad analysis that would draw on all the social disciplines, not solely on efficiency and business procedures, and finally to insist that sufficient work and thought be put into every survey report, every manual, every reform program so that the objectives could be whipped into a clear statement in simple terms. He insisted that manuals and reports not only should be comprehensible to the ordinary man, but should persuade him and command his active backing. To a technical expert, beating the air with his own special jargon, Beard often said: "Put it down, put it down, crystal clear. Until you do that I won't believe you have thought it through or understand it yourself."

Beard came at that point in the history of American political science when the legalistic, historical, and comparative constitutional approach was illuminated and expanded by the addition of four practical but upsetting new ideas. These were: (1) the idea that political science must also be explored as part of the struggle of mankind with complex economic and social forces; (2) the belief that political science cannot stand aloof from the daily affairs of practical citizenship, including local politics; (3) the conception that public administration is a branch of political science and is capable of advancement through dispassionate observation, research, and the formulation and testing of hypotheses; and (4) the conviction that governmental research, municipal reform, civic service, and skilled public administration offer a career, for which men and women can be educated and trained and in which they can find not only employment but also a lifetime of expanding social usefulness. Beard himself was one of those who contributed greatly to the popularization of these new approaches. This was particularly clear in his work with the New York Bureau of Municipal Research and its Training School for Public Service.

In all of this Beard's influence reached out far beyond the four walls of "261 Broadway," the home of the Bureau, and the Columbia campus, because he spoke frequently at conventions of reformers and researchers and because he never failed to lead, to inspire, and to transmit to his audiences something of his own belief in the efficacy of the struggle for better administration and better government. Many of his speeches are preserved in the proceedings of conventions and in the journals of the day, such as the *National Municipal Review, Public Management, Survey,* the *New Republic,* and the *New York Times Magazine.* Some of Beard's contagious ideas found their way in modified form into his lively texts on American national, state, and city government. Running through all these writings, however staid and traditional their outward appearances, are the dreams of the crusader and the passion of the reformer. Thus even Beard's textbooks served to train new generations of citizens who would understand something of democracy and would be prepared to back the cause of governmental reform.

The planners always found in Beard a strong ally in the early years of municipal research and reform. Beard's writings and addresses indicate that Beard became interested in planning because he found it a device through which streets, parks, traffic, water supply and sewers, zoning and land use programs, housing, health and education, and taxation and debts could all be brought together and integrated into a single logical program of action and reform. Here again in the field of planning as elsewhere Beard's influence brought a challenge to the social inadequacy and imaginative poverty of programs, for Beard called for the inclusion of all factors, "political, economic, and cultural," in any approach to future community action.

Beard's views on the economic foundations of national politics found further confirmation in the realm of urban politics where landowners, possessors of franchises, recipients of tax favors, bondholders, municipal bankers, private utilities, favored contractors, and liquor, gambling, and vice rings, as well as the politics-for-profit city machines, were struggling to keep and expand their political power because without it their economic enterprises would disappear. Many a municipal survey and reform program prepared under Beard's direction challenged one or more of these entrenched special interests. Beard's reform technique in these cases was doubly effective because, unlike some other research workers, he was quick to see the true underlying motives involved, and then to couch the language and the reasoning of the new program in the broadest terms of unassailable economic and political doctrine. However much he fulminated in private against "the interests," his method of destroying their hiding places and depriving entrenched privilege of its respectability was to appeal in his reports and reform programs calmly yet eloquently to facts, first principles, and practical deductions from them.

The best illustration is perhaps the Bureau's 1919 report on the traction crisis in New York City. At the end of a clear review of New York's traction history based on extensive technical studies by the staff, Beard came to this summary:

First, it must be conceded that the principles evolved by the American people in fifty years' experience in traction matters afford the basis for negotiation. These principles are (1) that perpetual franchises are intolerable, (2) that the capital in traction lines already established must not be inflated by manipulation, and that new capitalization must represent bona fide expenditures for services, materials and labor, (3) that a public utility company must be allowed to earn a reasonable return on the capital invested, (4) that all profits above this reasonable return should be divided between the company and the local government in such a way as to furnish incentive for efficient and economical operation, and (5) that the terms and conditions of municipal ownership should be explicitly set forth in agreements embodying principles 1-4.

Second, no increase of fare ought to be granted in New York City without a modification of the franchises and contracts of the existing companies in the public interest.

Third, the traction problem of Greater New York must be treated as one problem involving the entire system. The convenience of the traveling public and the cost of the general service, not the operating costs of single short lines should be the determining factors in fixing rates.

Fourth, provision must be made for unified operation with a view to effecting the economies which such operation promises, even though two or more companies might be embraced in the final settlement.

Fifth, the total capital upon which a return may be earned should be determined once for all and the slate wiped clean for future extensions, betterments and additions on a basis of bona fide capitalization. Furthermore, such extensions might conceivably be financed by being assessed on the property benefited.

Sixth, definite provision must be made for assuring to the companies consolidated a fair return upon their adjusted capitalization and upon additional capital hereafter raised for extensions and betterments—such a guarantee being accompanied by a division of surplus, if any, between the city and company or companies owning the properties.

Seventh, the way must be cleared for applying municipal ownership to the surface and elevated lines on definite terms and conditions as to acquisition and financing when and if such a step is desired by the people of the city.[1]

The devastating effect of these simple propositions, which played an important part in the ultimate unification of the system under municipal operation in 1940, can be appreciated only in the perspective of the titanic battle that was then raging over the right to profit from New York's transit system. Incidentally it should be stated for the record that the subway interests and their friends tried to suppress this report, not without vehement backing within the Board of Trustees of the Bureau of Municipal Research, but that the trustees as a group, under the leadership of R. Fulton Cutting, decided that the technical work of the staff was to be issued to the public regardless of the views of the Board, which had discharged its responsibility in the selection of a competent technical staff. This decision would certainly not have been reached but for the dispassionate character of the words and ideas through which in the traction crisis report Charles Beard stated the fundamentals of municipal reform.

Two famous survey reports, in addition to those mentioned above, show the unmistakable stamp of Beard's impress. One is the report of Governor Alfred E. Smith's New York Reconstruction Commission, with which Mrs. Henry Moscowitz worked as secretary to the legislative group and Robert Moses served as chief of staff of the technical group and Governor Smith's trusted adviser. The other is *The Administration and Politics of Tokyo* written by Beard in 1922-1923 when he was in Japan and published in that country under the auspices of the newly organized Tokyo Institute for Municipal Research.

The New York Reconstruction Commission's report was of course a group effort, produced by an extraordinarily fine staff[2] under the vigorous direction of Robert Moses. As the chief of staff and the research experts were drawn primarily from the New York Bureau of Municipal Research, it was natural that Beard should be brought in to advise on the strategy of reform and should be asked to draft the grand conspectus of the project and the broad summary of recommendations. In these opening pages the drive of the reformers was fused with the meticulous recommendations of the technicians to form an

effective weapon for Al Smith. Truly this report proved to
be one of the most influential reform documents in American
state history.

The important point to note is the way the report, under
Beard's hand, starts with "The Underlying Principles" as Chapter I and then skilfully boils down the whole program to three
interrelated objectives: "1. The consolidation of offices, boards
and commissions into a few great departments of government,
each of which is responsible for the conduct of a particular
major function. . . . 2. Vesting the power of appointment and
removal of department heads in the Governor; [whose term is
extended to four years, thus] making him in fact, as well as in
theory, the responsible Chief Executive of the State. . . .
3. [Establishing] a consolidated budget system with accounting
control over spending officers."[3]

The closing paragraph of Beard's part of the introduction is
reminiscent of the *Federalist* when he writes:

The only serious argument advanced against such a proposed
reorganization and budget system is that it makes the Governor
a czar. The President of the United States has administrative
powers far greater than those here proposed to be given to the
Governor. The Mayor of the City of New York appoints and
removes all of the important department heads, and citizens
know whom to hold accountable. The Governor does not
hold office by hereditary right. He is elected for a fixed term
by universal suffrage. He is controlled in all minor appointments by the civil service law. He cannot spend a dollar of
the public money which is not authorized by the Legislature
of the State. He is subject to removal by impeachment. If he
were given the powers here proposed he would stand out in
the limelight of public opinion and scrutiny. Economy in administration, if accomplished, would redound to his credit.
Waste and extravagance could be laid at his door. Those who
cannot endure the medicine because it seems too strong must
be content with waste, inefficiency and bungling—and steadily
rising cost of government. The system here proposed is more
democratic, not more "royal" than that now in existence. Democracy does not merely mean periodical elections. It means

a government held accountable to the people between elections. In order that the people may hold their government to account they must have a government that they can understand. No citizen can hope to understand the present collections of departments, offices, boards and commissions, or the present methods of appropriating money. A Governor with a Cabinet of reasonable size, responsible for proposing a program in the annual budget and for administering the program as modified by the Legislature may be brought daily under public scrutiny, held accountable to the Legislature and public opinion, and be turned out of office if he fails to measure up to public requirements. If this is not democracy then it is difficult to imagine what it is.[4]

When these introductory pages are compared with any prior efficiency survey one can see the two things Beard imparted to the work: the breadth of its democratic political philosophy and the simplicity of ideas and words into which the program is distilled.

Beard's *Administration and Politics of Tokyo* carries a subtitle, *A Survey and Opinions*. It is these opinions that are of special interest to the student today. As in the New York State report, Beard begins his Tokyo survey with a first chapter titled "The Criteria and Scheme of Municipal Science." The opening sentences follow: "Whoever undertakes the criticism of any particular administrative system, public or private, is under obligation to state the principles upon which he bases his criticism; in other words, to present the criteria upon which his judgments are founded. If he has in mind some ideal system evolved by a priori reasoning from an abstract concept, he is bound to state what that concept is. If, on the other hand, his approach is practical and pragmatic, he must indicate clearly the sources of his critical opinions."[5]

Beard then selects the practical and pragmatic approach for his Tokyo survey, rather than the philosophical, and presents his now famous formulation of the "criteria of municipal science":

The New York Bureau of Municipal Research in applying the criteria of municipal science to a particular city, evolved a general scheme or organization of standards. Although by no means rigid in character, this scheme usually embraces the following elements in one form or another:

1. A city government serves the people of a given urban district. For efficient functioning within that area, it should have legal jurisdiction over the entire urban district and within practical limits control the growth of the city.

2. By the nature of circumstances, certain responsibilities are imposed upon a city government, and its powers should be commensurate with its responsibilities.

3. The structure of a municipal administration should be determined by the number and variety of functions entrusted to it, all related functions being vested in the same department.

4. The city must carry on large financial transactions. These are closely related; therefore, the criteria for judgment as to appropriations, taxation, borrowing, accounting control, and reporting must form an *ensemble*.

5. The city in the discharge of its functions must purchase, store, distribute, and use an immense quantity and variety of material objects. The methods should conform to established standards.

6. The city must employ a large number and variety of persons ranging from skilled technicians to casual laborers. The standards of modern personnel administration should be applied.

7. The city must undertake functions which call for scientific methods and mechanical equipment. The technique should conform to the highest tested standards.

8. A city government is not an end in itself but an agent designed to serve the purposes of the community or certain groups in the community. Hence the scientific investigator is inevitably led into the examination of (a) the "social heritage" of the community, (b) the ways in which new characteristics are acquired, (c) the methods by which the agents of government are chosen and held responsible, and (d) the processes by which the community or the effective groups in the community arrive at purposes, formulate them, and secure their execution through the agency of the municipal government.

9. Modern civilization is industrial; industries are in the cities; the government of each city bears a vital relation to the

efficiency of the community viewed as a productive organism in an economic sense. The government should discharge the functions imposed by that relation.

Here then is the general scheme for the arrangement of data and the application of critical judgment.[6]

Beard's efforts to lead students of the problems of government to reduce their criteria and their hypotheses to systematic written form thus finally bore fruit in a report that he had to do alone, with his own hand, in a foreign land. But the effect on governmental research and on municipal reform in this country was significant. This is seen, for example, in the Cincinnati survey directed by Dr. Lent D. Upson in 1924, a survey that ushered in a notable era of good government in the Ohio city. In that survey Upson pressed every one of his team of experts to state explicitly his criteria of judgment, making the Cincinnati report one of the most outstanding surveys in print. Even more pervasive, however, was the effect of Beard's method of approaching municipal problems upon the thinking of those who were undertaking research into municipal problems.

It was against this background that the Bureau of Municipal Research and the Institute of Public Administration, into which the Bureau was transformed, undertook their first studies. These sought to establish measurements of administrative achievement in government as a foundation for testing the validity of the hypotheses and criteria that had long been implicit, and were, under Beard's influence, made more explicit in the thinking of those who were responsible for the American municipal reform movement. This drive for measurement has been pressed forward especially in the work of Arthur E. Buck, Clarence E. Ridley, Bruce Smith and the uniform crime reports, Donald C. Stone and the budget group in Washington, many of the bureaus of municipal research, and more recently by the psychological and sociodynamic approach of Elton Mayo, Fritz Roethlisberger, and Herbert A. Simon. It is interesting to note that, in the published record of a conference in Washington of the Society for the Advancement of Management (the former Taylor Society) in 1937 on the subject of work units, the opening essay was by Charles A. Beard. At that conference he called for the organization of a new national association to "include the most efficient workers" in public administration. He also urged the issuance of a journal of public administration that "would continually explore the philosophy and practice in the field of public administration and constantly apply the Socratic elenchus to all the thought and research that appears in the field of administration."[7] Beard's suggestion of a journal was fully realized when the American Society for Public Administration was organized in 1939 along with its excellent *Public Administration Review,* established in 1940. The further suggestion, however, of a continual application of the Socratic cross-examination lay dormant until Beard himself revived it. At a banquet in New York City in 1947 on the occasion of the Governmental Research Conference and the celebration of the fortieth anniversary of the establishment of the New York Bureau of Municipal Research, he proceeded boldly to challenge many of the well-worn phrases of reform dogma with the following thrusts:

IT IS NOT TRUE that the organization of any large legislative and administrative system can be "streamlined" and permanently put on a secure operating basis, without the aid of Politics and Providence.

IT IS NOT TRUE that the President of the United States, the governor of a state, or the executive of a city is necessarily a good administrator or a safe depositary of managerial powers or in fact more deeply concerned and better informed about honorable and efficient administration than all the members of the corresponding legislative body.

IT IS NOT TRUE that, at the federal and the state levels, all administrative agencies are *in* the executive department and *subject* to the direction of the chief magistrate; nor is it true that they should be so.

IT IS NOT TRUE that the executive powers are separate from the legislative and judicial powers, either legally or actually, and that the administrative system can or will operate according to a blueprint based on the assumption of separation.

IT IS NOT TRUE that in any system of government at a high level all functions which are alike or similar in nature should be grouped in the same department in the same interest of good administration.

IT IS NOT TRUE that centralization of administration automatically works for efficiency, economy, or the public welfare.

IT IS NOT TRUE that corporate management in the business world furnishes any safe guidance for the management of government, except in respect of routine procedures.

IT IS NOT TRUE that the spirit of and the capacity for self government are indelibly ingrained in the American people and will endure forever, no matter what they do or what activities and obligations may be undertaken by their elected agents and representatives in domestic and foreign affairs.

IT IS NOT TRUE that permanent civil servants are mere appendages to the executive and the legislature and that they will efficiently perform their duties if daily and indiscriminately castigated by politicians, the press, and citizens as "bureaucrats" and "subversive characters."

In closing this Socratic elenchus, which was intended to be more illustrative than complete, Beard said: "There are values in the formulas thus brought to the bar of judgment but the amount of truth in them is at best limited and they are dangerous if employed as the whole truth and pushed to extremes." He therefore went on to recommend to those engaged in governmental research and reform "an ever cautious consideration of the extent to which our operating principles are true and applicable in practice."[8]

The influence of Charles A. Beard in American municipal reform cannot be detached from the activities and ideas of the generation in which he lived and worked. His impress is found especially in the work of the National Municipal League, the Bureau of Municipal Research, the Civil Service Reform League, and the Training School for Public Service. These were the most important centers of constructive municipal reform in America's most dynamic era of urban governmental advance.

Beard's influence on governmental research and the surveys that offered in so many cases the charter of municipal advance stemmed from his constantly demanding two things: first, better scholarship with broader historical perspective, more thoughtful analysis, and the explicit formulation of hypotheses; and second, crystal-clear thinking and statement.

Beard was, moreover, as has been noted, the teacher of future administrators, research workers, reformers, and politicians. He taught them both directly at Columbia University, at the Training School for Public Service, and at the New School for Social Research, and indirectly through his texts and other writings. In all this work there never was a lecture, or a book, or a speech that did not raise the banner of civic responsibility and kindle the fires of reform.

Thus Charles A. Beard played a more important role in municipal and governmental reform in the years from 1909 to 1947 than the man in the street would ever understand, because Beard was scattering seminal ideas, challenging superficialities, demanding and formulating clear statements of truth, and ever giving to experts, and to citizens, confidence in human advancement through purpose, research, and political action.

GEORGE SOULE

Beard and the Concept of Planning

THE BITTER hostility with which American conservatives greeted *An Economic Interpretation of the Constitution* evidenced more than the difference of opinion among scholars commonly aroused by new academic theses. It is now difficult to recall the mood that stirred up heated public debate about Charles A. Beard's basic historical work, the editorials in the daily newspapers, the persecution of the author for what was regarded as a subversive attack on accepted fundamentals. So great has been the change in the climate of public opinion since the publication of the book that Americans no longer think of their Constitution as something remote from material considerations, or of the founding fathers as archangels without prejudices or interests of their own.

The stir caused by this introduction of economic motives into the writing of history was, on the surface, the shocked response of devotees of an American religion. Grimy hands, which had been digging in the muck of past self-interest, were being laid on the Holy of Holies; the shrine of 100 per cent pure American patriotism was being desecrated. If this sacrilege were to be left unpunished by a thunderbolt from heaven, the whole ethic of the American Republic was believed to be in danger. But the critics probably sensed vaguely a more real peril to their conceptual world than that the Constitution should be reduced to the status of a human and possibly defective document or that its framers should be regarded as mere statesmen rather than as prophets.

If in the case of the framing of the Constitution itself economics and politics were mixed, how could they ever be separated in lesser affairs? It was, indeed, Beard's ardent belief that they could not be, and it was his intention to convey that conviction to others by specific instance and inductive generalization. In a long lifetime of productive scholarship he never wrote political history without including its economic orchestration, and he never discussed economic problems without thinking of them as a function of politics. "Political economy," he insisted, not the more recently introduced "economics," is the proper term.

This attitude now seems a matter of routine; but even yet its implications have not been fully accepted either by all academicians or by many "practical men." In the American scene during the second quarter of the twentieth century, the idea stressed by Beard twenty years earlier that governmental and private economic activities are warp and woof of the same fabric has been powerfully dynamic, and it was correctly, though foggily, seen as such by critics of the first work in which Beard dramatized it for American readers. This idea gives, for instance, historical legitimacy to planning, a policy that some economists like Friedrich A. Hayek, who reject the role of political economist, have called the road to serfdom.

Beard's attitude toward public affairs was derived not merely from yellowed documents of the past. Moved by the startling idea that there is and must be a close connection between theory and practice, he soon set out to do research in municipal government and to make the results available for daily use. This was a field where the connection between economics and politics could not be ignored by the dullest observer. A good city government was not merely one in which political bosses ceased to pass out substantial favors in return for contributions or votes; it was one in which taxes, budgets, and debts were adjusted to clamorous needs for public services. Zoning and planning for development were employed to express the general interest as against individualistic anarchy and the pressure of property on the make. It was in this connection that Beard first began to use the word planning. City planning became widely accepted, at least as a formula, during the 1920's. Its growth was duly recorded in *The American Leviathan* before the Great Depression. On a national scale, however, the planning concept had not been formulated in the United States. Extension of regulations and controls by the federal government were regularly invoked for *ad hoc* purposes, but the idea that the national economy could be, or should be, understood and planned as a whole had found few advocates since the agitation for economic changes that had immediately followed World War I, and these few were on the extreme and uninfluential Left.

As Beard and other historians have shown, the forces that wanted governmental intervention and those that opposed it had locked horns many times and on many different issues. The philosophy of governmental nonintervention had been formulated even before the birth of the Republic, and was elaborated on occasion by some of the founding fathers, especially Thomas Jefferson. But the notion that this doctrine was consistently adhered to by any individual, any one party, or any economic group or section does not bear the test of the facts. Each wanted the power of government used to support his favorite measures. Anti-interventionism was hurled only against the measures he opposed. Even then it often took the form of arguing for the limitation of federal power as against that of the states, rather than of complete philosophical laissez faire—though nonintervention in the specific case was usually the object in view. Jefferson himself, after he became President, supported a gen-

eral scheme of internal improvements of the sort outlined in
1808 by Albert Gallatin, his Secretary of the Treasury.

It was during the bitter days when President Hoover was
resisting the demand for federal intervention on behalf of
unemployed workers and bankrupt farmers that Beard argued
this point most forcefully. A 1931 article in *Harper's* later
published as a pamphlet (1932) brought to bear on "The Myth
of Rugged American Individualism" the heavy batteries of historical precedent. Otto Kahn had just refurbished the old saw
that government should not interfere with economic processes,
and Hoover had asserted that notions about planned economy
came out of Russia. Such statements infuriated Beard the
patriot as well as Beard the custodian and interpreter of fact.
He demolished the opposition by citation of federal action concerned with railways, waterways, barges, canals, shipping, highways. He called into action references to the work of the
Department of Commerce, the Bureau of Standards, the Federal
Trade Commission, the tariff, the Federal Farm Board. Government, he pointed out, had intervened or lent a helping hand
on many occasions and in many ways, when politically influential forces of business, finance, or agriculture had wanted it
to do so.

"The cold truth," he concluded, "is that the individualist
creed of everybody for himself and the devil take the hindmost
is principally responsible for the distress in which Western
civilization finds itself." Never fully applied in the past, this
creed is above all "not applicable in an age of technology,
science and rationalized economy." The task was "to discover
how much planning is necessary" and "by whom it can best
be done."[1]

Planning is an omnibus word, and has been given a different
content by any number of its advocates, practitioners, and
opponents. In those days, however, its functional meaning
was sufficiently clear to men who urged it, including Beard.
It was used to denote opposition to those who advocated letting
economic forces take their course. The conservative attitude

was a blind faith in the automatism of the economic order. The traditional economist argues that private enterprise, if left to work out its own troubles, will tend toward an equilibrium in which supply equals demand at a level of full employment. Intervention in "natural" economic processes, whether by private monopoly or by public fiat, only upsets the necessary process of adjustment in detail. The historical basis of this thesis is an implied belief that somehow competitive private enterprise is decreed by Nature and that Nature is beneficent. Acceptance of the thesis involves a conscientious abstention from the exercise of foresight, purpose, or endeavor on the part of the political community. Against this negative and quietistic philosophy those who regarded it as superstition then reacted by an affirmation of the power of intelligence, the ability to foresee, the obligation to act collectively when individuals were helpless. Planning was as good a word as any with which to combat the rejection of the possibility that man, using his mind in the common interest, might improve his material state by collective action. And the term planning seemed to go to the heart of the matter without involving the proponent in endless arguments about specific panaceas. It stated the concept, implied the method, but left open the choice of means.

It should be noted, however, that even when the heat of the debate centered about whether the national government should or should not intervene further to rescue the people from the worst depression in their history, Beard was not oblivious to the need for a more positive definition of planning. "How much?" and "By whom?" were his questions; they revealed that he thought of planning as instrumental and limited rather than as total, and that he was concerned about the competence and power of the prospective planners.

In the *Forum* of July, 1931, Beard risked a concrete suggestion which, whatever its defects, showed that in his mind the prime necessity was to set up administrative machinery that might make control of the whole economy possible. According to this "Five-Year Plan for America" each industrial group was to be organized as a unit by a holding company, which should have the status of a public utility, with limited profits. Syndicates were to include even agriculture and marketing. At the top there was to be a National Economic Council, representing the various industries. In order to clear the way for common action, the Sherman and Clayton Antitrust Acts were to be repealed. And in order to develop the policies that were to be executed, there was to be an expert Board of Strategy and Planning.

The emphasis of the suggestion was not upon the economic policies that ought to be followed—that is, the policies about prices, wages, investment, taxation, public spending, distribution of income, and the like. These were left largely without discussion, perhaps in the hope that when the experts got to work and the industrial authorities faced the necessity for decisions, the relevant questions would be asked and the possible answers to them would appear. Nor—strangely enough for Beard—was there discussion of the contests for power or the organization of political pressures, which must be expected in any effort to govern. The emphasis was rather on the American origins of planning, embodied in the growth of city and state planning and the technological development of industry.

This was the period of blueprint national plans—a spate of which appeared and were widely discussed. In 1932 Beard edited *America Faces the Future,* a symposium including his own plan and others that bore a family resemblance to it—those sponsored severally by Gerard Swope of General Electric, the United States Chamber of Commerce, the American Federation of Labor, and Franklin D. Roosevelt. In an appendix appeared the La Follette bill for a National Economic Council, which embraced the planning but eschewed the over-all corporate organization of industry. Beard himself in a chapter of comment somewhat elaborated his questions. Planning, he wrote, we had already, at least in half-grown stature. What we had to find out was "how much planning, by whom, under whose auspices, and to what ends?"[2]

These were pertinent queries, in view of the fact that blueprints of the sort under consideration were not unlike the design of the corporate state introduced by the Italian Fascists. Hitler had not yet come to power in Germany, but Beard had no admiration for the realities of totalitarian rule. One-party dictatorship, suppression of civil liberties, governmental bossing of labor organizations, a permanent war economy, he would have fought to the end of his days. He did not expect that the essence of American democracy would be altered by what seemed to him a logical next step, an effort to quell the economic storm. What we needed, it appeared, was an industrial constitution, and the discussion in which he was engaged could be regarded as a contribution to a new *Federalist,* in which the groundwork for orderly economic government might be prepared.

Unfortunately the emergency was great, and the preliminary thinking was far from adequate. What we got was not a constitution to outlive the century, but the National Industrial Recovery Act, hastily thrown together by a bewildered but strongly activated Congress, and soon destroyed by the Supreme Court, to the relief even of many of its sponsors.

On the labor side, the innovations of the NRA did seem to be in the line of growth; at least they have endured to the present. The NRA established for the first time federally enforced minimum wages and maximum standard hours. It put the power of the government behind the right of collective bargaining, and gave an impetus to a remarkable expansion of the trade union movement. Business, however, was not so ripe for collective management. There were many violators of the codes in the industries where competition was the most anarchic, and the loud talk of "cracking down" on "chiselers" by the flamboyant General Hugh Johnson was hardly sufficient to bring compliance. Codes that were observed, in the better disciplined industries, usually revealed a lack of intellectual grasp and industrial statesmanship on the part of private enterprise.

Under the guise of an effort to eliminate cutthroat competition and boost the general price level there emerged restriction of output in the good old monopolistic vein and a dampening of the recovery that had made rapid progress before the NRA took charge. Planning, in the sense of a well-conceived strategy in the interest of the whole economy, was conspicuously absent. Meanwhile the consumers' representatives, without organized support in the community, struggled in vain to make themselves heard. Something better might have come out of the eventual reorganization, which gave more power to the experts representing the government, but their chance was cut short by the Court.

In *The Open Door at Home,* done under the auspices of the Social Science Research Council, Beard outlined in 1934 the major policies that he thought planning should execute. He blasted the superstition that the United States had exportable surpluses that were forcing the nation into an imperial career, or that the domestic problem could be solved by any other outward looking prescription such as lower tariffs, foreign loans, armaments, internationalism, or the adoption of foreign ideologies like communism or fascism. We should rather, urged Beard, center our attention on achieving the good life within our borders.

His model seemed perhaps to be the early agricultural and handicraft community as nearly self-contained as possible. To parallel it under conditions of modern technology he proposed taking as the central aim a decent standard of life, with security. Family budgets could be translated into a national production program, somewhat, one gathers, along the lines of the recent study by the Twentieth Century Fund, *America's Needs and Resources* (1947). The means of executing this program were, however, left somewhat hazy, except that Beard followed Veblen in the belief that the price system obstructed technology. He was concerned with avoiding too much capital accumulation and obtaining a better distribution of purchasing power, though like others at the time he was not equipped to avoid the hazardous shoals of the overinvestment thesis. Roosevelt's cold shoulder to the London Economic Conference met with his approval; the book foreshadowed the later neutrality legislation and suggested a centralized authority to conduct foreign trade on a barter basis. Though Beard disliked government subsidies, he favored the NRA techniques, even including the concerted regulation of prices and production by business.

In *The Old Deal and the New* (1940) by Charles A. Beard and George H. E. Smith, Beard did not disavow his intellectual paternity of this kind of planning. The NRA, he declared even at this late date, had been a bold stroke in the direction of a planned economy. It was American in its origins. It had occupied a middle ground between laissez faire and a governmentally directed regime. It had offered an opportunity to business leaders to show what they could do in management of the nation's affairs. To be sure, they had not done well, but experience was lacking. Obviously Beard believed not that NRA was an unfortunate error to be eschewed henceforth, but that it was a clumsy forerunner of something that might be tried again under better auspices. And he pointed out the benefits from many of the other New Deal interventions.

None the less, Beard did not renew so specific a proposal. Perhaps it was because the time was not auspicious; perhaps it was because his attention was drawn to the danger of war. He wanted the American society to fulfill its own promise in its own way; he bitterly resented the diversion of efforts and the distortion of ends that must accompany a plunge into the international maelstrom. He foresaw clearly enough that war would bring the prosperity that faltering domestic reform had failed to induce; gaining prosperity through war or preparations for war seemed to him an easy and disastrous evasion of the internal problem. We could for a while escape the struggle to create economic order and justice at home by becoming a great military power and pursuing what seemed to him will-o'-the-wisps abroad, but the ultimate reckoning would be all the more severe. Long before Pearl Harbor he observed to me that just as Wilson had abandoned the New Freedom to embrace war in Europe, Roosevelt would desert the New Deal for war in Asia. Most isolationists were moved by what they thought was the American past; Beard was thinking of his hopes for the American future. Like many of his other admirers, I disagreed with him about the need to fight the Axis and the motives of Roosevelt in doing so, but I deplored no less than he the turning aside from essential internal adjustment. The war was to me a defense of the possibility to advance; nevertheless it was a strategic retreat.

In the early New Deal days, I had written a book *The Coming American Revolution* (1934), the main theme of which was that this country was in the process of a gradual and long change in institutions, which could be called revolutionary, but that there was little prospect of a catastrophe such as the Communists were expecting. Beard's comment was that I had overlooked the effects of a possible war. War would strengthen conservatives, retard reforms, and increase the likelihood of domestic violence. This may sound like the view of a Marxist, but Beard explicitly rejected Marx's economics and his dialectic utopian philosophy of history. Like many intellectual leaders of the time, he was continually urged by eager young friends, who had been influenced by the conjuncture of the depression and a growing Communist agitation, to accept what they thought were the revolutionary implications of his position. He reread Marx, and thereafter made a point in his conversation of refuting Marxist principles.

In particular he rejected economic determinism. This was not at all what he meant by the connection between economics and politics. Political views were indeed affected by economic interests, but for that very reason a democratic state could express the economic interest of the people by political means. Man was not in the grip of a predetermined historical process; he could mold history, and it was the special genius of America to do so. The Communists almost gleefully predicted "imperialist war" leading to revolution and the dictatorship of the proletariat; Beard deplored war, tried to prevent it, abhorred dictatorship of any sort, and saw nothing inevitable about it.   Though he was a sympathetic student of the labor movement and supported many of the aspirations of the industrial workers, he never swallowed the perilous abstraction of an infallible and apotheosized proletariat.

In a new chapter added to a 1945 reprinting of an old series of lectures published under the title, *The Economic Basis of Politics,* Beard returned to his main thesis.   Incidentally he refuted the curious inversion of history made by Hayek in *The Road to Serfdom* (1944) that planning led to fascism rather than that dictators used planning for their own purposes.   Planning, Beard maintained, can serve democracy just as it can serve a war economy, a communist regime in Russia, or a Hitler in Germany.   Democratic planning cannot be identified with the decrees of a totalitarian order.   Hayek and his followers are as deterministic in their own way as the Marxists in theirs.   It is a falsification of history to assert that each resort to governmental intervention leads inevitably to another and that the foreordained end of this course is slavery.

What then, is the nature of democratic planning? Here Beard avoided organizational blueprints and rather described method in general terms.   Political government will employ systematic knowledge of economic institutions, Beard maintained.   It will make forecasts, reach informed judgments, and on this basis it will make decisions, take action, and submit the outcome to the test of human experience.   This is essentially a description of what is now done by the Federal Reserve Board and other governmental agencies.   It is what is aimed at by the Employment Act of 1946 and the Council of Economic Advisers, which that law established.

In the years since the agitation for national economic planning sprang forth during the depression as a protest against inaction, it has become apparent that what was most lacking at the time was a sufficient scientific basis for the guidance of economic decisions.   We might bring together councils, we might pass laws and adopt regulations. We might even have set up an expert strategic planning agency—though Roosevelt, who believed in improvisation rather than systematic analysis, did not use what planning agencies he had for the purpose of determining co-ordinated policy. But nobody could be assured by anything except his own inner light what was really the matter and how a given system of policies might improve the situation. Still less was there any consensus on the various policies proposed or the primary objectives to be sought. Was the remedy a rising price level? Was this to be achieved by business agreement, or by change in the gold value of the dollar, or by banking policy, or by fiscal policy? Or was a better internal adjustment among prices and incomes the chief desideratum? And what measures were appropriate for this purpose? Was it, for instance, proper to seek an increase of agricultural prices by restriction of output? These and other puzzles were debated, but there was no adequate conceptual framework in which to place them. The maze of theoretical difficulties was scarcely even visualized by those in positions of governmental or industrial power, who would have had to carry out any co-ordinated planning.

There is, after all, a science of economics, or at worst a vacuum where such a science ought to be. This science must be used by government, just as political science must be used, but it is not an intrinsic attribute of legislators or administrators, and it is not identical with politics. Beard's revulsion was against the type of economic theory that is little but a system of apologetics for a posited freedom of private business from governmental interference, a deductive elaboration of how and why a market economy would solve all public problems without intending to do so or being able to seek that goal by design. This theory had been under effective attack; the institutionalists had shown that it does not work as prescribed, and the depression had supplied stunning confirmation of their view. They were not yet ready, however, to substitute for it a valid theoretical system better grounded in experience. Yet the economist who wants to plan must know more than that the classical hypotheses are inadequate; he must be prepared to say what will follow from what is done, how the intricate economic network is actually affected by specific types of intervention. Beard was not an expert in this field, and he left it almost alone. Doubtless he assumed that once the function was assigned, the necessary techniques would be developed, as did others at the time. Yet he never seemed to accept the need for, or the possibility of, a valid social science except as one might be hammered out intuitively in the heat of action.

A new economic science is indeed beginning to take form, not altogether in direct response to public needs, since its basis has been the slow, careful accumulation and analysis of statistical measurements of economic forces that have been going on continuously in war and in peace, under conservative administrations as well as under progressive ones. It has been fertilized by the Keynes theories of employment and money, as well as by new studies of institutions. National income accounting, the empirical study of the business cycle, and other developments are supplying the planners with more reliable tools with which to work.

Little by little the focus of argument is being shifted, as understanding of the bases of policy is being achieved. While the economic stalwarts still attack the idea of planning and advocate sole reliance on automatic mechanisms, almost nobody takes their advice, while recurrent crises give rise to concerted action. The emphasis is no longer on the question whether we should plan. Nor is it on discussion of blueprints for planning machinery. Machinery can be improvised, altered, or abandoned readily as the occasion demands. The essence of the matter is not what combinations of initial letters one finds in a governmental directory. The emphasis now is upon arguments about what policies government should execute. The European Recovery Program—a continental, almost a world plan—is the result of one such argument. The Council of Economic Advisers, set up by Congress to develop policies for maintaining high employment, production, and purchasing power, has not often had its way in this country, but at least it makes a record of analysis and recommendation against which performance may and will be judged.

Beard's fight is being carried on, though not in the way he proposed. The long political struggle to maintain the general interest as distinguished from the particular is continuing as in the past, and with varying fortunes, but increasingly in terms of a viable concept of the national—and the international—economy. Planning for the common good becomes more feasible as the science that makes possible understanding of the economy gains bulk and texture—a requirement of which Beard was not sufficiently aware. The task is not peculiarly an American one, as Beard has supposed. But he was right that it has origins in the American past, and that progress in it is not alien to American talents. He himself did pioneer work in municipal planning in the second decade of the century. In the third and fourth decades he fought a spirited battle against the enemies of planning for the social good on a national scale, and helped to create faith that national planning was possible and salutary.

RICHARD HOFSTADTER

Charles Beard and the Constitution

IT IS NOW more than thirty-five years since the appearance of
Charles A. Beard's *An Economic Interpretation of the Constitution of the United States.*[1] The story of its reception and criticism is familiar;[2] a large part of its thesis has been absorbed
into the main body of American historical writing. Beard
himself has both defended it and expounded some of its limitations. While at first even informed and critical minds were
deeply shocked by its argument, they are shocked no longer,[3]
and although the book has not yet lost every vestige of its controversial urgency, it has entered calmly into history. It has
become less and less a book to argue over, and increasingly a
book that must be studied if we are to locate our own thinking
in the stream of intellectual events.

It is not my purpose in this essay to make another "evaluation" of the book—a task that can now be undertaken profitably
and without presumption only by someone who has done massive research in the period with which it deals. I am interested
rather in placing the ideas of the volume in their historical
context; in calling attention to some of its neglected method-

ological implications; in discussing a significant ambiguity in
its thought; and finally, in tracing the story of Beard's later
attitude toward the Constitution as a symptomatic fragment of
American intellectual history in the last three decades.

The most deeply rooted of the sources of Beard's economic
interpretation and emphasis on class conflict can be found far
back in American history. There had been a long tradition of
economic materialism and consciousness of class in American
political thought, deriving in good part from James Harrington
and embracing such writers as James Madison (to whom, of
course, Beard was especially indebted), John Adams, Daniel
Webster, John C. Calhoun, Orestes Brownson, and Richard
Hildreth. It would be claiming too much to impute equally
to all these writers a systematic espousal of the economic interpretation of history or of the other ideas that formed Beard's
early work; but no one thoroughly familiar with American
political writing could fail to find in them frequent marginal
suggestions of a kind that would point toward Beard's inquiry.
Such late nineteenth century writers as Alexander Johnston,
John Fiske, Woodrow Wilson, William Graham Sumner, and
Henry Jones Ford had seized upon such suggestions, and each
of them anticipated in some respect the thesis that we identify
with Beard.[4]

A second source of Beard's ideas, in the more immediate
background, was the Populist movement and the rise of western
self-consciousness. The Turner school of historical interpretation was, in a broad sense, the product of a revolt of the West
that found its political expression in Populism, its cultural
expression in the Chicago World's Fair of 1893, and its literary
manifesto in Hamlin Garland's *Crumbling Idols*. Garland de-
claimed against the provincialism and colonialism of eastern
writers and predicted that Chicago would replace Boston and
New York as the literary capital of the United States; Turner
argued: "The true point of view in the history of this nation
is not the Atlantic coast, it is the Great West." Populism and

Bryanism had thrown the clash of debtors and creditors, the antagonism of sections, into bold relief; projected backward into American history, western self-consciousness encouraged concentration on sectional struggles and the history of currency and fiscal policy.

When Beard began work on his book, the Turner school had already produced important monographs, among them William A. Schaper's *Sectionalism and Representation in South Carolina*[5] and Charles H. Ambler's *Sectionalism in Virginia*,[6] both of which contained data of importance to his thesis. But the most relevant product of Turner's seminar was Orin Libby's careful study of *The Geographical Distribution of the Vote of the Thirteen States on the Federal Constitution, 1787-8,* which appeared in 1894. In a preface to this work Turner pointed to the artificiality of state as opposed to sectional boundaries in the study of American history and complained that "the economic interpretation of our history has been neglected." Turner anticipated that a series of studies of "natural economic groupings" in American history would be invaluable in studying the political past.[7]

Libby's study, which Beard drew upon heavily, put much emphasis upon the debtor-creditor conflict under the Articles of Confederation. Libby found that the state system under the Articles had acted "as a shield for the debtor classes," that opposition to the Constitution was confined to the interior where "interests were agricultural as opposed to commercial, rural as opposed to urban," that a fundamental reason for calling the Constitutional Convention of 1787 was "a desire to provide for the public necessities a revenue adequate to the exigencies of the Union," and that the victory of the new Constitution was won "by the influence of those classes along the great highways of commerce . . . and wealth."[8]

The social thought of the Progressive era and the intellectual climate encouraged by muckraking constituted a third source of Beard's ideas. Many of the Progressive thinkers, carrying over the old Populist antinomy of the masses versus the classes, were disposed to apply it to the past. V. L. Parrington, whose outlook was shaped by Populism and Progressivism, later declared: "Considered historically perhaps the chief contribution of the Progressive movement to American political thought was its discovery of the essentially undemocratic nature of the federal constitution."[9]

The most important articulation of the Progressive spirit, in this respect, was a book with which Beard was quite familiar—J. Allen Smith's *The Spirit of American Government*—which discussed at length the philosophy behind the Constitution. "Democracy—government by the people, or directly responsible to them—was not the object which the framers of the American Constitution had in view, but the very thing which they wished to avoid," Smith argued. He saw in the document a compromise between the undemocratic aims of the framers and their need to produce a constitution that would be acceptable enough to be ratified. The Constitutional Convention, he concluded, was attended by many illustrious men with a genuine desire to further the welfare of the country as they understood it, but they represented "the wealthy and conservative classes, and had for the most part but little sympathy with the popular theory of government."[10] Although Smith's view of the Constitution anticipated some aspects of Beard's, it was far less circumstantial. Smith approached the Constitution essentially as a problem in political theory; he hinted at the economic base of the movement for the Constitution but made no attempt to elaborate upon it.

Changes in the social sciences also influenced Beard profoundly. The seminal thinkers of his generation, revolting against the formalistic approach of their predecessors,[11] were reaching out to allied disciplines with fresh enthusiasm and perceptivity. The historical method was gaining ground in law and economics. Advocates of sociological jurisprudence like Holmes and Pound were drawing upon a wide acquaintance with sociology, philosophy, and the history of law. Veblen was studying economic institutions as a sociologist, social psychologist, and historian of ideas. Dewey was elaborating an evolutionary and historical approach to philosophy and arguing for a cultural naturalism. The men of this generation felt themselves united by a common effort to tear through the veil of formalistic speculation—Veblen in his attack on abstract and deductive economics, Pound in his criticisms of static and formalized law, Brandeis in his fight to get the facts of life into the meditations of the Supreme Court, Dewey in his war against formal logic, and Beard in his assault on the juristic approach to the Constitution.

Beard was fully persuaded of the value of this effort to break down the barriers between disciplines. In his study of laws and constitutions he not only used economic and geographical methods then being developed by other historians like William E. Dodd and Frederick Jackson Turner, but also came to the writing of history with a conceptual framework much enriched by such legal and political theorists as Arthur F. Bentley, Frank J. Goodnow, Roscoe Pound, and others.[12] "We are coming to realize," he wrote in 1908, "that a science dealing with man has no special field of data all to itself, but is rather merely a way of looking at the same things—a view of a certain aspect of human action. The human being is not essentially different when he is depositing his ballot from what he is in the counting house or at the work bench. In the place of a 'natural' man, an 'economic' man, a 'religious' man or a 'political' man, we now observe the whole man participating in the work of government."[13]

The incongruity of old legal theory and the changing legal practice of the Progressive era compelled many thoughtful jurists to become aware—as Holmes had long been—of changes in the social foundations of law. There was a growing tendency to interpret the judicial process—and after it every other type of juristic event—in the light of the social and psychological forces that underlay it. As Roscoe Pound wrote in 1910, "Public thought and feeling have changed, and, whatever the law in the books, the law in action has changed with them." "The history of juristic thought tells us nothing unless we know the social forces that lay behind it."[14] The sociological movement in jurisprudence turned away from first principles and static generalizations to "pragmatism as a philosophy of law," making human situations, rather than logic, central.[15] Students of law were driven to the conclusion, as Frank J. Goodnow put it, that a kind of legal opportunism was more likely to be productive of social good than "adherence to general theories which are to be applied at all times." "This feeling," he continued, "which has influenced philosophy through the writings of the pragmatic school, has been strengthened by the theory of the economic interpretation of history, which of recent years has been received with so much favor."[16]

A comparable tendency, in political theory, was the drive to reduce theories of the nature of the state to clashes of concrete social interests rather than clashes of mutually inconsistent abstract dogmas. Beard was familiar with Arthur F. Bentley's *The Process of Government,* a vigorous book that traced all legal and political processes to struggles among interest groups. "Law," Bentley wrote, "is activity, just as government is. It is a group process, just as government is. It is a forming, a systematization, a struggle, an adaptation of group interests, just as government is." And everything that could be said about law could be said about constitutions, for "constitutions are but a special form of law."[17]

But if legal and constitutional ideas could be unmasked and reduced to interests and pressures, what would become of abstract juristic theories of the state? Plainly they would be supplanted by empirical inquiry into the origins and development of actual states, not as theoretical repositories of sovereignty but as administrative and coercive agencies, whose control was fought for by conflicting social groups. "How," Bentley asked, "can one be satisfied with a theory that comes down hard on the federal Constitution as primarily a great national ideal, in the very face of the struggles and quarrels of the constitutional convention for the maintenance of pressing social interests?"[18]

It is clear that liberals were formulating their own theory of the state, and that Beard's book was in part an attempt to document this theory out of American experience. The liberal theory occupied a middle ground between older formal theories which treated the state as the product of abstract doctrines and beliefs, and the Marxian theory which described it as the naked coercive instrument of the ruling class. To the liberals, as to the Marxists, the state was a coercive agency which expressed social and economic pressures; but the liberals differed from the Marxists in that they did not minimize the importance or possible efficacy of pressure upon the state by groups outside the ruling class. They were satisfied with the more pragmatic conclusion that the state in a parliamentary democracy offers a sort of fluctuating barometric reading that registers all the force brought to bear by various interest groups. "It would seem," wrote Beard, "that the real state is not the juristic state, but is that group of persons able to work together effectively for the accomplishment of their joint aims, and overcome all opposition on the particular point at issue at a particular period of time. . . . Changes in the form of the state have been caused primarily by the demand of groups for power, and in general these groups have coincided with economic classes which have arisen within the political society."[19]

Marxian socialism, although it had no prominent exponents in academic circles, was winning wider interest in the years after the turn of the century. Most Progressive writers ignored Marx's economic analysis of capitalism and his apocalyptic social predictions but absorbed and used his approach to history. Those later critics of Beard who thought to discredit his work by coupling his name with Marx's[20] were guilty of more than the obvious demagogy of attempting to refute an idea by invidious association; failing to understand the era in which his important early books had been written, they ignored the congeniality of the economic interpretation of history to the Progressive mind. In 1902 E. R. A. Seligman, soon to be Beard's colleague at Columbia, published a sensible and popular little book, *The Economic Interpretation of History*, in which he observed: "Wherever we turn in the maze of recent historical investigation, we are confronted by the overwhelming import-ance attached by the younger and abler scholars to the economic factor in political and social progress."[21] Seligman favored a qualified version of the economic interpretation of history (described by Beard eleven years later as being "as nearly axiomatic as any proposition in social science can be"[22]), which he predicted would in the future "occupy an honored place in the record of mental development and scientific progress."[23]

Some socialist writers had produced works that Beard thought "deserved study,"[24] among which he named A. M. Simons' *Social Forces in American History* and Gustavus Myers' *History of Great American Fortunes* and *History of the Supreme Court*. Simons' book contained a crude but clear anticipation of Beard's thesis. "The constitutional convention," he asserted, "was little more than a committee of the merchants, manufac-turers, bankers, and planters, met to arrange a government that would promote their interests."[25]

It is clear that by 1913 the time was ripe for a thorough pres-entation of the new thesis on the American Constitution.[26] What was still needed was a student of politics and history pos-sessing a bold and free mind, capable of applying systematically the insights of current critical thought, who could turn up fresh data and combine them with a general history of the con-stitutional period. Beard discovered just such a body of data when he unearthed Treasury Department records that had lain unused for well over a century.

The subject of method can be dealt with briefly in passing. Previous discussion of Beard's book has been purely substan-tive; both the general economic interpretation of history and Beard's specific version of the struggle over the Constitution have been endlessly debated, but no attention has been given to one of the work's greatest achievements. Methodologically it is a triumph of systematic intelligence. Historical method in America has never taken adequate notice of Beard's technique of illuminating a historical movement or event through a composite, quantitative account of the economic and social backgrounds of the personnel involved in it.

What Beard was trying to do in his famous chapter on the economic backgrounds and fiscal holdings of the members of the Convention was to locate their social position as a group, and from this add to our understanding of the adoption of the Constitution as it related to the class structure of late eighteenth century America. He collected information not only on the holdings of the framers in the public debt, but also on many other relevant factors in their background: the occupations and economic interests of their fathers, their own educations, professions, landholdings, political offices, business interests, marital connections, and social status. He was using in 1913 a somewhat rudimentary form of the systematic career-line study, which political scientists and sociologists have begun to use only recently and which American historians have hardly used at all.[27]

Beard's method was unrefined in details, but the broad beginning he made was in itself remarkable. Had his technique been seized upon by his own generation and refined and applied systematically to the major events and movements in American history, the resulting contribution to historical understanding would have been immense. Historical writing today—and I refer here not to the narrative art but to the great body of monographic investigation whose tradition is that of the social "sciences"—is still wanting in method, in no small part because of a curious failure to explore the vistas opened by Beard forty years ago.

The undercurrent of ambiguity in Beard's book is worth dwelling upon at some length, not for the sake of a textual criticism of the volume, but because it may enlarge our understanding of the Progressive mind. This ambiguity is most evident in Beard's long chapter on the economic position of the founding fathers, which stimulated more heated criticism than

any other part of his book. Was he saying that the fathers
framed the Constitution because they expected to profit by it?
Or was he merely saying that the ways in which the fathers made
their profits predisposed them to look at political and constitutional issues from a certain perspective? Was he, as Max Lerner
has asserted, "making the economic interpretation theory of
men's motives rather than of men's ideas"?[28] Or was he simply
trying to show that property holdings were broadly relevant to
constitutional and political attitudes?

It was possible to argue either position from the text of the
volume itself. At one point Beard asserted: "The overwhelming majority of members, at least five-sixths, were **immediately,**
directly, and personally interested in the outcome of their labors
at Philadelphia, and were to a greater or lesser extent economic
beneficiaries from the adoption of the Constitution."[29] At another point he stated: "The Constitution was essentially an
economic document."[30]

But there were also passages in which he carefully expressed
a much larger view of the matter (passages which his critics too
frequently chose to ignore). At the outset of his examination
of the economic holdings of the fathers, he wrote: "The purpose of such an inquiry is not, of course, to show that the Constitution was made for the personal benefit of the Convention.
Far from it. . . . The only point here considered is: Did they
represent distinct groups whose economic interests they understood and felt in concrete, definite form through their own personal experience with identical property rights, or were they
working merely under the guidance of abstract principles of
political science?"[31] Again, in summarizing his conclusions at
the close of the chapter, he did not declare that the fathers
were working to make money for themselves, but simply that
they were not altogether "disinterested"; that they "knew
through their personal experiences in economic affairs the precise results which the new government that they were setting
up was designed to attain. As a group of doctrinaires, like the
Frankfort Assembly of 1848, they would have failed miserably;

but as practical men they were able to build the new government upon the only foundations which could be stable: fundamental economic interests."[32] These passages were undoubtedly entitled to more respectful attention than many critics gave them.

If one were primarily concerned to present a lawyer's case for the book, one could rest it upon these explicit delineations of purpose, arguing that they, rather than any incidental overstatement, should govern the interpretation of the volume. But the presence of the ambiguity goes deeper than this; it is built into the very structure of Beard's research. If he had been primarily interested in the formation of the founding fathers' ideas on politics, taking the perspective of their class only as a clue, why was his chapter on their political ideas such a literal-minded compound of scattered quotations from the debates in the Convention? Why was the chapter on the property holdings and economic position of the fathers so carefully worked out in the context of the economic and political situation of the Confederation, while the formation of the fathers' ideas on democracy was ignored and the content of these ideas retailed without any effort to place them in the framework of eighteenth century thought? As between ideas and interests, it is interests that have the foreground in this volume.

Behind this ambiguity in statement, then, lay a real ambiguity in thought; and behind the ambiguity in thought lay a certain dualism in Beard's position. Something, no doubt, can be attributed to the fact that when revisionist theses appear in the writing of history, they are usually overstated. Something, too, can be attributed to the fact that Beard was a scholar who naturally wished to exploit to the full an enterprising and resourceful discovery among old Treasury Department records. But what was it in the beginning that led him to unearth these dusty records, untouched for more than a century? What was it that made him feel closer to "reality" among old 6 per cent securities than in the volumes of eighteenth century political speculation? The answer must be found in the fact that Beard was not simply a scholar; he was, and remained his life long, a publicist with an urgent interest in the intellectual and political milieu in which he lived. As a young man, in both England and the United States, he had shown himself in sympathy with popular causes and with the current impulse toward social criticism.[33] He could hardly fail to absorb the style of thought of the Populist-Progressive-muckraking era; the limitations, as well as the best insights of that style of thought, left their impress upon his book.

As the most enlightened scholars and journalists of that period saw it, selfish interests had made use of the government to serve private ends, and in so doing had subverted democracy. The problem of journalism and scholarship was to find out how they had done this, to expose the ideas that drew a cloak of protection about them, and to show how their illicit activities had rendered false the genteel picture of society drawn in conventional economics, conventional political science, and conventional fiction. The iconoclasm of the period was concerned with the motives and activities of the rich and established classes. For the most part, it failed to go far in showing how the spirit of gain that had been so rampant in America had extended to the Progressive elements themselves, to the little businessmen and farmers whose discontents gave the movement its vital surge.[34]

This was, then, an extroverted not an introspective movement. It was much more concerned with examining and destroying the declining ideas of an earlier age and a discredited order than in evaluating its own. But skill in dealing with the human context of ideas is in large part a by-product of self-evaluation, in which alone the full personal urgency and the psychological dialectic of ideas can be felt. The highest pitch of understanding of the formation of ideas is not likely to emerge in a climate of opinion where intense self-examination has not yet begun. To use Karl Mannheim's terminology, the best thought of the Progressive era was in a transitional state between the theory of ideology and the sociology of knowledge, and in any such age of transition a certain fruitful ambiguity of thought is to be expected. Before one could go far in examining *how* ideas and interests were related, the point had to be established, and established against considerable resistance, that they were so intimately and universally related that no phase of political life could be exempted from the principle—that a sacred symbol like the Constitution could, at least in this respect, be treated in the same light as a railway franchise.

The common preoccupation of the Progressive political critics, the muckrakers, and the early realistic and naturalistic novelists was the search for "reality." But what, to them, *was* reality? At bottom, I think, it had three characteristics: It was rough and sordid; it was hidden, neglected, and, so to speak, off-stage; and it was essentially a stream of external and material events, of which psychic events were a kind of pale reflex.[35] Reality was the bribe, the rebate, the bought franchise, the sale of adulterated food. It was what one found in *The Jungle, The Octopus, Wealth versus Commonwealth,* or *The Shame of the Cities.* The imagination of the era was more fundamentally conditioned by reporters and literary journalists than we usually recognize, and its characteristic goal was "the inside story." That is why Beard's book, when it appeared, was so quickly seen to fit into the political context of the twentieth century. It may also help to explain why Beard's rather casual treatment of the political ideas of the founding fathers seemed so much more representative of current political argument than of the intellectual climate of the late eighteenth century.

With the coming of World War I and the passing of the Progressive enthusiasm, the American intellectual climate changed drastically. For different reasons, however, the critical views that had become identified with Beard's work continued to be relevant and appealing to a large public. The Progressives had criticized the American past because they hoped that in the future America could be remade; the intellectuals of the twenties continued to criticize because they needed to explain to themselves why they had lost this hope. Progressivism had extended muckraking backward into the past in order to purify the present; the alienated mood of the twenties accepted muckraking simply because America seemed so wonderfully and extravagantly vulnerable. At a time when such an unsparingly iconoclastic book as W. E. Woodward's study of George Washington—an ideal model of an attack upon the father-image—was being widely read, Beard's critical view of the Constitution period was still appreciated. The two major historical works of the twenties, the Beards' *Rise of American Civilization* and Parrington's *Main Currents in American Thought,* were ideological residues of the Progressive era, and in both Beard's thesis about the Constitution took a central place.

The growth of a still different intellectual temper in the period of the Great Depression and the New Deal found the Beard-Parrington synthesis, at the zenith of its appeal, a pervasive expression of the American liberal mind. The class struggle was rediscovered; the vigorous liberal outlook of the Beard-Parrington synthesis and its use of the economic interpretation of history were congenial to the day of popular-front Marxism and sociological literary criticism. In 1938 when the editors of the *New Republic* conducted a symposium on "Books That Changed Our Minds" and asked a number of American liberal intellectuals to suggest titles that ought to be discussed, the two most frequently mentioned titles were Beard's *An Economic Interpretation of the Constitution* and Veblen's *Theory of the Leisure Class,* followed by works of Spengler, Freud, Henry Adams, John Dewey, and Parrington. Harold J. Laski wrote that the works of Beard and Parrington had "opened windows for me into the significance of the American tradition as no other books since Tocqueville."[36]

In 1935, when Beard's book was republished with a new introduction, he naturally felt that it had met the test of time. He pointed out that readers had been warned in advance of its theoretical bias and its emphasis, that its very title had suggested its limits, and that no pretension to completeness of interpretation had been made. He denied that he had ever been committed to "economic determinism," and added, in a curiously casual but sweeping concession to relativism, that his book did not "explain" the Constitution or "exclude other explanations deemed more satisfactory to the explainers." Praising the founding fathers for their profound insight into political realities, he urged that they be emulated in their effort to ask, whenever theories of national power or state rights are propounded, what interests lie behind them and to whose advantage change or stability would operate. "By refusing to do this we become victims of history—clay in the hands of its makers." In December, 1937, at a meeting of the American Historical Association celebrating the sesquicentennial anniversary of the Constitution, Beard once again repudiated the notion that "economic considerations determine or explain all history," but argued the case for a realistic approach to constitutional ideas. The next task of constitutional scholarship, he suggested, would be to treat the constitutional attitudes of both interest groups and historians as problems in the sociology of knowledge.[37]

However, the intellectual milieu was already changing, and on this occasion Beard's view of the Constitution changed with it. The rise of fascism abroad had already caused Americans to look more and more favorably on their own political institutions, and the Nazi-Soviet pact delivered a stunning blow to Marxism. The rise of the New Deal at home had revived interest in reform, and by making the state a patron not merely of the disinherited classes but also of many artists and writers, had helped to foster a literary and intellectual nationalism that was raised to a still higher pitch during World War II. As the ugly picture of the United States of the twenties faded from view and the far uglier outlines of the twentieth century world became painfully clear, the American past took on an increasingly roseate light. The re-embracement of America that followed became as intense as the earlier vogue of criticism and expatriation. Van Wyck Brooks, whose *America's Coming of*

Age (1915) had struck the dominant note of the disillusionment of the twenties, now turned to the sugary cycle that began
with *The Flowering of New England;* John Dos Passos turned
from *U. S. A.* to *The Ground We Stand On;* Sinclair Lewis from
Babbitt and *Main Street* to *The Prodigal Parents.* Even H. L.
Mencken in his autobiographical volumes struck a note of
sentiment and nostalgia.[38] The fact that Beard, at the moment
of growing international consciousness, moved toward a more
intense isolationism has obscured the essential conformity of
his heightened nationalism with the main trend of the early
forties.   When the defense of the United States, as he understood it, became his primary concern, his vision of the American past softened perceptibly.

Writing under the shadow of militarism and dictatorship,
Beard became increasingly preoccupied with the task of preserving a form of government that clung to civilian control and
decentralized authority. As his original view of the Constitution
had taken shape in an age of domestic conflict, his final view
was fashioned in an age of world conflict.[39] The struggle of
classes seemed less important; the process by which constitutionalism could be preserved more vital. *The Republic,* which
appeared in 1943 as the nation was preparing for the final effort
of the war, reflected his essential satisfaction with the American
form of constitutionalism, which he attractively defined as "the
civilian way of living together in the Republic." Exploring the
historical merits of the American political system, Beard put
much weight upon its effectuality in preventing undue concentration of political power and dominance by the military.
Considerations not important to him in either edition of *An
Economic Interpretation of the Constitution* now seemed to
demand a material restatement of the political outlook and
aspirations of the framers. "Leaders among the framers of the
Constitution," Beard observed, "regarded the resort to Constitutional government instead of a military dictatorship as their
greatest triumph.   In my opinion they were entitled to view
their achievement that way."[40]

At first, Beard explained, he had paid scant attention to evidences of a movement for military dictatorship in the years before the drafting of the Constitution, but as time went on he had found evidences of its importance accumulating in his files. This brought him to "a somewhat different view of the movement for the Constitution." In 1943 he wrote: "One of the interpretations now generally held is that the Constitution was the outcome of a conflict between radical or agrarian forces on the one side and the forces of conservative or capitalistic reaction on the other. That conflict was undoubtedly raging, and the advocates of the Constitution were involved in it. But I am of the opinion that there were three parties to the struggle. Besides the radicals and the conservatives there was an influential group on the extreme right of the conservatives—a group that was ripe and ready for a resort to the sword. . . . Had the movement for forming a new Constitution by peaceful processes failed, there is no doubt in my mind that the men of the sword would have made a desperate effort to set up a dictatorship by arms."[41] Thus the Constitution appeared not merely as a victory of conservative republicanism over democracy but also of republicanism over military dictatorship—a pertinent theme in 1943.

The best measure of the change from Beard's original view of the making of the Constitution to his later view may be had by comparing the Beards' chapter on the subject in *The Rise of American Civilization* (1927) with that in their *Basic History of the United States* (1944). The two narratives have a great deal in common, but there are significant omissions in the second account and entirely different verbal formulations. The change in tone is epitomized in the titles; in the first book the account of the struggle over the Constitution is called "Populism and Reaction," in the second, "Constitutional Government for the United States." In the first the authors speak of the political purpose of the framers of the Constitution in erecting a system of checks and balances as "dissolving the energy of the democratic majority." In the second, checks and balances are described as preventing "the accumulation of despotic power in any hands, even in the hands of the people who had the right to vote in elections."

The first, in summarizing the political attitudes of the founding fathers, says: "Almost unanimous was the opinion that democracy was a dangerous thing . . . to be given as little voice as possible in the new system." The second describes balanced government as one which would allow "the persistent will of the majority" to prevail; "yet at no time could the 'snap judgment' of a popular majority prevail in all departments of the federal government." The first observes that "More than half the delegates in attendance were either investors or speculators in the public securities which were to be buoyed up by the new Constitution. All knew by experience the relation of property to government." The second characterizes the Convention personnel as a conservative body of "merchants, lawyers, and planters," but refrains from mentioning public security holdings. The first argues that the division of the voters in the ratification of the Constitution ran along economic lines. The second indicates that "a tempest of public debate" raged over the merits of the document, but labels its critics in general terms as "radicals" and "friends of liberty," and characterizes its proponents only as "able defenders." The first closes with an exposition of the economic interpretation of politics and group struggle expressed by Madison in the *Federalist,* Number 10. The second drops Madison and closes with the observation that, "without drawing the sword in civil war, without shedding a drop of blood, a new plan of government had been proposed, framed, discussed, and adopted."[42]

WALTON HAMILTON

Fragments from the Politics

. . . A SYMPTOM, but not a mere symptom.* It is true, of
course, that a loyalty test has little, if anything, to do with real
loyalty. Its imposition is itself a symptom of "the sickness of
an acquisitive society." The significant thing is that a question
should be overt that in a healthy society would never be raised.
A protest so insistent that it cannot be confined within the
bounds of the process of free discussion and breaks into open
political revolt is a symptom of an unhealthy state of the nation.
But, once officially and insistently raised, it makes its way into
the intellectual climate and thus becomes dangerous by assuming a causal role. The malady lies far beyond the reach . . .

. . . a word of compelling force, and little concrete meaning.
Standing alone loyalty is a word at large. To signify, it must
be set down as "loyalty to what." All of us have a number of
loyalties; and try as we may, they torment us by getting into
conflict. To the rational man, there is no escape from a scheme
of priorities among loyalties; and even this will not stay put,

* This manuscript, or rather fragments of the manuscript that appear here,
by a strange chance fell into my possession. The story of how I came by it is too

for rank among them must vary in terms of the situation that presents the problem. And, even for the irrational man, there is no escape from the priorities; he seems to escape only because he lacks the intellectual integrity to keep the scheme put. In the old days of test oaths, the custodians of other men's beliefs were able sharply to define the orthodoxy from which they would tolerate no departure. They might have a "short way" with the heretic; but they were specific about his heresy. We have produced a modern version of an up-to-date cruelty by asking vaguely, or not at all, to what . . .

. . . not to the administration; for with us criticism has always been regarded as the most wholesome of procedures, and nothing is more American than "to vote the rascals out of office." And certainly not to the government; for it is the most respectable of doctrines that the government is the instrument of the general welfare, and that "we the people" have a right—and a duty—to change it when it flunks its job. To the country, maybe—but, with a diligent regard to the obligations we bear to other countries. And this includes the need, so far as our own conduct will allow, of remaining at peace with them. From earliest days the test of love of country is a burning desire to make it a better country. It cannot be loyalty to our economic system, for the national economy under which we live was

long to be told here even if this were the proper place. The manuscript bears every mark of recent vintage; but what accidents befell to reduce it to its current state I cannot tell. Three things, however, stand out clearly: First, although the title has not survived, the internal evidence makes it clear that the fragments are from The Politics; second, the surviving parts are a mere fraction of a far larger whole; and third, the manuscript is obviously a first draft. The author would doubtless on revision have sharpened phrases, made meaning more precise, and straightened out the lines of argument. A number of passages would also have received the benefit of second thought. The rather abrupt breaks have worried me, as well as the incomplete sentences here and there. It was my intention, had Providence been more considerate of the affection of the rest of us, to serve some interrogatories upon Charlie Beard. But since his guidance is no longer to be had, the editor concurs with me that the manuscript, fragmentary as it is, should be published exactly as it has survived. This is not out of reverence to Beard's memory—for reverence is the last thing he would want—but because any tampering or tinkering with the word as here written would be speculative; and speculation is a game which every reader should be permitted to play.—WALTON HAMILTON unknown to the framers of the Constitution and is largely a post–Civil War, even a twentieth century, creation. In strict and American terms, the test of disloyalty is taking up arms against the United States or giving aid and comfort to its enemies. But so historically sound a definition of loyalty would never . . .

. . . setting up weights and measures for opinion. The freedom of the mind to think daring thoughts, to form images of that which has never been, yet may well be, is the most important of our national assets. For the feat of mind that frees from an ancient bondage, that discovers in inert stuff resources long ago locked up there, that invents techniques by which we can form a more perfect union, there can be no standards. In the late Middle Ages rigidly formulated criteria of belief gave or denied access to the sacrament and Christian burial. A while ago, test oaths were predicated upon clearly enunciated articles of faith. In our age of enlightenment . . .

. . . confusion of words. Under the pretense of giving us security, they employ a test called loyalty to take from us our freedoms. It is obvious that "security" and "loyalty" are not plain words that carry their own meaning, but rather crude terms of art. Security has little to do with making the country strong or stripping of their strength those who would attack it. As our thoughtful military men are well aware, 95 per cent of all the know-how with which a war is fought comes from the fund of common knowledge. The field of legitimate secrecy, confined largely to war plans and "miracle weapons," is amazingly small. The policy of holding knowledge of a new art or process under tight control may easily defeat its purpose. Science and the useful arts are not advanced by human beings working in isolation. To exclude from general use cuts off the process of experimentation. Our military men are strong on security, but weak upon what it is that they wish to make secure. Among us security has no concrete reference. It is in kind like a grand seal that confers power upon its possessor and as occasion . . .

. . . like other symbols of government. There is always an urge, even in the most popular government, towards a display of irresponsible authority. Among persons in power there are always officials who love to shield their acts alike against publicity and review. Such individuals seek constantly for a screen, blessed with a sanction, behind which they can operate. A war, or even an emergency, is likely to provide opportunity for putting such sanctions into play. Anyone experienced in government is aware of a host of papers that travel from desk to desk, bearing designations running from "confidential" to "top secret." The great bulk of such miscellany, save that it confers a pseudo importance upon those who handle it, might just as well be published to the world. A person who for fifteen years has occupied strategic positions in the federal government reports that although he has handled hundreds of documents so marked, he has still to encounter one that needs to be kept secret. Its effect is to create a host of insular offices within . . .

. . . the most effective of them. But, to be realistic, the matter needs to be put in terms of procedure. The question is not whether in fact, a given act or thing imposes a hazard to security. It is rather what officials of government are vested with the right of invoking "security" at their own pleasure to smear a person, to veto an action, or to brand an organization. For the power to invoke security is in itself an immunity from having to shape official conduct to conform to the requirements of due process. In a republic the rule should be that no official or department should be allowed to invoke security in behalf of its own activities; for no person should be allowed to impress his own work with the sanction of irresponsibility.

. . . a peacetime successor to "the war effort." The use of the term "war effort" to secure to the privileged immunity to the law is recent history. A moratorium was granted to big business from the antitrust suits instituted by the Department of Justice. The argument was that corporate executives, consecrated to the national defense, must not be harassed while we

were at the enemies' gates. Yet no such indulgence was given
to little business; and the war period remained an open season
during which the same executives were not too occupied with
national defense to continue annoying the lesser brethren
in their trades with a vast array of lawsuits.

A single instance, typical of its kind, will reveal the easy
transition from war to peace. As the war effort went forward,
the question arose as to the proper payment to the railroads
for the carriage of military supplies. The War Department
contrived its own procedure for the solution of the problem.
In order that the decision should be thoroughly informed, it
called in a group of railroad executives. Half the group was
told that it represented the carriers. The other half was put
into uniforms and told it represented the government. The
two groups were then told to bargain with each other. It
chanced that the Undersecretary of War fell a little short of
omniscience in dividing the executives into two groups. For,
as destiny would have it, all the good horse traders turned up
in the group representing the railroads. The result was not
only that a level of rates was fixed decidedly higher than that
set by the Interstate Commerce Commission. In addition the
schedules were fixed in oblivion, by the two groups, of the
federal statutes governing the subject.

Since the coming of peace the Department of Justice has
been insistent upon a re-collection of the overcharge. In answer
to an inquiry of a United States senator, a ranking official has
written that he would make diligent inquiry as to whether the
finances of the railroads are in good enough condition to allow
them to make the refund . . . prepared by the Department
of Justice. But the War Department has objected to the filing
of the suit on the ground that it is a hazard to national security.
In like manner . . .

[The next fragment is torn somewhat deeply at the left. But
the duty of the editor is clearly to present what has survived,
rather than to attempt to reconstruct.]

. . . carry on in peace as if we were still at war. Men do not easily . . . by a renaissance of the old mercantile doctrine that a peace is a truce be . . . enables officials, by saying the proper incantations, to carrying on in irrespon- . . . sion of the symbol "war effort" into "national security" was a brilliant inven- . . . would have served nobly Richelieu or Talleyrand in days when war was a marginal . . . are fought with economies as well as armaments, it is nothing short . . . no area of the industrial system, however humble, is beyond . . . to give to the military a primacy among agencies of . . . although co-ordinate in rank, to exercise a veto power over other depart . . . in fact, an authority never set up by law to grant immunities from the obligation to obey . . . increase in number of these islands of absolute power within the federal estab . . . ating apart from and in defiance of our system of representa-tive . . . confuses and corrupts the institution we love to call the democratic process. The voice of . . . under such a usurpa-tion of power, the *vox ex machina* an extension . . . has al-ready made the writings of Bagehot and of Bryce fictional . . . commonwealth . . . the very nature of the American federal system as molded by such influences, is revealed in . . . and as is . . .

. . . is the bother, the inevitable bother, with every resort to war. In its nature war is an instrument. Its task is to serve the ends of statecraft, not to create objectives of its own. Yet, if history teaches anything, it makes it clear that war is the most unruly among all the instruments of national policy. Once there is resort to arms, the "winning of the war" becomes an all consuming purpose, and the reasons that compelled arbitra-ment on the field of battle move into the background or are even driven to the sidelines. When in Stuart times the Parlia-ment, in its quarrel with the King . . .

. . . to go back to these ancient examples. In World War II, there was a repetition of an often written chapter in history. The objective was clear—for the second time to make the world safe for democracy. But, even before the ink was dry on the declaration of war, the objective was being compromised. The military moved into a position of authority; and, since the administration believed that it could not fight upon two fronts at once, a truce was effected with the lords of the national economy. The result was a working arrangement between the war lords and big business. The theory—it was never tested—was that because war supplies must be had fast and in quantity, orders must go to the large corporations. A small number of companies, which in general were permitted to write their own tickets, secured 90 per cent of the orders. Small concerns were brought in only as subcontractors of the huge corporations. Here, too, the big fellows dictated the terms, and the relationship was feudal in character . . . fact, in winning a chance for the democratic process abroad, the war was carried on in such a way as seriously to compromise the operation of democracy at home.

. . . agency after agency, the high command had little sympathy with the aspirations of the people. The very group that repeatedly the voters had rejected at the polls held the strategic posts. The War Production Board can most exactly be defined as a House of Delegates from American industry. Although officials from within fought against it, the whole trend of official events was toward the concentration of economic wealth and power. The fortunes of small business entrusted to . . .

. . . did no more than accelerate and make explicit a situation in the body politic that had long been in the making. Quite a while ago Arthur T. Hadley, then President of Yale, elaborated the thesis that the real division of power in the government is between the people who go to the polls and the owners of property who possess other channels through which to assert their power. It wasn't a novel thesis; James Madison had argued to the same effect and in the framing of the Constitution had sought such a balance of interests within the commonwealth as to relieve the political process of a stress and strain not to be borne. The balance of interest was intended to make orderly the operation of the political process and to

provide a buffer against revolution. The machinery of government, even though it was contrived by his celestial omniscience
itself, would be of no avail, unless within the commonwealth
the several interests . . .

. . . the effect of the pretense either that such interests do
not exist or that in the politics they do not signify. The result
is the creation of the antithesis recognized by Hadley and Madison. We have moved steadily toward universal suffrage; and,
even though no more than half of us are desirous of exercising
our right, the voice of the people is more articulate than ever
before. Yet, somewhere between its expression at the polls and
its emergence in government-in-action, that voice becomes that
of an alien. The people insistently demand housing, personal
opportunity, the maintenance of purchasing power, a relaxation
of the insistent pressure of higher prices upon income. Yet
measures designed to serve these worthy ends somehow manage . . .

. . . nonconductor of the public will. For, the will of the
people must find its expression within the enveloping ways of
thought; and, where the climate of opinion is itself so largely
a creation of the small group that commands the press, the
movies, and the radio, popular political demand can hardly be
transmitted in its purity . . . beats somewhat uncertainly upon
the ordinary senator or congressman. He is a far from inert
instrument for its expression. He is usually not exactly insensi-
tive to the interests—outside his state or district as well as inside—that contribute to his campaign fund. If he comes from
a state or district safe for his party, he enjoys a large freedom
from his voters. The well-fleeced interest has its megaphone,
and he may mistake the voice of the few for the voice of the
multitude. He is not indifferent to the imperatives of a rising standard of life and of his own career. In a pecuniary
culture . . .

. . . no defined channel of articulate expression. As a result
these special interests impose their pressures wherever they can
and by whatever means promise to be effective. The lack of
an appointed place for them within the political order, and the

failure to provide avenues of expression, means that a pressure, left uncontrolled and too strong to be subdued, corrupts the whole process of representative government. Its *sub rosa* expression means that it is never clearly stated; that the public is told only what the interests desire to tell them; and that decisions of the utmost importance in the operation of the national economy are habitually made without ever being subjected to that critical scrutiny which is . . . Such a dualism . . .

. . . enough. But as with the growth of the nation the responsibilities of government increase, this lack of balance within the republic becomes doubly dangerous. The affairs of state can no longer be carried on by the Executive and his Secretaries, in response to the decrees of the Congress. A host of matters, of the most varied kinds, has come to demand the continuous oversight of the government. This can be given only by a series of administrative agencies with special competence for the several tasks that have to be performed. The high commands of these agencies—Agriculture, Commerce, ICC, SSA, FCC, CAB, and what not—are not elected by the people. In general they are appointed by the President with the advice and consent of the Senate. As has been shown, the democratic process does not carry the will of the people in its purity. The work of these agencies is of too technical a character to be subjected to a popular referendum. Nor can the people approve, amend, or veto an administrative policy whose formulation is implicit in a continuous series of everyday decisions. The operation of the administrative agency lies a step beyond, or even outside of, the reach of representative government. Its very indirection exposes . . .

. . . ever intended that it should be so. As an answer to the question of railroad rates or of adequate air transport or of the maintenance of fair competition, or of providing security against the great hazards of life, the administrative agency was never carefully designed. It is instead an expedient, a kind of *ad hoc* answer to a problem that could no longer be denied. The general type has to some extent, but far from neatly, been shaped to the many distinctive tasks it is called upon to perform.

Thus, to limit the discussion to just three typical examples . . .

. . . invented no techniques for imposing responsibility upon the agency. The stream of popular opinion has been beaten
upon by many forces before ever it reaches the agency. It is
out of the question to secure a revision or a veto of its work
at the polls. The institution of judicial review was never contrived for such a use. Judges, like administrators, are themselves appointees, holding offices presumed to be above popular
clamor. They can hardly be called upon for the needed task
of accommodating what an agency does to the popular will.
An administrative decision must be commuted into a justiciable
question—an alien sort of thing—before a court of law will
touch it. The agency, supervising an activity that moves with
quick step, is not helped by a judicial review that moves at the
tortuous pace of due process. Such a device for imposing
responsibility has been tried with disastrous results. To tell
the agency to impose responsibility upon itself is to make of
it a priestcraft. For the exercise of irresponsible power there
can be no place in the republic. Here is the necessity for political invention, an art whose neglect has been visited . . .

. . . the people cannot watch, it does not follow that the
agency goes unwatched. On the contrary, its every move is subjected to the most critical scrutiny of the interest—always a minority group—whose activities it is supposed to keep within the
tolerance of the law. If the public gets no chance at the agency,
the interest or the industry gets in its licks every day. The public interest in its work is usually dormant, not articulate, widely
diffused. The regulated group is small, compact, mobile, and
keenly interested. As occasion offers, its forces are concentrated
at the point where decision is to be made. Techniques for applying pressures have appeared in a brilliant series of inventions; and neither the public nor the government has succeeded
in inventing counter techniques. Against the reiterated beat
of the everyday pressure, the still small voice . . .

. . . rust into impotence. The organization comes to be a
series of petty principalities; the head of a Bureau or Division,

to be a little Czar, sensitive to his perquisites and his jurisdiction. The process of decision comes to be frozen into ritual; and it is more important that the ceremonial be performed than that a sensible answer be found. Habits of thought and of action grow up that are as rigid as the folkways of a savage tribe. New blood is about as welcome as . . .

. . . But a far greater danger is that the agency be captured by the very interest it was set up to regulate. The oldest of such agencies, the Interstate Commerce Commission, presents the classic example. At first, the railroads objected to governmental interference; then they discovered that regulation could be employed to serve their own ends. The Commission, once a vital, has now become a servile body. It stands ever ready to lend its authority to private interests; and, in sanctioning rate increases, puts official approval upon a riot of inefficiency and waste. Its function of late has come to be to load upon the public the costs of the refusal of the industry to put its house in order . . .

. . . no easy escape. Every appointment is watched. A host of letters and telegrams reaches the White House in support of the acceptable candidate. The industry has its effective ways of preventing the reappointment of the Commissioner who has refused to go along. And the process of shortcircuiting, if not sterilizing, initiative . . .

. . . like a human soul, can go astray, and help to defeat the very purpose for which it exists. Nor is decay or captivity an affair of time. It has taken the Civil Aeronautics Board only a few years to throw off its loyalty to the public and to put on the livery of a vested interest. The Board has made no serious attempt—as the Act under which it operates requires—to create an air transport industry adapted to the needs of the country and its commerce. On the contrary, air carriage, whether of persons or of cargo, has been allowed to develop as a luxury service within the reach of only a small fraction of the people. No incentive to efficiency has been provided. On the contrary the manipulation of mail pay has been made to provide a sub-

sidy for sloth and waste. Whatever the certificated carriers do,
the government is called upon to bail them out. The favored
carriers are protected against competition. A public release of
the agency announces that "public convenience and necessity"
becomes a term of art that has nothing to do with the convenience and necessity of the public. And a former chairman of
the CAB—his inability to disregard the public interest rendered
him ineligible for reappointment—has accused the agency of
usurping the office of financial underwriter to the chartered
companies. Seldom in so short a time has so complete a cap-
ture . . .

. . . none too subtle form of bribery. For the industry can
do far better by the bright and ambitious young official than
can the government itself. It demands no formula of multiple
terms to explain how it came to pass that a head of a section
concerned with milk control resigned to go to a large milk dis-
tributing company; a patent commissioner, to enter the employ
of a large patentholder; or the Secretary of Agriculture to defend in court a statute that the Congress passed in behalf of the
sugar trust. One wonders, if in these, as in other things, responsible government officials are led by an invisible hand to promote . . .

. . . indifferent to a clash of loyalties. Anyone of them would
resent it if accused of not being a patriotic American. Yet in
this whole series of instances public officials have by their
deliberate decisions sacrificed the welfare of the public to private interest. If the word loyalty has any substantive content
in respect to the obligations of officials of the government . . .

. . . a great and unanticipated constitutional charge. The
guarantee of the right of petition has been converted into the
established institution of lobbying and the grievances that the
lobbies seek to have redressed are deficits in the privileges that
they seek. As yet the art of the counterlobby . . .

. . . fact of first importance. These special interests have the
power, and easily acquire the will, to make it extremely un-
comfortable for any agency of government unwilling to accept
their dictates. If at the polls they are too few to have much to

say, they have the wherewithal, by making the worse appear
to be the better reason, to persuade the masses. But, far more
important, they command many channels through which to
influence official action and they demand to be appeased . . .

. . . a quack sort of medicine or surgery timidly practiced.
An analysis of an ill in the body politic may be objective, clean
cut, and beyond the slightest peradventure. But in government
diagnosis is in only the rarest case the key to remedy. What
needs to be done—what has to be done if health is to be restored—is at the mercy of what will not stir up too much opposition. The result is that far too often to solve a problem is
only to restate it. And just as often the treatment gets no
further than the symptoms, and the heart of the disease is left
undisturbed. The "Spirit of 1912" for example, found expansion . . .

. . . the right to tinker. We are a nation of tinkerers, fond
of gadgets and mechanical contrivances. The flood of grants
from the Patent Office may not bear testimony to a continuous
thunderstorm made up of countless flashes of genius. But it
does bear evidence to our love of gadgetry. It is, therefore, not
strange that we love to tinker with the mechanisms of government. At one time or another we have gone all out for the city
manager system, the popular election of senators, the initiative
and referendum, and a score or more of kindred measures. In
such reforms there is nothing wrong; on the contrary, it is imperative that the exercise of power be connected with its popular source, and that the channels through which the will of the
people is conveyed be unblocked. But all such improvements
will fall far short of their goals, so long as such tinkering is
allowed to provide an escape from attention to other problems.
For if the interests that make up the commonwealth are out of
balance, or if the lack of harmony between a democratic political process and an economy marked by the concentration of
power is . . .

. . . an axiom. Only the novice in Albany, Harrisburg,
Austin, Springfield—or for that matter Washington—endows
truth with the virtue of self-realization, or expects a reform to

make its way on its own merits. This does not mean that the hell-raiser of old has no place in the modern order. But it does mean that he must work through channels; that he must employ the pressure groups if he is to be heard. He may go to his senator or congressman; but the better—in fact the only sure—strategy is to enlist the help of those who are professionals at that sort of thing. The special interests have each its institution of persuasion. These are established affairs, well financed, ably staffed, fitted out with every resource. The art of shaping legislation has a tradition, involves numerous and varied techniques, is constantly enriched by invention, and demands a highly skilled priestcraft for its practice. The reform groups, far less adept, are learning from the interests. The place for the solo reformer is now back of the lines. His task is to get the progressive organizations busy. It is only as he does so that . . .

. . . the power to compromise, or even to nullify, the will of the people as expressed . . . no checkmate has as yet been invented. Nor is invention possible . . . for the problem lies in the lack of harmony between . . . within the social order. And so long as that unbalance endures, the trouble lies beyond the reach of . . .

. . . revolution to provoke a counterrevolution. In an industrial society the lions could not be expected to lie down and be controlled by the lambs. That the lions should be subjected came to be accepted doctrine, even among the lions themselves. All they insisted upon was that the control should be in "competent hands." And, it was sheer common sense that those who knew most about—and understood best—the acquisitive pursuits of the lions were the lions themselves. So what so natural as that the regulated should take over the machinery of regulation. Herein lies the great revolution of our times. Its course can be . . .

. . . Sidon, Munich, or Appomattox. A third aspect of this revolution was the conversion of controls into sanctions. Hardly an industry or area of the national economy has been free from this impact. As a milk farmer in New Milford, Connecticut

. . . witness in a single scheme of regulation, a great historical movement in epitome. In the name of public health, a system of inspection has been imposed upon milk, and no milk from anywhere within the milkshed—notice the political term—is permitted to enter the market that does not meet standards of purity appointed by law. But the industry quickly saw that inspection was too useful an institution either to give up or to be left to public-minded officials. So, sanctified as an instrument of health, it remained to serve another purpose. Inspection could be used, not only to admit into or to exclude from the industry, but also to dictate the terms under which members of the industry could lawfully carry on. In time, about the elementary fact of inspection, an elaborate code of regulation was woven. In this way a private control as complete as . . .

. . . and procedures constitute the most elaborate of systems. In most of our cities an elaborate building code has been set up. Its terms are flexible enough to exclude the alien and to throw most, or even all, the construction work to local . . . warranted in the learned professions. But trades, once little more than vocal or manual, have aspired to the dignity of professions; and, solicitous for the public, they have persuaded the legislature to set up standards of competence. So today, the aspiring youth who would become a barber or beautician, a realtor or mortician, must secure a certificate from a board made up of his competitors. The school of pedagogy—a discipline that is still a great mystery—is able to market its pseudo wares by securing state laws that make of teaching a privilege lawfully to be conferred only upon those who have been certified as proficient in "education" . . . the liquor trade, the most regulated of all—with every statute written in the name of public morals. That such regulation is an asset is demonstrated by the lack of a demand for its repeal. In fact, without regulation, the vendors of distilled spirits would beat . . . protective tariff, which enjoys prestige only because it is venerable, is in terms of modern politics, a back number.

The rise of the corporate estate—the single most important historical fact of our times—has set the stage for the conversion

of controls into sanctions. Let us, with actual yet adequate
illustrations, conduct a brief inquiry into the devices by which
the corporate estate is established, the armament used in its
defense, and the weapons and strategy by which it is expanded.
The imperium . . . a greater empire than any Caesar or Napoleon ever knew . . . steel . . . glass bottles . . . aluminum
. . . ethical drugs—the term is an arresting one . . .

. . . the dominant and most arresting use of such sanctions.
In fact the letter-patent is a beautiful example of this type of
political phenomenon—namely, an institution which, in classic
words, has come to serve an end that is no part of its intent.
The Congress was, by the Constitution, given the power, not
to issue patents, but to "promote the progress of science and
the useful arts." The exclusive right conferred upon the inventor is the instrument of that public end. By lawyer's invention,
and by a development quite outside the statutes, "the patent
system" has been erected upon the patent grant. The first of
these inventions is assignment; the inventor deeds over all his
rights to a corporate estate. Thereby the invention changes
worlds; it passes out of the world of science and technology into
that of business enterprise, where a different system of values
and of mores prevails. The second is the patent license, an
instrument through which the patent owner imposes its corporate controls upon those who put it to use. For the owner
can decree the terms upon which he will permit the use of
industrial devices or processes to which he holds patents; and
if such devices or processes are essential to the production of
a marketable commodity, it is only by the license of the patent
owner that another person can enter the business. The similar-
ity of this corporate permission to . . .

. . . most ingenious. For the right conveyed by the grant
comes to be divorced from the right granted by the letter-
patent. A corporate estate usually gathers all of the patents it
owns into a "portfolio." It does not usually license companies
to make use of particular grants. Instead it grants to its licensee the right to use the inventions covered by all of its

patents within a particular field. Again, usually it does not grant a general permission in respect to the techniques covered; instead the recipient of the grant may make use of the inventions only in the fabrication of specified products. Thus the rights conferred by many patents are pooled, redivided, and assembled for sale to manufacturers. The life of a letter-patent is seventeen years; a patent license, providing for a limited use of many grants, may run for half a century. As old patents expire, and new ones are granted, the inventions that are covered by the grant constantly change.

In fact, the license—or package of rights—that the producer buys from the patent owner is a synthetic . . .

. . . this power to fix the terms under which a series of inventions, along with the know-how, is put to use. The patent owner can determine who is to have a license, and who is to be excluded; the field within which it is to be recognized; the methods to be employed; the amount to be produced; the territory within which the resulting product is to be marketed; and the price to be charged. The patent owner exercises dominion of an industry whose strategic technology it controls. Its patent license is a set of statutes for the good government of the industry. The relation of patent owner to licensee can be cast only in terms of industrial feudalism. The licensee as a matter of business must supply the patent owner with accounts and reports by which any infraction of the law of the industry can be discovered . . . a system of private police . . . if the licensee violates any term in the license, he is using the patent beyond the limits of the grant and thus his act gives a basis for a suit for infringement. Thus the federal courts are enlisted in enforcing a system of private government. It is a far call from James Madison and Charles . . .

. . . a typical corporate estate, which, through the operation of its elaborate patent licensing system, exercises a dominion over men and affairs that the United States Supreme Court, in the *New State Ice* case, was unwilling to entrust to a sovereign state of the union.

The number of such sanctions . . .

. . . far beyond the reach of the Constitution. For no convention of the fathers has been called to ordain, or even to sanction, this fundamental change in the character of the political order. We the people have never solemnly decided that, as an agency of industrial control, the free and open market should pass into eclipse. We have never decreed that in an industry a number of competing firms should be succeeded by a corporate estate. We have never highly resolved that the play of economic forces should be superseded by the formal government of an industry. Yet area after area of the economy has been withdrawn from the self-regulation of the market and little by little a series of private industrial dominions, under a single overlordship or a number of corporations acting in concert, has arisen. In our century, the economy is dominant, and our vital politics has come to be the politics of industry. Apart from, it is stronger than, the state; and its political systems far neater, more articulate and more powerful, than any formal government. So swift has been the change, and so little planned that . . .

. . . find ways of securing the ancient liberties within the corporate estate. Of equal importance is the problem of devising ways and means of insuring response to democratic pressures within the institution called, for lack of a better name, The Political Order of Industry. The task of fastening responsi- . . .

. . . though, which has lingered after fact has departed. The demise of price controls at the end of the war attests this confusion of mind. They were lifted in the face of a reality that demanded their retention; for it was obvious that as yet most goods were not in free supply and that the effect of the Act of Congress was to turn markets over to the sellers and to strip the buyers of the protection of competition. It was all done in the grandiose manner of removing restraints and making men free. But, in the great majority of industries affected, the market has long since been replaced by a political organization. The result was to put off public regulation and to take on a regulation established by private industrial government. In a word a system of control responsible to the people was exchanged for a system of control responsive to the will of the industrial . . .

. . . no such thing as an international patent. But invention has done quite well with the material at hand. The corporate estate takes out a patent, in the name of one of its captive inventors, in every country in which it expects the invention to be put to use. The sum of these various national patents is in effect an international patent. As at home, the corporate estate seeks to gather all the patents covering an art into a single portfolio. Then this portfolio is drawn upon to carve out licenses, each for limited uses and each with conditions attached, to as many corporations as may be desirable. It may happen that the patents that together make up an art are in different hands. In such an event a "treaty" between the various corporate estates is made to "pool" the patents and to establish a government for the industry. The items are aggregated into the whole and the whole is carved up into distinct parcels of rights. An imperium comes into existence that is worldwide in its orbit, and in which national frontiers are only boundaries between marketing provinces.

The salubrious climate of Switzerland has often been remarked. The picture of a German, an Englishman, and an American meeting by the blue waters of Lake Geneva to resolve the world market for aluminum into three huge proprietary domains is . . .

. . . the political order caught in a pincers between the two great modern movements. The one is the trend, underlined by Versailles, to fractionalize Christian society into competing nations. The other is the pursuit of gain, revitalized by the rise of the corporate estate, which drives toward its universal goal and refuses to be stayed by frontiers. Between the wars nationalism scored a partial victory in imposing physical barriers in the way of the movement of goods. But patent rights and other equities are intangibles that, witnessed by legal documents, pass through customhouses with impunity. The result is a strong trend toward the organization of industries on a world basis; nations, as stated above, constitute provinces within an international industrial order . . .

. . . dualism of state and economy. The antithesis presents the great fault line, to borrow a geological figure, in modern culture. Along this fault line . . .

. . . significant that it is in industries most strategic to war that the corporate *entente cordiale* is most apparent. The patent owner may license or refuse to license. If a foreign corporation holds United States patents, yet refuses to license an American corporation to "make, use, and vend," it can prevent the new product or method from going into production in this country. If an alien nation exercises a rigid discipline over its corporations, it can decree that no United States corporation shall be licensed. If none the less an American concern goes into production, using the forbidden technique, it exposes itself to a suit for infringement. Here is the Achilles' heel in our armament program. The policy of the state is at the mercy of the politics of industry. If the alien patent owner does license, he is entitled to full reports upon the volume of output in which the patents were used. Thus, if the alien becomes the enemy, it has in routine reports access to complete and accurate information. It would be impossible to devise so reliable an . . .

. . . a dynastic pitted against a democratic state. The dynastic state exercises close supervision of its corporations; the democratic state employs a deliberate negligence. If corporations of the two countries move into lockstep, the alliance is far from equal. In the industrial tie the dynastic state possesses an instrument with which to paralyze the war potential of . . .

. . . creates a new paradox for loyalty. The real votaries of the acquisitive arts are zealous in the pursuit of gain. If advantage lies that way, they do not hesitate to make alliances with corporations in alien countries. And, when war is on, they will so far as they are permitted continue "to trade with the enemy."

They intend no conscious harm to their own country. Whatever befalls in suppressing inventions, or in leakage of information, is an unfortunate incident, to be regretted but outside the scope of their calculations. If country and interest go hand in hand all is well—as when for business enterprise fat government contracts are in sight. But, when advantage moves in one direction and national loyalty in another, the real clash comes. Advantage is tangible, national loyalty far from concrete; and the man of affairs is usually not good on abstractions. In the last war testimony . . .

. . . no evidence that it makes for efficiency. But even if it did, some of us would not like it. At all costs the dynamic impulse must be kept alive; and it cannot be done in an economy made up of a series of corporate imperia. For all history shows that when an institution ceases to be dynamic and freezes into establishment, it takes the road to decay . . . So it has happened with corporation, empire, . . .

. . . antitrust, although it has in word at least been a fetish with us, is only an instrument. But, in the backward art of politics, it is the best weapon that as yet we have devised for putting members of an industry on their toes, giving them an incentive to get ahead by doing things better and differently, and keeping alive that vital spark that makes for progress. For in an economy of corporate estates, the politics of industry has largely replaced the market process, and the conduct of every firm is regulated by the law of the industry. Whereas in a competitive system, the minority, even the single concern, can think and act boldly; and if its innovations prove themselves, it can, as the price of their survival, impose its innovations and its more progressive ways . . .

. . . not really a matter of the economy. For, as wealth and power are diffused, the number of points at which judgment is to be exercised is increased. And, instead of authority being exercised at a few strategic points, discretion is carried far down the line. The number of persons who must make intelligent decisions is enlarged. The points at which creative thought and action may emerge are multiplied. And a system in which duty cannot be discharged by routine, and in which responsibility for decision reaches down even to menial tasks, alike gives release to the human spirit and offers incentive to thinking freshly and boldly. The case against monopoly, establishment, the corporate estate, rests, in last analysis, upon its stultifying effect upon the capacities of the human being for creation. The politics cannot ignore . . .

. . . lack of health. But its service is not in the individual. The political lords of our corporate estates are mostly men of good will. It is true that they respond, even in a tropismatic way, to the usages of the institutions that play upon them. If they did not, they would presently lose their places to corporate officials whose zeal in the pursuit of gain was purer, and who were more sensitive to the rigorous demands of business enterprise. But guilt is in no sense personal. If a philosopher were to be cast in the role of a tycoon . . .

. . . back to the fundamental fact of the great antithesis between the character of the national economy and our faith in the democratic process. The progress of science and the useful arts needs release from captivity. The progress of knowledge should be the creature neither of big business nor of the nationalistic state. The whole course of events dictates an end to the separation of state and economy, and so long as this dualism . . .

. . . for our generation. The great problem of the politics is to discover the way, and to invent the means, for the return to a political economy that responds to the will of the democracy whose servant and instrument it should always be. . . .*

* EDITOR's NOTE: This was written not by Beard but by Walton Hamilton as he believed Beard would have written and Hamilton would have approved it. Had he lived, Beard, his friends had hoped, was going to write his *Politics*. "My idea had been to write in this area in which Beard and I shared something of the same ways of thought and of faith," Walton Hamilton explained. "It was really hard to hit upon an art form for this venture. I first tried dialogue form and though I found that there was less difficulty with this than I had expected, I discovered that it used up space very rapidly. . . . After one or two other trials I hit upon the device of the fragments." Walton H. Hamilton to Howard K. Beale, December 17, 1948.

HOWARD K. BEALE

Charles Beard: Historian

BY ANY STANDARD Charles A. Beard ranks among the most significant historians of the first half of the twentieth century. Many loved him; many hated him. No one could deny his importance. To analyze the qualities that gave him so unquestioned a position is not easy. He had the dramatic quality of a James Westfall Thompson. He was erudite as were only a small group like Ferguson, Haskins, Schevill. He had the same wide contacts with historians and materials that made J. Franklin Jameson remarkable. He had the breadth of understanding and the capacity to pioneer in new fields that made Frederick Jackson Turner so significant. He stimulated students and provoked thought and historical curiosity as perhaps only Turner and Dodd among American historians could do. Like Turner in the history of the West, Dunning in Reconstruction, Bolton in Latin American history, Schlesinger in social history, and Curti and Gabriel in intellectual history, so in his emphasis on economic motivation Beard headed a school of historians and influenced younger men. Like Carl Becker, Henry Commager, and Samuel Morison he wrote with a style that com-

manded attention for anything he produced. Like Parrington
and Preserved Smith he had a gift for synthesis that few possessed. Like Parrington he was of a philosophic turn of mind
and wrote trenchantly on the history of ideas. Like his friend
and collaborator James Harvey Robinson he was deeply concerned with the meaning and purposes of history. More than
any other historian of his generation he sought to apply history
to the problems of his time and sallied forth from his Connecticut farm to do tireless battle persuading his fellow citizens
that the promise of American democracy could be fulfilled, if
only the lessons of history and philosophy were applied to public problems. Others have possessed one or several of these
talents. In combining in a single person so many and such
various qualities Beard was unique. Besides, in all American
historiography, only one other—Bancroft—has at the same time
enjoyed an outstanding reputation among scholars and been
so "popular" in his own day and so widely read by laymen.
More than any historian of his half century Beard stimulated
or antagonized historians and laymen into thought about historical problems and the place of history in the contemporary
world.

Beard wrote in all forty-seven volumes of history including
his textbooks, thirty-three if the latter are excluded. They are
individually discussed in a bibliographical note at the end of
the volume. Taken as a whole they cover a wide span of time
and a great range of subject. They embrace European as well
as American history, the philosophy of history, and history's
place among the social studies. Among them are several that
rank with the most important of the half century. In sheer
quantity they are impressive; in quality they are even more so.

Quite as important as Beard's books, however, are the ideas
he promoted in American historiography.

More than any other historian Beard stimulated an interest
in economic interpretation. Turner and Hildreth, as Beard
readily acknowledged,[1] had emphasized this principle earlier.
Turner, in Beard's own time, had applied it in his writing and

teaching, but in regard to an economic interpretation, Turner had failed to strike the historical imagination as Beard did, and he never had so wide an audience. Beard believed that economic factors play an important part in human motivation. Men's actions and ideas and hence their institutions are determined in large measure by their interests, he insisted. Of the various forces in history, the struggle for food, clothing, and shelter is the most important. In 1906 Beard had said, "The general direction of the political movements and legislation in Great Britain during the last one hundred years has been determined by the interests and ideals of the three great economic classes: landlords, capitalists, and workingmen."[2] In 1913 he declared: "Economic elements are the chief factors in the development of political institutions. . . . The whole theory of the economic interpretation of history rests upon the concept that social progress in general is the result of contending interests in society—some favorable, others opposed, to change."[3]

Beard formulated his views most clearly in lecturing to Amherst students in 1916. "There is a vital relation," he told them, "between the forms of state and the distribution of property, revolutions in the state being usually the results of contests over property." To the Amherst students he explained: "A landed interest, a transport interest, a railway interest, a shipping interest, an engineering interest, a manufacturing interest, a public-official interest, with many lesser interests, grow up of necessity in all great societies and divide them into different classes actuated by different sentiments and views. The regulation of these various and interfering interests, whatever may be the formula for the ownership of property, constitutes the principal task of modern statesmen and involves the spirit of party, in the necessary and ordinary operations of government."

"In other words," Beard believed, "there is no rest for mankind, no final solution of eternal contradictions. Such is the design of the universe. The recognition of this fact is the beginning of wisdom—and of statesmanship."[4]

Again and again Beard interpreted history in terms of this principle. He applied it to constitutional development in medieval England and France, to the later constitutional history of Sweden, Austria, Prussia.[5] In provincial America, too, political and social functions had an economic basis.[6] The American Revolution came, according to Beard, because "American business and agricultural enterprise was growing, swelling, beating against the frontiers of English imperial control at every point." Colonial assemblies and English royal officials Beard dubbed "the political knights errant in a great economic struggle that was to shake a continent."[7] Beard saw the conflicts over political principles during the period of the Confederation as a clash of economic interests. Desire for protection of manufactures, for security of investments in Western lands, for safeguarding American shipping on the seas, and for a stable monetary system were impelling motives that led people to favor the political theory of strong government.[8] Thus "the Constitution was not created by 'the whole people' . . .; but it was the work of a consolidated group whose interests knew no state boundaries and were truly national in their scope"; it was the "product of a conflict between capitalistic and agrarian interests." Support for its adoption "came principally from the cities and regions where the commercial, financial, manufacturing, and speculative interests were concentrated and the bulk of the opposition came from the small farming and debtor classes, particularly those back from the sea board."[9]

When the new government was established Hamilton and Jefferson as the leaders of rival parties were the "spokesmen of capitalistic and agrarian interests." The Republicans by "declaring war on the rich and privileged drew to themselves the support not only of the farmers, but also of a considerable portion of the smaller tradesmen and mechanics of the towns, who had no very great liking for the 'rich and well born.' " Jeffersonian democracy, however, "did not imply any abandonment of the property . . . qualifications on the suffrage or office-holding." It "simply meant the possession of the federal government by the agrarian masses led by an aristocracy of slave-owning planters, and the theoretical repudiation of the right to use the Government for the benefit of any capitalistic groups, fiscal, banking, or manufacturing."[10] Even in the area of foreign policy, Beard believed, Jefferson's "deep antipathy toward capitalistic interests in general was partly responsible for his opposition to Hamilton's conciliatory policy in dealing with Great Britain." Throughout the controversy over foreign policy from 1805 to 1815 "the division between the commercial and the agricultural interests . . . was clearly discernible." "From the beginning to the end it was the merchants and ship-owners who took the lead in opposing the policies and measures of the Republican administration."[11]

So, too, in later history Beard saw economic forces. For Jacksonian democracy and its Whig opposition he saw an economic basis. Mid-century imperialism, Beard believed, was not created merely by a slaveowners' plot, but by "economic forces equally potent: the passion of farmers for more land, the lure of continental trade, and the profits of New England traffic in the Pacific Ocean."[12] So, too, in more recent imperialism, the Spanish-American War, and World War I Beard saw economic forces at work.

Sectional conflict, too, Beard attributed to economic factors. Men of the several sections, he pointed out, "were of the same race, spoke the same language, worshipped the same God, and had a common background of law, ethics, and culture." Yet soil, climate, natural resources, and the resulting labor systems were different, and out of these differences men developed "differences in sentiment, patterns of thought, and linguistic devices—social psychology." In consequence, America developed what Europe had never had, "a highly developed group of capitalists, a large body of independent farmers, and a powerful landed aristocracy each to a marked degree segregated into a fairly definite geographical area." Each such class produced leaders who formulated political programs and ethical justifications for each geographical area and planned attacks on other areas dominated by rival classes, and this conflict, essentially a clash of economic interests, constitutes what is called sectionalism.[13]

The resulting struggle that led to civil war Beard interpreted as primarily economic. Neither slavery nor yet state rights principles would have produced the conflict. "At no time . . . did Garrison's abolition creed rise to the dignity of a first rate issue." Tariffs rather than antislavery agitation first provoked the South to formulate secession principles. The roots of the controversy lay not in slavery but "in social groupings founded on differences in climate, soil, industries, and labor systems, in divergent social forces, rather than varying degrees of righteousness and wisdom or what romantic historians call the 'magnetism of great personalities.' "[14]

The Civil War itself, Beard says, was a Second American Revolution, "a social war, ending in the unquestioned establishment of a new power in government." This conflict, like other revolutions, brought "vast changes in the arrangement of classes, in the accumulation and distribution of wealth, in the course of industrial development, and in the Constitution inherited from the Fathers." "The core of the vortex," Beard pointed out, lay not in "the fleeting incident" of military conflict, but "in the flowing substance of things limned by statistical reports on finance, commerce, capital, industry, railways, and agriculture, by provisions of constitutional law, and by the pages of statute books."

All that two generations of Federalists and Whigs had tried to get was won within four short years, and more besides. The tariff . . . a national banking system . . . the policy of lavish grants from the federal treasury to aid internal improvements so necessary to commerce . . . the construction of the Pacific railway . . . the Homestead Act . . . innumerable grants to railways . . . allotments to the states in aid of agricultural colleges . . . [and] as a counter stroke [to avert] the danger of higher wages, threatened by the movement of labor to the land . . . an extraordinary law which gave federal authorization to the importation of working people under terms of contract analogous to the indentured servitude of colonial times.

In fact, one of the main results of "the salvation of the Union with which so many lofty sentiments were justly associated" was to assure to industry "an immense national market surrounded by a tariff wall bidding defiance to the competition of Europe."[15]

Indeed, if Beard is correct, the political conflict between Coolidge and his opponents in the 1920's and the clash between McKinley and Bryan in the late nineties both represented the same basic contest of business and farming interests that was symbolized by Webster and Jackson and, in an earlier day, by Hamilton and Jefferson.[16]

Three features of Beard's economic interpretation of history are worthy of note. First, it was influenced by Marx, but was in no sense Marxian. Beard had read Marx as an undergraduate at DePauw and while he was at Oxford; he read him again in the 1930's. He had read, in fact, not only the *Communist Manifesto* and *Das Kapital* but letters and other writings by Marx, and he often insisted that many American Marxists did not understand nor appreciate Marx because they had not properly explored these other writings. Yet Beard's ideas did not stem from Marx. Indeed, he was attacked by Marxists like Richard Enmale on the ground that as a "liberal bourgeois historian" he had partially seen the light but had failed to appreciate fully "the class dynamics of historical development."[17] Beard admired Marx for his "amazing range of . . . scholarship and the penetrating character of his thought," his "wide and deep knowledge," and his "fearless and sacrificial life." He was ready to learn from Marx and advised students to do likewise.

He denied, however, that there was anything in the nature of an economic interpretation that compelled one to use it for Marx's purposes or for any partisan or doctrinaire purpose whatsoever.[18] Beard refused to use "Marxian" as an epithet of either praise or condemnation.[19] At the same time he saw between his and Marx's interpretation of history a "collision . . . as cleancut as the antagonism between the Enlightenment and Prussianism." "Dialectical materialism," protested Beard, "represented history as all deterministic; like Hegel's system, fate without ethics. Marx took the mechanical god which Hegel had created and turned to the service of the Prussian State, and transformed this god into a materialist god operating on the same plan in making history—thesis, antithesis, and synthesis— in the service of the urban proletariat." Beard could conceive of no future state of society, classless or otherwise, that would remain static. Conflicts between opposing interest groups would develop even in the classless society of the communist utopia. Indeed, with the dialectical class-struggle view of history he had no truck. It was unreal. Furthermore, it left no place for the play of the individual will, for the power of ideas, for chance, or for ethics, all important to him even when he was most impressed with the power of economic forces. In Beard's view history was "a continuous process involving ethics no less than necessity; . . . a struggle within human personalities no less than within and between classes—a struggle pointed toward a higher objective for humanity, enlisting all the powers of men and women for progressive, civilizing purposes, yet with no final act for the drama of history, thus giving room for endless creativeness individual and social."[20] Rather than from Marx, Beard had gleaned his economic interpretation of history from Aristotle, Machiavelli, Hobbes, Locke, Hamilton, Jefferson, Webster, the English Fabians, a Civil War colonel, James Weaver, who had taught him as an undergraduate at a small midwestern college, and most of all from James Madison.

Secondly, Beard rarely exaggerated the importance of economic motivation as his opponents charged and as his friends sometimes did exaggerate it. In 1906, writing on British history, he insisted that securing new markets for manufactures and opening new areas for the profitable investment of capital were great impelling forces in imperialism, but he added that religious sentiments and philosophical conceptions concerning the world's civilization were also important.[21] In 1927 in stating his economic thesis he again ascribed great importance to political, religious, and personal emotions. After describing the role of slavery and of profit in the westward expansion of the midcentury, he warned that neither fully explained the movement but that an idea—Manifest Destiny—was important. Similarly, after portraying the economic and social aspects of the sectional conflict, he pointed out the importance of "sentiments of a moral nature."[22] In the book that gave vogue to the economic interpretation he guarded himself against exaggeration of the thesis. In the preface of the original edition he stated that the study was "frankly fragmentary," that his purpose was "to suggest new lines of historical research rather than to treat the subject" exhaustively. The use of the article "an" in his title pointedly suggested tentativeness. He insisted further that it was not his purpose "to show that the Constitution was made for the personal benefit of the members of the Convention." Nor was he interested in the amount of money the members made from the formation of the new government. Only one point was important: "Did they represent distinct groups whose economic interests they understood and felt in concrete, definite form through their own personal experience with identical property rights, or were they working merely under the guidance of abstract principles of political science?" He warned that there was "considerable danger of attempting too much in making generalizations."[23] Later he explained to his students at Columbia that he had emphasized the economic approach not because it was the only valid one, but because it was important and had been neglected.[24] I well remember, in a smoking room discussion on the Pullman returning from the 1929 meeting of the American Historical Association at Durham, North Carolina, the emphasis with which Beard told a group of us: "I never said that economic motives explain everything. Of course, ideas are important. And so are ethical concepts. What I have always said and all that I have said is that, among the various motives impelling men to action, the struggle for food, clothing, and shelter has been more important throughout history than any other. And that is true, isn't it?—ISN'T IT?" In reissuing his treatise in 1935 he denied that he had "accused the members of the Convention of working merely for their own pockets." He denied that he had ever undertaken to show that "the form of government established and powers conferred were 'determined' in every detail by the conflict of economic interests."[25] These denials he repeated in Constitution Hall in 1937.[26]

Thirdly, Beard *did* change, if not the nature of his economic interpretation, then certainly his emphasis upon it. In thus changing he was not alone. Like Beard, so historians collectively, some more and some less, in the period between World War I and the middle 1930's, stressed economic motivation. Thereafter a number of things happened that challenged the dominance of economics among the forces that made history and led to more complex concepts of motivation that included new social forces, emotions, ideas, ethical considerations, and the influence of dominant personalities. Beard shifted ground too. In 1935 he felt compelled to defend and re-explain his old thesis. In 1943 in *The Republic* he dealt with the great ideas of the Constitution rather than the economic interests of those who had framed it. In the *Basic History* the famous economic thesis about the Civil War disappeared entirely, and the writings of Julius Pratt and others forced a repudiation of what he had said earlier about economic causes of the War with Spain. Interests and ideas were still intertwined, but interests were less important and ideas more so.

In 1945 Beard re-examined the economic basis of politics and explained the changes in the world that had forced him to modify the emphasis of his historical interpretation. Recent events connected with the rise of totalitarianism and war had affected human history. Two world wars had "altered the social, intellectual, and moral setting in which the theory of the economic basis of politics" had been discussed. Beard, like political theorists ever since Aristotle, had recognized that "economic forces operate freely only in the absence of military force." Now since 1914 "the military man" had "again entered into full competition with 'the economic man' and 'the political man' for power over the state and its fortunes."

"Purely economic interpretations of the rise, growth, and nature of Fascism" Beard called "oversimplifications." Economic interests, he protested, do not universally furnish, as some assume, the sole or even the most powerful "impetus to political action for the conquest of power in the state," nor are motivations the same in war, civil or foreign, as in peacetime. The world of 1945 led him to give more importance than formerly to noneconomic aspects of human motivation. The ambitions and force of unique personalities, the activism of men searching for "adventure and power in the war-torn world," "the passion for destroying, killing, and dominating" that still filled some returned soldiers were now important. So, also, resentment, craving for revenge, racial doctrines. "Antisemitic diatribes" affected human events as did "virulent abuse of 'democracy' and 'civilization,' exaltations of irrationality and violence as masculine virtues, and the systematic formulations of Sorel, Mosca, and Pareto in criticism of the masses and popular government." These as much as economic forces had induced the rise of fascism.[27]

In Communist countries, too, the basic conditions of history had changed. In Western Europe of the nineteenth century economic interests had "enjoyed a high degree of freedom and independence as against the state," and hence it was easy for men of property to wield political power. Now, however, Beard pointed out in 1945, "the political man" can often order "the economic man" about instead of taking dictation from him. "There has been a large-scale revival of belief in, quest for, and exercise of unlimited power in government as an end in itself or as a means to class, national, and imperialistic ends." Beard retreated to a relativistic definition of his economic interpretation of history. Economic motivation is important, but it can function freely, he now pointed out, only under conditions such as existed in Britain and America in the nineteenth century; it is only one of the many forces that make history; ambitious men and military power can destroy the climate in which normal motivations operate. In any event, the finite human mind cannot grasp or determine the causes of human history; as for laws of history, there are none that man can discover. Hence in history, as in the world, man can only grope, formulating only the most tentative hypotheses. One of these will still be that economic interest is an important force in history when the "economic man" is not overpowered by the "military man" in war or preparation for war or by the "political man" in totalitarian nations.[28]

In constitutional history, also, Beard challenged traditional attitudes. He denied that either the framers of the Constitution or later justices of the Supreme Court were dominated primarily by great "principles of justice." To understand the legal theories they defended one had to inquire into the economic interests of the group to which they belonged. The framers created an instrument that would serve the best interests of society as they saw them and then formulated political theories to support that instrument. Their opponents erected rival theories to protect rival interests. As interests changed, constitutional principles were modified, sometimes reversed. Even justices of the Supreme Court, Beard insisted, were influenced in the decisions they handed down by what they deemed "possible and desirable."[29] This was the period when Holmes and Pound were applying relativism to legal theory and Brandeis was basing legal practice on the need of acquainting judges with social and economic realities. Similarly Beard was exploding the judges' own contention that historically they had always merely applied the law and was showing that actually judges had molded the Constitution to what they deemed desirable and then had searched for legal precedents to justify the ends.

Beard's relation to constitutional history is typical of his historical career. He wrote his important works on the Constitution at a time when most historians and constitutional lawyers accepted the tradition of Bancroft and Curtis, of Kent, Story, and Miller, that great principles governed the framing and interpreting of that document. Beard slashed unmercifully into their pretensions. He piled fact upon fact upon fact to produce a devastating effect. The great of both professions denounced him. But the future was Beard's. The denunciations died away. The next generation largely incorporated Beard's view into its history. Practicing lawyers began following Brandeis's lead in presenting economic and social facts to instruct the justices on the realities of the world about them so that their practical judgments on what was "possible and desirable" might reflect actual conditions.

Beard was an iconoclast realistically battering down the judicial bulwarks of conservatism. He was a pioneer breaking new paths of interpretation. Yet he was also a part of the progressive trend of his time and greatly influenced by it and by his wide readings in European theorists. Von Jhering, Menger, and Stammler were telling Europeans that law does not develop through "natural" growth but is "made" to serve interests that can be objectively ascertained. A few great legal authorities in America, Pound, Freund, and Goodnow in the classroom and Brandeis in active practice, were approaching the application of constitutional law as Beard was its history. Furthermore, as Beard later pointed out, he was supported in "the association of economic ideas with judicial interpretations" by high authorities: Justices Holmes, Taft, and Stone.[30] Actually, Holmes and Pound were applying relativism to the theory of law as Beard was to its history. What Beard could not know but what he would have chuckled to learn was that conservative, respectable John Hay, the very model of an old-school gentleman and the darling of interests whom Beard's views on constitutional history scandalized, had abandoned the traditional view. Eight years before Beard exploded his bombshell Hay had confided to his diary: "Even the Constitution . . . is seen now that we have the journal of the convention, to have been the result of discussion mostly puerile, dictated by ignoble motives."[31]

Beard, however, did not accept the view of Hay and of his own detractors that to recognize the fathers' awareness of the association of ideas and interests was to brand them "ignoble."

To Beard this merely proved the fathers to be political realists, and Beard respected realism far more than fine-sounding principles detached from reality. Beard was proud of America, particularly proud of her Constitution, which he regarded as among the greatest creations of all time, and proudest of all of the Americans who had had the wisdom to create it. He persistently quoted Madison—that "profound student of politics"; he gloried in the fact that Madison, an American, grasped profound truths decades before Karl Marx began to discover similar forces in history.[32] Even before Beard wrote *The Republic* he had pointed with pride to the fact that the fathers had "regarded government and economics as things intimately associated, not as separable and separated."[33] Beard regarded the "wonderful piece of argumentation" in which Hamilton, Madison, and Jay presented their appeals to various economic interests as "the finest study in the economic interpretation of politics which exists in any language." The support of conservative groups won by such appeals to their interests he regarded as a "sound basis" on which to rest "the superstructure" of the Constitution.[34] In 1927 he wrote: "Among the many historic assemblies which have wrought revolutions in the affairs of mankind, it seems safe to say that there has never been one that commanded more political talent, practical experience, and sound substance than the Philadelphia convention of 1787."[35] And in 1935 he declared:

It was largely by recognizing the power of economic interests in the field of politics and making skillful use of them that the Fathers of the American Constitution placed themselves among the great practicing statesmen of all ages and gave instructions to succeeding generations in the art of government. By the assiduous study of their works and by displaying their courage and their insight into the economic interests underlying all constitutional formalities, men and women of our generation may guarantee the perpetuity of government under law, as distinguished from the arbitrament of force. It is for us, recipients of their heritage, to inquire constantly and persistently, when theories of national power or states' rights are propounded: "What interests are behind them and to whose advantage will changes or the maintenance of old forms accrue?" By refusing to do this we become victims of history—clay in the hands of its makers.[36]

Beard's importance as an economic and social historian is too well attested by the majestic sweep of economic forces through his works and the penetration of his social analyses to need elaboration. Less known is his pioneering in these fields while he was still writing European history. When more famous scholars were still concentrating on political and military history or the best among them were exploring constitutional and institutional development, Beard at DePauw was studying the elder Toynbee and economic forces under a teacher who "emphasized the social content and the social implications of whatever it was he and his students were investigating,"[37] and then, both before and after a half year at Cornell, he went to England, studied economic history, and gained practical experience in the British labor movement. When he returned to America and applied for a job he could point to two years of teaching of history and *economics* for Co-operative Educational Committees in England and Wales and could claim as his special field not only English constitutional but English *economic* history, in which he had "made a special study of the industrial developments of the XIXth Century."[38] It is significant that his first book, published before he entered Columbia's graduate school, was *The Industrial Revolution,* along with the elder Toynbee's, one of the earliest historical treatments of that subject. Beard had been schooled in the prevalent institutional history and theory of Teutonic origins, first when as an undergraduate he translated Stubbs's charters, then under Powell, Dicey, and Poole at Oxford, where he learned paleography and intensively studied Gneist and Fustel de Coulanges, and finally when for a Columbia Ph.D. he dug into medieval British local history. Perhaps it was in protest against this emphasis that in his next book, published in 1906, he pronounced economic activities an important part of the life and thought of medieval man, and indeed of men of all times.[39] When in 1908 Beard and Robinson joined to write European history, the usual political, military, and institutional narrative yielded a considerable segment of each volume to long treatments of social and economic developments. In the first decade of the twentieth century it was an innovation to present in history books full and sympathetic treatments of labor, concomitant reform movements and socialism, the economic effect of inventions and new scientific knowledge, the industrial revolution, and imperialism.

The authors were interested in social history too. "Scientific discoveries produced a spirit of reform" and gave the Western world "its first hopes of future improvement." Inventions were "destined to alter the habits, ideas, and prospects of the great mass of the people" more than "all the conquests of Napoleon."[40] Here were early evidences of Beard's concern about social forces, which in his later histories led him to point out the social effects in the East of the growth of the West, to emphasize the social results of the Civil War, to explore the subsequent "triple revolution" in American agriculture, "no less Sibylline in its social implications than the conquest of manufacture by science and the machine," to concern himself with the "social forces" that "finally breached the philosophy of 'Let us alone,' " and to explore the social implications of shifts in the structure of American classes.[41] We have the witness of a colleague of both men and a student of Robinson's, James T. Shotwell, that "the increased attention to economic history, especially the industrial revolution" resulted from Beard's influence on the joint work.[42] Robinson himself testified: "There are plenty of signboards along life's pathway, but the directions are only visible when one has passed them. . . . Beard had trotted down the trail and peeked around the sign when he included 'imperialism' in our old edition."[43]

In the history of ideas, too, Beard broke new ground. The Beards' effort[44] to discover in *The American Spirit* a central idea and trace it through American history was a thought-provoking undertaking, even though not entirely successful in execution. *The Republic* is uneven but is at its best excellent. *The Idea of National Interest* and *The Open Door at Home* are models of large-scale treatment of the growth and conflict of ideas. The portions of *The Rise* dealing with ideas, arts, science, religion, and literature elicited high praise. Yet more significant and often forgotten is the fact that in 1915, ten years before Parrington published his great work, Beard wrote passages on the philosophy of Hamilton, Jefferson, Madison, Adams, and John Taylor that were not surpassed even by Parrington. And in 1908 he and Robinson devoted as much space to the "new history" of ideas, religion, and culture as to the "new history" of economic and social forces. Radium, bacteria, the atomic theory, Darwinism's effect on religion and secular thought, a full and fair treatment of the Catholic church, the intellectual ferment of the French enlightenment, and the social consequences of the idea of progress—all these were treated.

Beard constantly pointed out the effect of technological and economic forces upon ideas. Thus he showed how the "grand political ideas" of Jeffersonian democracy were modified by the revolution in technology, which did "more to shatter the old patterns of speculation and unfold vistas of endless progress for democracy than all the upheavals and renaissances of the centuries that had gone before." "Once the industrial revolution was fairly started," Beard wrote, "its effects upon culture—upon intellectual interests, aesthetic appreciation, and the institutions for the distribution of knowledge—were swift and cumulative."[45] He lauded Dodd and Turner for discarding righteousness and unrighteousness as the basis of the clash of ideas between North and South and for substituting geographic and economic factors.[46] He insisted that to understand democracy one had to get beneath political forms "into the real basis of American civilization, into the forms and distribution of property which conditioned, and to some extent determined, the rise and growth of any democracy that existed."[47] "Triumphant business enterprise . . . gave the dominant tone to the intellectual and moral notes of the nineteenth century's closing decades."[48] The 1929 depression created an economic climate that led to "a general surrender of the doctrine that poverty and unemployment come only from the improvidence of the poor." It led, too, to repudiation of "the Darwinian law of the jungle by seeking to eliminate through concerted action . . . innumerable practices of competition once deemed right and just."[49]

Yet Beard also believed ideas had been powerful in their own right. As he watched fascism spread he declared, "The world is largely ruled by ideas, true and false. . . . [An idea] contains within itself a dynamic power to move individuals and nations, to drive them in the direction of effecting the ends and institutions implicit in it. . . . Ideas . . . frequently arise from obscure sources, are cherished for a term by the weak and unimportant, and finally make headway against indifference and suppression to a place of dominance in a whole epoch of civilization." Of all ideas the most dynamic in the history of thought was "the idea of progress or the continual improvement in the lot of mankind . . . by the attainment of knowledge and the subjugation of the material world to the requirements of human welfare. . . . Violent differences of opinion over ways and means could not obliterate the conviction. Nor could economic depression destroy it. It remains, and will remain, a fundamental tenet of American society."[50]

Esthetic and ethical concepts, Beard found, also had been powerful in history. The ethical factor is one of the points at which he quarreled with Marxian interpretation. Men that make decisions choose what they consider desirable, and desirability involves ethical or esthetic assumptions, "however vociferously" men "may repudiate them as irrelevant and odious." Beard believed indeed that the crisis of thought in the 1930's, by opening "the way to emancipation from two delusions of certainty . . . the theological and the scientific," had brought "an imperative call . . . for the deliberate assumption of ethical and esthetic responsibility, a freedom to dare and experiment."[51] Still, Beard did not, even in his late emphasis upon ideas and ethics and esthetics, abandon his belief that interest was important. In 1939 he pointed out that "the covering of interest by ideology had been a common custom in ages past." Yet Beard believed that determining the true relation between ideas and interests, "the relation between individual and mass thought and action on the one side and total environment on the other," was a chief concern of historians. Beard was no mechanistic determinist, theological or materialistic. To him "necessity and ideal, interests and ideals" seemed "inextricably interwoven." Both developed in time; both interlocked. "Wherever ideas appear," he insisted, "interests are attached; wherever interests appear, ideas are associated with them."[52]

Always intrigued by the problem of power, Beard often speculated on the relative importance of individuals and impersonal forces. For the most part he thought in terms of "forces." He could not believe "that the election of Blaine instead of Cleveland in 1884 or Parker instead of Roosevelt in 1904 would have made much difference in the economy, social life, or general culture." Though legislative acts were associated with McKinley, Roosevelt, Taft, Wilson, Harding, Coolidge, "it would be difficult," he thought, "to find a single statute which any of them originally conceived in general or in detail and made a party issue." Presidents and legislatures came and went, but legislation was produced by social forces that were continuous. So, too, he felt that the final triumph of business enterprise resulted not from the qualities of particular leaders but was made inevitable by the juxtaposition of "a vigorous ingenious race" and "marvelous natural resources."[53] Even in 1936, in *The Devil Theory of War*, he still protested against oversimplifying history by blaming leaders for circumstances that had been created by underlying forces and the people themselves. Politicans do not "wilfully lead us into war." "War is not the work of a demon. It is our very own work, for which we prepare, wittingly or not, in ways of peace." Even here, though, he was protesting more against the presumption of saying why men acted or what "caused" events than against the claim that a leader like Wilson had shaped events.[54]

As totalitarian dictators arose to menace the world, Beard shifted his position. He did not abandon his effort to understand them in terms of the social and economic forces that made them, but he became much more impressed with the power of individual men than he had been earlier. Men were far more important in *The Republic,* published in 1943, than they had been in *An Economic Interpretation.* In his last two books, too, Roosevelt's personal role was more stressed than Hamilton's had been in his early writings. His old historical tenets remained applicable to the conditions that had prevailed in the nineteenth century, but new conditions dominated the world. The military and political man had conquered the economic.

His quarrel with Franklin Roosevelt centered in the problem raised by this new importance of man vis-à-vis forces. Beard pointed out that Roosevelt's defenders made contradictory claims. Some of them defended him against the charge of maneuvering us into war by insisting that the war was "thrust upon" him. Others claimed that Roosevelt "as a perceptive statesman foresaw, in advance of the American people, the great end to be attained" by America's entry into war and ultimately won the people to his position. If one accepted the first contention, then, Beard asked, "were President Roosevelt and Secretary Hull merely victims, and not makers, of history?" Beard himself broke with his old contention that forces and not men make history and accepted the second view, but then questioned the means through which Roosevelt took the unwilling people to war. The means Roosevelt used Beard believed could be upheld only on the principle that the end justified the means. This principle Beard refused to accept.[55]

Yet his major objection went deeper. Even if Roosevelt's means could be ethically justified by the importance of the end he served, still there remained to be faced "the relation of the means, as actually employed, to the Constitution," and all it signified for "limited government, consent of the governed, democratic processes, and political ethics." This issue, Beard believed, rose above parties and personalities and was "timeless in its reach for the American people, perhaps for the people of the whole world." Beard's final legacy to the historical world was a warning that Roosevelt had established "the theory that the President of the United States possesses limitless authority publicly to misrepresent and secretly to control foreign policy, foreign affairs, and the war policy," and that the Rooseveltian precedents had endangered the future of representative government under the Constitution.[56]

Fully as important as his economic interpretation of history was Beard's insistence throughout his writings that "domestic affairs and foreign affairs are intimately associated with each other." "Often," he said, "both are but different aspects of the same thing. Separating them into distinct compartments, if pursued to the logical conclusion, results in misleading conceptions concerning the processes of national life and their actual ramifications throughout the texture of world societies."[57]

Foreign policy had traditionally been determined, Beard insisted, by the exigencies of domestic affairs. Sometimes foreign policy has been molded by pressure groups—munitions makers promoting larger armament sales, bankers wishing new investments or protection for old ones abroad, shipping interests wanting foreign trade, manufacturers desiring foreign markets, investors seeking foreign territory to exploit or chauvinists craving territory to boast of, or officials and citizens living in American communities abroad who are able to persuade their government to sponsor their special interests. Frequently problems at home have controlled men's actions on overseas issues as when, during the Napoleonic wars, such domestic issues caused both Jeffersonians and Federalists to take positions on foreign policy that were contrary to what might have been expected. Jefferson's hatred of England, Beard believed, stemmed from domestic

economic reasons. Sometimes foreign policy has been decided
by a desire for escape from a domestic crisis; sometimes by the
pursuit of a positive philosophy that domestic prosperity is
created by solving international problems and creating an orderly, prosperous world without trade barriers; at still other
times by the pursuit of imperialist or power politics theories
that prosperity at home will result from world domination. So
economic depressions such as those that threatened in 1914 and
1937 were averted by events abroad. So, too, Beard accepted
Hobson's thesis that "the primary force in the rivalry of nations
for market outlets . . . is the inefficient distribution of wealth
at home . . . the enormous accumulations of capital that cannot find high profits in domestic expansion and must go abroad
or burst."[58] Indeed, Beard insisted that tariffs, armaments,
merchant marine, and immigration, always rigorously withheld
from international action because they are "of purely domestic
concern," none the less constitute "outward thrusts of power
which produce repercussions in various parts of the world, as
surely as do trade promotion, investment protection, and dem-
onstrations of force in the national interest."[59]

Yet even as domestic concerns have influenced foreign policy,
so also have foreign conditions affected domestic affairs of nations. In 1906, in his first book touching foreign policy, Beard
pointed out that in every European country domestic policies
were complicated by imperialism.[60] Even Jefferson's agricultural interest in his relatively simple America "depended for
its prosperity upon . . . the markets of the Old World. . . .
American agriculture vibrated in its fortunes with every turn
in the European balance of power." World War I destroyed
any easy assumption that domestic policy was not at the mercy
of happenings abroad. The prosperity of the 1920's was so
intertwined with events all over the world that it crashed in
part because of conditions in other countries; and neither the
American navy, foreign investments, the world power of American bankers, nor far-flung imperial possessions had been able to
prevent it. Indeed, "the economic world" in which Americans

lived, "the intellectual climate on which they relied for ideas and phraseology," and "the setting for capitalist operations had been radically altered by . . . the transformation of Europe in peace and war."[61]

What most concerned Beard, however, was the effect of foreign policy, particularly imperialism and war, upon domestic institutions fundamental to our democracy. "Foreign policy in action," he warned, "is more than the exchange of polite notes." It stirs "domestic interests, passions, and frustrations to the very deeps."[62] Lincoln and Wilson fighting wars for freedom had been forced to deny at home freedom that was in Beard's mind basic to American democracy. Beard had himself lived through disillusionment over what war could do to American liberties. A passage on Jefferson that is often overlooked throws light on his later attitude toward Roosevelt's foreign policy. In 1927 he had written: Jefferson dreaded "the social results of armed conflicts." "War," Jefferson exclaimed, "had transformed the kings of Europe into maniacs and the countries of Europe into madhouses while peace had 'saved to the world the only plant of free and rational government now existing in it.' Corruption and tyranny, in his opinion, flowed from armed conflicts, whereas 'peace, prosperity, liberty and morals have an intimate connection.'" Yet Jefferson was forced into war. "The fateful course of events in Europe, beyond the will and the purpose of Jefferson, . . . drew him and his immediate followers into domestic policies more autocratic and sweeping than Hamilton's boldest enterprise; hurried them, pacific as they were in intention, into a struggle not of their own deliberate making; compelled them to resort to hated measures of revenue and finance."[63]

There is an innate consistency, then, in Beard's basic interpretation of the interrelation of foreign and domestic policies and the point of view of his last two books on foreign policy. Beard could not dissociate the two aspects of Roosevelt's policy. As his researches convinced him that Roosevelt had led the country unnecessarily into war, his old convictions about the historic effects of war upon domestic institutions aroused him to dismay, for he saw a "needless" war endangering the hope of preserving democratic freedoms and of fulfilling the promise of American democracy.

Beard always urged a closer interrelationship between history and the other social studies. He had himself early studied European history and economics. He had read a great deal of political theory and philosophy. All his life he was a student of the problems of education. His standing in political science was as important as in history, and he had taught "politics" involving something of both. Indeed, it was the breadth of his culture that made him so great an historian. He was at home in a variety of fields and in any one he utilized the others. He knew not only America but Europe, not only the present but the past. He knew not only American historians, but he had read widely in Fustel de Coulanges, Maitland, Stubbs, Toynbee, Vinogradoff. He had studied legal theorists like Goodnow and Pound at home and von Jhering, Menger, and Stammler abroad, philosophers like Dewey, Royce, and James at home and Comte, Croce, Hegel, Mannheim, Pascal, Spencer, Vaihinger abroad. He had been influenced in political philosophy not only by Madison and other early Americans and a later American like Arthur F. Bentley, but by Plato, Aristotle, Machiavelli, from whom he drew much, More, Hobbes, Locke, Rousseau, Condorcet, Bagehot, and Graham Wallas. He had been profoundly affected by Seligman and Veblen in economic theory, but he also knew Smith, Ricardo, Mill, Marx, Marshall, and John A. Hobson at first hand. In search of a philosophy of history he had read John, Brooks, and Henry Adams, Anaximander, Buckle, Droysen, Hegel, Heussi, Mannheim, Marx, Mueller-Armack, Ranke, whom he vigorously attacked, Riezler, and Spengler, but had probably been most influenced by E. W. Hobson, Sombart, and Croce. Beard had the background, then, for broad cultural history, what he called "history as actuality," history that attempted to include "all that has been done, said, felt, and thought" in one great "seamless webb."[64] Max Lerner rightly called it *Kulturgeschichte* and paid Beard high tribute when he declared:

To write this kind of history the historian . . . must be economist, politician, administrator, military- and foreign-affairs expert, geographer, educationist, sociologist, lawyer, scientist, literary and artistic critic; and he must finally be part of and yet detached from the ways in which the American masses spend . . . their income and their leisure. To do this well is the privilege of only a few. Some . . . lack gusto for it, others . . . are not well enough rounded. To say that the Beards fall down at some points is therefore not a damaging criticism. What is amazing is . . . that on the whole the competence of any authors should be so well sustained.[65]

Beard never ceased to struggle against the compartmentalizing of the social studies. He served on various committees, wrote widely on the subject, gave four years to the work of the Commission on the Social Studies in the Schools. He protested the "transformation of political economy into mere economics." He admitted that excluding "politics" from "economic activities made 'thinking' about those activities simpler, for it eliminated all impinging and penetrating realities which might interfere with the pleasant, arm-chair operation of deducing 'economic laws' from undisturbed major premises," but he insisted that "by barring government, national policies, and the social contexture of economic transactions from their thought, writings, and teachings, American economists helped to take all sense out of the idea of civilization."[66] Obviously for purposes of work and thought, the broad field of the social studies had to be delimited. Yet, Beard warned, "specialization in particulars, cut off from wider relations, leads to mere thoughtless scholasticism."[67] In his last appearance before the political scientists Beard pleaded with them "to reduce, if not break, the tyranny of specialization and alleged expertness over the human spirit and enlarge the power of informed and discerning judgment in the conduct and study of public affairs." He repeated the warning of Burgess that "the divorce of political science and history . . . would break contacts with long human experience in the conduct of government and thus furnish no seasoned standards for making those epochal judgments which constitute the highest acts of statesmanship so fateful for the life and death of nations."[68]

All his life Beard was seeking a philosophy of history. He had been struck by the statement Bury made in 1904 that he could not imagine "the slightest theoretical importance in a collection of facts or sequences of facts, unless we can hope to determine their vital connection in the whole system of reality."[69] In 1934 Beard rejoiced because historians were at last recognizing that "in their selection, classification, and treatment of cold, stubborn facts" there was "a shade, color, or dash" of their own philosophy. Paraphrasing Croce he warned social scientists that "an ostentatious expulsion of great philosophy at the front door usually means that a poor little vulgar philosophy of prejudices and passions is smuggled in at the back door and controls the selecting and emphasizing operations in historical writing." However distasteful "empirical historians" might find this need for a philosophy of history it was none the less real. For Beard's part, he believed a conscious philosophy was "an indispensable corrective for the adding machine type of historical 'manual,'" and warned that "all serious efforts to be informed about history and historical writings" must take the problem of a philosophy of history into account.[70]

The philosophy Beard finally adopted under the influence of Croce and others is termed "relativism." Beard himself defined it as his belief "that no historian can describe the past as it actually was and that every historian's work—that is, his selection of facts, his emphasis, his omissions, his organization, and his methods of presentation—bears a relation to his own personality and the age and circumstances in which he lives." Or again, "All schemes of historical construction are relative to time and place and are destined to pass with the passing of the circumstances—ideas and interests—in which they originate." But

Beard, always realistic even about himself and his own doctrine, warned: "If all historical conceptions are merely relative to passing events, to transitory phases of ideas and interests, then the conception of relativity is itself relative. When absolutes in history are rejected the absolutism of relativity is also rejected."[71]

Beard's relativism was, however, a philosophy not of despair but of hope. In giving up absolutes Beard felt he was bringing historical interpretation into the realm of the possible and the useful. The relativist could offer interpretations helpful in understanding the present without waiting to determine final and absolute truth. Hence he was not estopped entirely from interpreting, as the seeker of absolutes was. Beard was content with "the utmost truth attainable to us." This more modest relativist truth Beard continued to pursue. It was in his answer to a criticism of Theodore Smith, however, that Beard gave his most explicit statement of his confidence in relativism. "We do not acquire the colorless, neutral mind," he warned Smith, "by declaring our intention to do so. Rather do we clarify the mind by admitting its cultural interests and patterns—interests and patterns that will control, or intrude upon, the selection and organization of historical materials." Beard urged his fellow historians to consider seriously what they thought they were doing when they wrote history, what philosophies and interpretations were open to them, which of these they actually chose and practiced and why, and what methods and processes would best enable them "to bring the multitudinous and bewildering facts of history into any coherent and meaningful whole." To ask such questions would not extinguish but increase hope of fulfilling the "objective" historian's "noble dream of the search for truth." But, warned Beard, to ask these questions will make historians human beings, not immortal gods.[72]

Corollary to his relativism is Beard's belief that the social studies are not "sciences" and that to assume for history the qualities of a natural science is merely to confuse and mislead.

Like others of his generation he was schooled in "scientific" history. In 1908 he warned against bias, eschewed all temptation to "praise or condemn," and set as his goal the procurement of data "by scientific investigation," which the theologian, the teacher of ethics, and the patriot might then use for their several purposes.[73] In Beard's youth he gloried in being freed by the new scientific approach from the older natural rights doctrines, racist explanations of history, and belief in divine intervention in human affairs.[74] Gradually, however, he became convinced that it was impossible "to describe the past as it actually was, somewhat as the engineer describes a single machine."

He still believed that "historical scholarship" had "wrought achievements of value beyond calculation," that the "scientific method," which alone could provide "accurate knowledge of historical facts," had illuminated "once dark and confused" phases of history. The "enquiring spirit of science" provided, too, "the chief safeguard against the tyranny of authority, bureaucracy, and brute power." But utility of the "scientific method" as a tool does not, he warned, make history a science. "The idea of exact determination" applicable to physics cannot be applied to "all human action, thought, and aspiration." The idea of organism borrowed from biology only distorts history. Ideas of the physical sciences provide "analogies, not accurate descriptions of historical occurrences and relations." Unlike the physical scientist, Beard insisted, the historian is not an observer of what he describes. He must depend upon a variety of records that are at best only a portion of the data, and he can never know how much or how important a part is lacking. He cannot set up controls and test hypotheses. Furthermore, the social studies deal with "ideas, aspirations, hopes, conceptions of possibility, resentments, hatreds, and passions that are not open to the eye, that cannot be weighed and measured." Ideas are not fixed but constantly changing. Conflicting social forces make human tensions impossible to measure. Into ideas and other social forces enter values, "ethical and esthetic," impossible of measurement, and "contingency, chance, and choice in changing affairs."[75] No, protested Beard, the historian who writes history does not practice science but "consciously or unconsciously performs an act of faith as to order and movement. . . . In writing he acts and in acting he makes choices, large or small, timid or bold, with respect to some conception of the nature of things." The historian's faith, Beard contended, "is at bottom a conviction that something true can be known about the movement of history and his conviction is a subjective decision, not a purely objective discovery."[76]

Beard was unable to find in history "a body of axioms or laws which enables a master of them to predict with a high degree of assurance what will happen when a series of events is set in motion under any particular law." No one had found "laws" of all history. Henry Adams had tried and failed. Spengler had tried and Beard found him unsatisfying. Marx had gone further than others, but left Beard unconvinced.[77] Eight months before his death he told the Political Science Association, "I have come to the conviction that we have no justification whatever for regarding our universe as a unified process under law and hence reducible to an exact science, either physical or political; and still less justification for supposing that, given the nature of our minds, we can grasp the scheme of things entire in its three-dimensional fullness."[78]

At the beginning of his career Beard had noted "a persistent attempt to get more precise notions about causation in politics," and had felt that this effort was "destined to have a high practical value." "A thousand experiences of political life bear witness," he had written, "that a treatise on causation . . . would be the most welcome contribution which a scholar of scientific training and temper could make." He himself assigned causes to many events and movements. Yet ultimately he came to believe that the term "cause" should never be used. "A search for the causes of America's entry into the war," Beard pointed out, "leads into the causes of the war, into all the history that lies beyond 1914, and into the very nature of the universe of which history is a part; that is, unless we arbitrarily decide to cut the web and begin at some point that pleases us." "Where historians are concerned," he said, "as they should be, with consequential and coexisting relations between events and personalities and interests, which are intimate in nature and have the appearance of necessity, they can describe such relations in terms more precise than those of causality; without using the word 'cause' or 'causes'—'ambiguous and difficult' terms, 'of varied and complex meaning.' "[79]

In view of Beard's concept of the nature of history and historians, it was natural that he should always inquire into a writer's "frame of reference."[80] As he used to tell his students, "The hand is subdued to the die in which it works" and "A man sees that which is behind his eyes."[81] A man's "frame of reference" as Beard used the concept was "composed of things deemed necessary and of things deemed desirable." "The thinker who deals with chemicals and stars stands outside the objects observed," Beard admitted, but in the social sciences "the thinker floats in the streams of facts, so-called, which he observes" and "his thoughts are parts of the thing thought about." The social scientist is not "an abstract human being timeless and placeless" but an American, Englishman, German, or Japanese at a given time in history. Within his country he belongs to a geographical area and a class, group, or profession concerned about its security and welfare. In limiting his subject and selecting and organizing the facts of any given bit of history the historian necessarily makes arbitrary choices that are controlled by his frame of reference. "The frame," Beard warned, "may be a narrow class, sectional, national, or group conception of history, clear and frank or confused and half conscious, or it may be a large, generous conception, clarified by association with the great spirits of all ages. Whatever its nature the frame is inexorably there, in the mind."[82]

In Beard's judgment the key to sound history was for the historian to determine his own attitudes that affected his writing of history and then take them into account. Beard realized how difficult and dangerous interpreting history was. It was easier and more comfortable deliberately to evade facing the problem of one's own frame of reference by eschewing interpretation altogether. Or to avoid conflict and the hazards of thinking the historian might "confine his attention to some very remote and microscopic area of time and place, such as the price of cotton in Alabama between 1850 and 1860, or the length of wigs in the reign of Charles II."[83] As early as 1913 Beard had described to deplore the "school of historical research" that "have resolutely turned aside from 'interpretation' in the larger sense, and concerned themselves with critical editions of the documents and with the 'impartial' presentation of related facts."[84]

Beard himself always urged men to examine and avow their frames of reference and then, as fair-mindedly as possible within them, to essay an interpretation of history.[85] "Does the world move and, if so, in what direction?" he challenged the members of the American Historical Association. "If he believes that the world does not move, the historian must offer the pessimism of chaos to the inquiring spirit of mankind. If it does move, does it move backward toward some old arrangement, let us say, of 1928, 1896, 1815, 1789, or 1295? Or does it move forward to some other arrangement which can be only dimly divined—a capitalist dictatorship, a proletarian dictatorship, or a collectivist democracy?"[86] When Theodore Smith attacked Beard for destroying the ideal of "objective history" for which Smith said the American Historical Association stood, Beard replied that Smith's "objective" interpretation of the framers of the Constitution excluded arbitrarily all interpretations but its own, that it failed to explain their acts since it did not tell how the opposing ideas got into the heads of the framers and their opponents, and that it hurled the epithet "Marxian" at those who pointed out economic motives. But Beard also charged Smith with violating the "objectivity" he was defending against Beard. Smith insisted the struggle over the Constitution was "a contest between sections ending in the victory of straight-thinking national-minded men over narrower and more local opponents." "An economic interpretation," said Beard, "does not inquire whether men were straight-thinking or crooked-thinking. It inquires not into their powers of mind or virtues, but into the nature and effects of their substantial possessions." Then it also tries to explain *why* "some men were national-minded and others were local-minded."[87]

Again when he reviewed Arthur M. Schlesinger's *Rise of the City* Beard attacked the whole school of "objective" historians for evading interpretation and refusing to acknowledge their implicit assumptions. After listing at length a miscellaneous series of topics that Schlesinger dealt with, he commented:

Whether this movement and uproar meant anything then or means anything now, whether it had any center of gravity or was merely chaos floating in chaos, whether it had any direction, Professor Schlesinger does not venture to say. He steers clear of all interpretations—economic, political, and philosophical. Apparently he thinks interpretations are wrong, that none is possible, and that impressionistic eclecticism is the only resort of contemporary scholarship. He may be right. But that, too, is an interpretation, with profound philosophic implications— for those who care to go into the metaphysics of historiography. We may shut our eyes to the abyss of thought that yawns devouringly at our feet, so perilous; the abyss remains.

Beard himself did not mind criticism. He throve on historical argument. What he minded about the attacks on his last books was the presumption and lack of scholarly realism in his critics' claims that his frame of reference was bias and their point of view constituted "objectivity."

Beard always emphasized the importance of pointing history up to current problems and throwing the light of the past down the path of the future. He wished to avoid the error of the nineteenth century, which was "too arrogant to recognize its dependence upon the eighteenth, from which it derived most of its inspirations as well as its aversions."[88] At a time when it was the fashion to study history "with no other aim than that of learning about bygone events and famous men long since dead," Robinson and Beard called attention to the "inexorable dependence of the present upon the past." "Existing forms of government and social life are not to be understood," they declared, "by simply examining them," but by taking the trouble to discover their origin and to follow their gradual development. History can explain almost anything from a state constitution to the presence of useless buttons upon a man's coat sleeve. In their book Robinson and Beard in 1908 announced that they would dwell especially on those events, conditions, and public persons that have made the governments, politics, industries, and intellectual interests of Europe what they are today.[89]

In his review Sidney B. Fay questioned whether this emphasis on contemporary problems was wise but concluded that Robinson's and Beard's book was itself "a strong argument in the affirmative," for "it is as solid and informing as it is interesting and clever." "It may shock some conservative temperaments," Fay warned, "but by many others we suspect it will be hailed as a new evangel."[90]

Beard who had been schooled in the ideal of "objective" history deplored in *Politics* in 1908 the efforts of many writers to bend the pursuit of learning to a vindication of their own preconceptions. Politics he then felt should be separated from theology, ethics, and patriotism. Its function was not to praise or condemn institutions but to understand and expound them; to provide scientific data and then leave it to the theologian, the leader of ethics, and the patriot to judge the past.[91]

Gradually, however, Beard found himself reversing his earlier position. He discovered that if history was to shed light on current problems, someone had to judge and criticize past efforts to solve those problems. Who was better qualified than the historian who knew the past experience of mankind as no one else did? Passing judgment, however, involved possessing values by which to judge. In the meantime, while he was discovering that history was not a science and that the work of "objective" historians was determined by points of view that they held but merely refused to admit or avow, he became convinced that, to make history meaningful, it was necessary for the historians to evaluate the success or failure of oft tried expedients or principles. Hence in 1934 he contradicted his 1908 ideal of history.

He now reminded historians who insisted on having nothing to do with value judgments that even if avoiding such judgments was practically possible, they would do well to remember two unequivocal facts. One was that the greatest among their colleagues from Plato to John A. Hobson, from Aristotle to John Maynard Keynes, have faced the realities of their subject with wide comprehension and have not shrunk from making value judgments themselves. The other was that, if those who are most informed about the data of the social sciences will make no such judgments deliberately, thinkers and doers in actual life, confronting competing values, will and must make decisions. "Human desires, interests, hopes, admirations, dislikes, and resentments," Beard warned, "will not disappear because social scientists refuse to take them into consideration and ostentatiously decline to express any opinions respecting them." "Humanity," Beard insisted, "will continue to make history, although the skeptical historian can find no reason why it should be done."[92]

Beard always held to the rigid use of scientific tools. He often expressed contempt for the man who distorted history by reading his own views back into it. His belief was that history should instruct the present and that current and passing values of those writing history should not be permitted to mold the past. Only by reconstructing the past accurately could it be made useful to the present. Yet he came firmly to believe that the historian should subject the past to value judgments, always keeping facts and opinions clearly differentiated, and that, since all historians in plain reality did just that anyway in selecting and arranging the facts, it was better to be conscious of it. His relativism saved him from any illusions about the permanence of either his value judgments or his interpretations, but he felt the attempt at evaluation enlightened the present. He himself had an amazing capacity, often remarked, to describe fairly past points of view and interests and values that were not his own and to subject to rigorous criticism men of the past who had shared his. For to Beard forming value judgments involved no self-justification of the present out of the past but a never-ending search through the past for truth that could guide the present. Hence in his history he was constantly preoccupied with forces that seemed important to the present: the motives of men, the ethical and esthetic values they lived by, the idea of progress, the meaning of democracy, the long fight for the freedom of the individual, economic rivalries, imperialism, war, and particularly the concept of power, what produced it, who exercised it, and safeguards against abuse of it.

From the belief that history had use only if it were given meaning through interpretation and that the experience of the past could help solve the problems of the present, it followed that the man who knew most about the past—the historian—should participate in the present. The scholar could enlighten contemporary statesmanship. The scholar had a public duty to offer society the benefits of his discoveries of truth. In theory, then, as well as by temperament, Beard deplored the ivory tower scholar. For him scholarship and public activity were inseparable. Beard not only produced more scholarly works than most scholars who never leave the academic cloister; he spent more time in genuine public service than do most public men. He felt that history could best be illumined by a man actively tackling human problems about him and that public problems could best be solved by a man intimately acquainted with the experience of wise men of the past. Hence historical truth and the commonweal both benefited by the union of concern for both in a scholar who was at the same time an active citizen. Of this ideal Beard was himself the epitome, and the result was a vitality in his history that would otherwise have been impossible.

Indeed, the quality of Beard's history and the quality of
Beard the man are inseparable. Several characteristics combined to give the peculiar Beardian touch. Most obvious is his
style. There is a majesty about it that Max Lerner has described as "a blend of Olympianism and the concrete."[93] Great
forces and movements flow through Beard's books and blend
with other forces into crescendos, diminuendos, characteristic
rhythms, and oft repeated themes in many variations, producing
moving harmonies and startling dissonances, to make at last a
synthesis like a great symphony. Beard combines dispassionate
description of facts with moving concern about values. His
style is crisp, vivid, incisive, vigorous, stimulating, refreshing,
often brilliant. It is frequently original, never trite. It has
clarity without thinness or triviality. It is thorough, systematic,
painstaking, but never dull. Beard's books could not have been
written by an Englishman or a New Englander of the genteel
tradition. His style has a flavor of the American Middle West.
It is rugged, homely, forthright, but never provincial or vulgar.
It is subtle without being obscure, often dramatic without becoming cheap. As Max Lerner puts it, here is "no dilution of
the strong stuff of history" but "sweep, learning, depth, tough-
mindedness."[94] And when his anger is aroused by a threat to
democratic values, or by fraud or injustice, particularly when
human freedom is endangered, his wrath becomes devastating,
magnificent. Besides all this he demonstrates a power of synthesis that re-creates in the end what looks to ordinary mortals
like the "seamless web" of history as actuality that he always
protested could not be reproduced.

Beard's education had given him a breadth of view that en-
compassed many fields and Europe as well as America. He had
been lucky in an undergraduate teacher who stimulated him
to wide reading and serious thinking. Colonel Weaver at
DePauw had raised many of the problems that Beard spent his
life pursuing.[95] Beard responded to the stimulus, won highest
honors, demonstrated "fine ability," exhibited "the highest
moral character," excelled all other students in history and

forensics, and, as an undergraduate, showed such marked ability in historical research that Professor Stephenson "insisted from the first that he give his life to this line of work." Professor Weaver described the undergraduate Beard as "full of zeal, fond of investigation, . . . eminently fitted for . . . original research," and possessed of "a keen insight into truth." His leading professor at Oxford, Frederick York Powell, commended him for his application, industry, ability, and judgment, and reported that this first-year graduate student had "enthusiasm and the power of exciting it in others." Moses C. Tyler at Cornell perceived at once Beard's "unusual intellectual and personal gifts and his special aptitude for historical research and exposition" and regretted Beard's declining a fellowship that was offered him. Tyler found him "a high-minded and gifted young man, moved by generous impulses, and worthy for talent and character of all confidence, friendship, and co-operation."[96] Contact with leaders of his profession at Cornell, Oxford, and Columbia influenced him profoundly. Some of his graduate professors, such as Goodnow, stirred great thoughts in him, and several others, such as Burgess, seem to have influenced him by provoking him to refute them. Indeed, several of his most important contributions, such as his economic interpretation and his repudiation of racist doctrines, were contradictions of what some of his best-known graduate teachers stood for. In any case his training grounded him thoroughly in the best of orthodox scholarship of the day. Perhaps the most important parts of his education were his experience as editor of a small-town Indiana paper and his activity in the Independent Labour Party in England, where he enjoyed contacts with both Fabian theorists and practical organizers in the ranks of labor. The combination of labor organization experience, cloistered scholarship, and Midwestern editorship that comprised his education created one important Beardian quality.

Beard not only formulated from history theories about public affairs, but he translated them into action. History led him to believe that wars endangered democracy, that overseas posses-

sions and empire threatened domestic well-being, that power
politics menaced civilization.   Hence he worked out a policy of
"continentalism," battled for it, appeared before congressional
committees to advocate it.   Militarism he feared, and one of
his last public acts was to warn a Senate committee that peacetime conscription would endanger democracy.   Repelled by the
chauvinism of World War I, he proposed that the New York
School of Social Work, on whose staff he was instructing, should
institute a course teaching the right kind of Americanism.   He
devoted much time to training social workers.   He pioneered
in municipal reform and drew up practical programs for New
York, Tokyo, and Yugoslavia.   History revealed to him the evils
of laissez faire; in consequence he became a leading proponent
of municipal, later national, and finally international planning.
He served on countless committees concerned with educational
and other public problems, but he refused to let his name be
used unless he could contribute actively to the work.   In Connecticut he helped terminate a strike and then helped organize
the milk farmers to greater strength.   History taught him the
methods of railroad reorganization; so he sued to prevent Morgan's reorganizing the rights of bondholders out of existence;
so, too, he testified in Washington against railroad practices.
History convinced him that personal freedom was important
in preserving democracy; hence he became a crusader for civil
liberties, resigned from Columbia in protest against Butler's
violations of academic freedom, fought teachers' oaths, helped
Senator Cutting draft his petition of 1930 against customs censorship of "dangerous" and "impure" thoughts in imported
literature, and traveled to Atlantic City publicly to attack
Hearst for interfering in the schools.   Consequently, when
Beard wrote about any of these matters in the past, he wrote
with experience of an active participant.

   Beard brought to history a philosophical bent that led him to
speculation about life and about what made the wheels of history go 'round.   Coupled with this was an intellectual curiosity
that led him into obscure places where time after time he struck
pay dirt.   Merrill Jensen, who more than any one of this gen-

eration has explored the decade of the formation of the Constitution, says that the evidence supporting Beard's economic interpretation makes Beard's thesis an understatement and that, as Beard knew, the same thesis could have been applied more broadly to other aspects of public life of the time. Indeed, Jensen says that students have only begun to mine the riches that Beard's explorations in old records have revealed. His curiosity and his habit of questioning orthodoxy led him to pioneer in ways that often engendered denunciation. He was one of the early promoters of revisionism in the history of World War I. No one who recalls the vigor of the attack made on the earlier new interpretations sponsored by Beard and the later much wider acceptance of those interpretations can help wonder whether Beard's usual intuition failed him as he wrote his last two foreign policy books, or whether time will again prove him to have been prophetic in sponsoring anew an unpopular thesis.[97] Beard was always provocative, fatal to complacency, and hence admired by the young and disturbing to the well established, who did not like to be forced to rethink their positions.

Beard was never trivial. Human as he was, endowed with a keen sense of humor, loving a good story, he still had a seriousness of purpose that banished banalities from any talk in which he participated. His presence insured good conversation. He thought great thoughts, and cheapness and triviality were so incongruous in his presence that even cheap and trivial minds forebore from uttering their commonplaces.

Beard was courageous. Fear of denunciation, of personal loss, of offense to powerful persons never caused him to be silent if he believed truth or justice demanded that he speak. He loved his friends. He knew his last two books would cost him many previously devoted ones. In full knowledge of the hurt and loneliness he was preparing for himself he went doggedly ahead just as he had once defied Columbia's mighty trustees and Hearst's power to destroy. It was a grim and in the end a lonely courage, but on occasion it could scale magnificent heights of the human spirit.

His impress upon his America was extended far beyond those who read his histories by his wide human contacts in committees, with lecture audiences and readers of his articles, with countless friends and admirers, with scholars whom he counseled, and particularly with young people whom he befriended. Beard was perennially young in spirit. He appealed to the young. That was because he was interested in young people and their ideas. Of my own contacts with Beard three stand out that reveal the secret of the peculiar affection in the term "Uncle Charley" by which many younger historians knew him. The first was a talk in Chicago in 1933. After a morning, afternoon, and evening of discussion in a smoke-filled common room of Judson Court at the University of Chicago where the Commission on Social Studies was in session, Beard sought out Merle Curti and me, young and little known, from the distinguished members of the Commission whose meetings we were attending merely because we were writing books for them. "Let's take a walk." We walked to the lake and back. On our return Beard insisted we come to his room and talk some more. He gave us the only two chairs while he sat cross-legged on the bed. We talked until after midnight. As we left, stimulated by a hundred new ideas, Beard thanked us for coming and told us how much *he* had enjoyed talking with *us*. "You know," he said, "I learned years ago to seek out at meetings the *young* men and talk to them. I knew twenty years ago what those old fellows think. What I want to know is what you youngsters are thinking." The second episode was a party Merle Curti and I had in the Harvard Club in New York after the annual dinner at the 1940 meeting of the American Historical Association. We each invited twenty guests ranging in age from our contemporaries down to young graduate students. Then we wrote Beard and told him the guests were mostly young men whom we should love to have know him if he could possibly come. Beard came up from Baltimore, stayed quietly in his room in the hotel where the great of the profession would have given him a place of honor at the Association's annual dinner, slipped out to the party at the Harvard Club, where he was the center of exciting conversation until one A.M., went to a Johns Hopkins breakfast the next morning, where there were more unknown young men, and then returned to Baltimore with the important historians still unaware that he had spent the night in the hotel in which they were meeting. For all of us the evening was one of those unforgettable events. But Charles Beard, surrounded by young men, drawing out their thoughts and expounding his own, was enjoying it all as much as the youngest graduate student. The third event occurred in 1941. I drove past to spend the night with the Beards on their Connecticut farm before proceeding northward for the summer. A student who was with me, before driving back to the village to spend the night, stopped long enough to inquire when he should call for me next day. The Beards characteristically insisted that he, too, be their guest. He was an undergraduate physics major, who had not been much out of North Carolina and had studied no college history. At first overawed, he was speedily put at ease by Beard's simple friendliness, which soon drew him into the conversation with questions about his state. The evening was for the student an exciting intellectual experience, for Beard a chance to pick up new information and learn what a Southern undergraduate in physics was thinking. As we drove away next morning, the student remarked, "Golly, I didn't know so great a man could be so simple." Then after a pause, "Maybe that is why he is so great."

The simplicity the student sensed was one of Beard's greatest qualities. He had, besides, an element of universality about him. He was very much a part of the stream of progressivism that marked the early years of the twentieth century. He applied to contemporary America the truths he gleaned from history. Yet the immediacy of his ideas was mixed with something that was timeless, without geographic limits, universal.

Beard was intensely American, yet never chauvinistic. The great irony of his life was that a man who early and constantly stressed our interrelations with the rest of the world[98] and who

did so much to make other Americans conscious of Europe, her
scholars, and her contributions, should at the end of his life
have been denounced as an "isolationist." His devotion to
America was not a devotion of ignorance of the rest of the
world. With excellent contacts among the people, great and
obscure, he had traveled widely in Britain, Germany, Yugoslavia, Hungary, Greece, Albania, Japan including Formosa,
and China including Manchuria. He did have a profound
faith in America, in her institutions, in her future. He distrusted the slogans of nationalism. Yet his "continentalism"
was based on a belief that America's way of life and her democratic institutions held out the best hope for mankind. His
constantly critical treatment of much of America's record represented the desire of an ardent admirer to see America's faults
corrected so that she might fulfill her democratic mission. The
vigor of his opposition to Rooseveltian foreign policy stemmed
from his determination that America's chance to use democracy
for the creation of a better society should not be destroyed by
involvement in war. In 1927 he had quoted with approval
Charles E. Hughes's warning that "we may well wonder, in view
of the precedents now established . . . whether constitutional
government as heretofore maintained in this republic could
survive another war even victoriously waged."[99]

Beard had a deep concern about human beings, a profound
respect for human dignity. Hence he battled tirelessly to preserve the freedom of the individual. His hatred of totalitarianism was born of its disregard for human dignity and for
individual rights. His lifelong obsession with the problems of
power stemmed from his fear lest uncurbed power destroy the
free individual. Consequently, he was concerned about the
power of corporations, the power of government, totalitarian
dictators, the threat that he saw in the growing power even of a
democratic executive. He sought to understand power, to
explain the realities of power, so that we might preserve human
liberty in the face of it. A month before he died, in the last
item he was ever to write for publication, he redefined in "our

time of turbulence and groping" the problem he had spent his life trying to solve. It involved the "underlying tenets of the Constitution." With solemnity he warned that "if . . . society is to depend, even during the gravest crisis . . . on reflection and choice rather than on force and accident," then the issue must be faced and a solution found. This "greatest of political issues" is: "How to maintain a government strong enough to defend society against external and internal foes and yet so organized as to protect, by supreme law and its administration, the liberties of the people against oppressive actions by public agents or popular tumults."[100]

Beard outgrew many of the orthodoxies of his youth. But one conviction of the 1890's he never discarded, and that was his faith in progress. He saw progress not in some automatic approach to utopia, but as the evolution, through constant struggle and effort, of a better society. His guess was that that better society would be a "collectivist democracy," which would control many of man's economic activities through planning for a more abundant life, but which would control them for the sake of preserving and enlarging, not destroying, human free- dom. Beard admired Franklin Roosevelt's contribution to "humanistic democracy," which "had been a powerful dynamic in American civilization and culture." Indeed, when in 1939 Beard was most critical of Roosevelt's foreign policy, he still wrote of the domestic scene: "In his numerous discourses Frank- lin D. Roosevelt discussed the basic human and economic prob- lems of American society with a courage and range displayed by no predecessor in his office." He thrust the challenges of these problems into "spheres hitherto indifferent or hostile," said Beard; "he both reflected and stirred the thought of the nation to the uttermost borders of the land." Beard placed his own faith in the "humanistic wing of American democracy" that was seeking "to provide the economic and cultural foundations indispensable to a free society," seeking to fulfill the promises of America's democratic heritage and aspirations. Indeed, Beard felt that important as leaders were, America's destiny did not turn on personalities or political parties, but lay in "great movements of history, manifesting forces of thought and action that had created America's heritage and were working for her future."[101]

It is difficult to measure influence or assess greatness. Certainly, however, Beard's claim to both rests in part on the basic human qualities of Beard the man that profoundly affected both his history and his influence. Certainly, too, what he said was so fundamental to an understanding of America's problems and was so arrestingly said that, whether it inspired admiration or provoked anger, it could not be ignored. Max Lerner has perhaps most aptly analyzed Beard's impact upon the public. Of Beard's economic interpretation of history, he wrote: "What was maddening to those who raged against Beard was that he could not be ignored. . . . What was galling about him was that he used all the paraphernalia of scientific method, which had been considered a monopoly of smugness and the *status quo.* . . . The research he did was a real *tour de force;* it could put to shame on the level of sheer scholarship anyone who sought to challenge it from his Olympian heights. The technical flaws that could be picked were few and unconvincing. . . . What could you do with a man like that? You could not ignore him. You could only rage against his indecency, question his patriotism, accuse him of fomenting class hatred— and bide your time."[102]

Beard then became one of the two or three great figures of American historiography of the first half of the twentieth century because of a peculiar combination of qualities. He stimulated his fellow historians through his constant probings for the meaning of history; yet he could at the same time present history in terms comprehensible and stimulating to the layman. His scholarship was profound, but he had a wider audience than any popularizer of his day. He was living proof that scholarship and popular appeal were not mutually exclusive, but at their best were inseparable. In learned discussions he provoked historians to consideration of economic interpretations and a new balance of human motivations. He challenged traditional views of constitutional history. He pioneered in social and economic history in an age obsessed with political and institutional matters. He set men to speculating on the relative importance of striking personalities and impersonal forces in the making of history. He broke the habit of treating foreign policy and domestic issues in insulated compartments and forced upon men a comprehension of their interdependence. He smashed the barriers that departmentalized the social studies by making himself an expert in several departments and then refusing to be confined within any one discipline. He delved into philosophy and gave the profession "relativism" to argue about. He attacked the concept of "objectivity" and made reluctant colleagues conscious of their frames of reference, and he attacked as misleading the notion that history was an exact science analogous to the physical sciences. He deplored using history to support current opinions but pleaded for the use of history to find answers out of human experience for baffling modern problems. He provoked heated discussion and violent attacks. He distressed adherents of traditional and popular and official points of view and hence stimulated intellectual ferment, for his learning and his force of character were such that he could never be ignored. At the same time, he symbolized as did no other man of his generation the scholar applying what he had learned from the past to problems of the present and descending into the thick of combat unafraid, determined, braving the wrath of the mighty, using his powerful pen and the evidence of history to battle for basic American freedoms wherever he felt they were endangered. For admiring young scholars disillusioned by the futilities of ivory tower scholarship and by safe-in-the-classroom critics of society, Beard became the embodiment of scholarship made vital in public affairs, of the scholar concerned to make his learning effective in actual life. To succeeding generations of young historians discouraged by the complacency or defeatism of their elders, Beard, himself one of its finest products, seemed an eloquent argument for faith in that American freedom-loving democracy that his histories made vivid to millions of readers.

GEORGE R. LEIGHTON

Beard and Foreign Policy

CHARLES BEARD, one of the most vigorous and influential American intellectuals of his time, was born in Indiana of a prosperous rural family who were skeptics in religion. It was a family in which the discussion of ideas and of affairs was as much a commonplace as a solid Sunday dinner. To be born into such a family meant to be given a running start. Given the running start, Beard improved upon his advantages. The story of his life is that of an able and energetic man who, having attained popularity as a teacher and distinction as a historian, threw his career overboard on a point of principle and thereafter achieved a new and remarkable status. He became an attorney with a brief and with his country as his client.

Having accepted the brief, he argued the case for the rest of his life. The intensity with which he regarded his cause may be seen in his statement to the Armed Services Committee of the Senate, made on April 3, 1948, just five months before he died.

Universal military training, so-called, represents an attempt to implant in the United States a well-known curse of the Old

World [said Beard]. I have studied it on the ground there and in the melancholy history of the nations brought to ruin or servitude under its degrading influence, gross and subtle. This system of conscription would violate every liberty to which our Nation has been dedicated since the foundation of the Republic. It would destroy the freedom which our ancestors, having fled from the despotism of Europe, established for themselves and their posterity on American soil. It would create a monstrous military bureaucracy drawn from the upper and middle classes. It would enslave the sons of plain people—farmers, industrial workers, and all other laborers who toil with their hands for a living. It would exalt the military above the civil and thus would work for the overthrow of the first principles upon which the Constitution of the United States is based.[1]

Beard was a participant, a circumstance that set him off from such intellectuals as Henry Adams and Turner and Veblen. Adams, who was given a running start too, was forced to the sidelines and ended his life in a sort of disconsolate resignation. Beard was incapable of resignation. Turner spent years as a professor at Harvard, unhappy in the Cambridge atmosphere and longing to be back at Wisconsin. Beard would never have put up with such a state of affairs; he would have been up and out of there and on his way. As for Veblen, one cannot imagine Beard reaching the state of misery and discouragement that prompted Veblen to say, just before he died in 1929, "Naturally there will be other developments right along, but just now communism offers the best course I can see."[2] Beard was often discouraged, but his fits of depression didn't last long. There was a hardy self-reliance about him that was always sending him back into action. His ideas about foreign policy were inseparable from his ideas and attitudes toward the United States and toward himself.

From what he said and did as an attorney for the Republic and from what he wrote and taught as a historian, the evidence shows that Beard regarded himself first of all, and seriously, as an American citizen. Though to him this meant being a citizen of no mean nation, there was nothing of the bigoted nationalist about him. Citizenship confers upon the holder certain rights, privileges, and responsibilities. Beard's personal history showed that he was aware of the privileges, that he was never slow in asserting the rights, and that he was not dilatory in assuming the responsibilities. Once he was routed out in the night and asked to go help settle a milk strike. He went. The strike was settled. Once I saw him when he was pulling wires and putting on the pressure to have a professor restored to the job from which he had been fired. The truth was that the professor had been sacked because of his own senseless folly. Beard knew it. "It's hell," he said, "spending time and effort to save the life of a fool. But it has to be done."

Beard knew the value of a dollar and never talked bunk about money. Asked why Veblen wrote such tortured prose, Beard replied: "That's easy. Veblen's ideas were disturbing and he never knew where his next meal was coming from. If he hadn't written obscurely he never could have spoken his mind at all. I've always known where my next meal was coming from and that makes a lot of difference." For him economic determinism was something besides an argument in a book. If he wanted a good price for his wares—both his manuscripts and butterfat from his dairy—he never pretended otherwise. I never heard of his being caught in the pose so frequently observed in successful authors of disdaining money in public while grabbing for it in private.

Beard had no patience with a sloven, and as a scholar, his own information was so admirably organized that he was a deadly adversary. I once saw him demolish a vociferous assertion about Pareto by snatching down a volume of Pareto and then and there translating a passage that blew up his, Beard's, opponent.

A formidable antagonist, Beard was subjected to savage abuse and it is remarkable how some strain of sweetness in his character kept the malice in him—and he had plenty of that, too—from turning, as it did with Veblen, to pure vitriol. Much of the abuse sprang from common, ordinary jealousy. Beard had proven that he could go it alone, make a living and tip his hat to no man. Not only could he do this, but simultaneously he could achieve a prestige—in the conventional sense—that was immense. This was more than many people could endure. William James used to talk about "the bitch goddess Success," but there is success and success, just as there is nationalism and nationalism. Joseph Gurney Cannon, Speaker of the House of Representatives, once said that "America is a hell of a success." Beard, too, was a hell of a success, and it always struck me that he enjoyed his success plenty.

Though Beard was once described as "a compound of Indiana Populist, New York Marxian, and Crocean philosopher," it was the Indiana hard nut with humanitarian ideas that persisted. When Beard was eighteen his father bought him a weekly paper, the Knightstown *Sun,* and Beard and his brother ran it successfully for nearly four years before Beard went to DePauw College.

Beard started off as an *owner,* as a *proprietor.* The United States was no geographical expression to him; it was a going concern in which he had a share, a *stake,* and damn the man who, for reasons of frivolity, ignorance, irresponsibility, or simply a desire to throw his weight around, jeopardized the Republic's prospects. When Beard had a chance, in his Oxford days in the late nineties, to get in on the ground floor of the British Labour Party, he didn't take the chance; he came home. Back in this country, later on, he threw over the Socialists before he set to work to investigate the Constitution. I am sure that this investigation must have had a powerful effect upon him. It had taken tremendous ability, energy, and determination to organize the United States. And now, look, he was a part owner of it.

Beard harped incessantly about the pragmatic character of American thought. When he talked about the military establishment he talked as one familiar with it and highly critical about something into which his proprietorship extended. Beard's reiteration that the powers of Congress to investigate must not be restricted wasn't just an attitude. It was practical.

When, in 1935, J. P. Morgan & Company refused to pay the interest on Beard's Missouri Pacific bonds—though the Morgans had the money—Beard did some research himself and then went to Washington to argue before the Senate Interstate Commerce Committee for an investigation of the Van Sweringens. The investigation was made, though Beard wasn't the only one who wanted it, and in the end he got his money. But it would be hard to tell what infuriated him the more: having his own money withheld or having railroad thimbleriggers loose in the country.

Finally, he had nerve. I would not say he never trimmed his sails, nor dodged in a tight place—"I'm not God," was an old trick of his when cornered—but it was the fact that when called upon to stand and deliver, Beard made no bones about delivering. And when he delivered, he delivered both as one of the proprietors of the United States and as its attorney protecting its democratic institutions.

His ideas about the United States may be summed up substantially as follows:

Restless energy, the search for fortune, the desire to escape religious and political absolutisms, blind chance, and a variety of other reasons gave a handful of people a new start on the American continent. Here, a century and a half ago, a group of remarkable men organized the government. Many of them were acutely conscious of what they were doing. As Washington said in his first Inaugural: "The preservation of the sacred fire of liberty, and the destiny of the Republican model of Government, are justly considered as deeply, perhaps as *finally* staked, on the experiment entrusted to the hands of the American people." Here, under a remarkable politician, poet, and dreamer had been fought an enormous Civil War. Here, at last, a remarkably close-knit middle class society—despite the difficulties of blending many immigrant races—had been built up with numerous common goals and ideals. Indeed, said Beard, "it is hardly going too far to say that, in theory, America has one class—the petty bourgeoisie—despite proletarian and plutocratic elements which cannot come under that classification, and that the American social ideal most widely expressed is the *embourgeoisement* of the whole society—a universality of comfort, conveniences, security, leisure, standard possessions of food, clothing and shelter." This America is intellectually homogeneous; it is "republican, secular, and essentially economic in character. It is not feudal, clerical, monarchial, or 'spiritual' in the European sense of that term. . . . American nationality has no mythological traditions, rooted in a distant past, but is hard, factual, and mechanical and has been built up in the full light of recorded history."[3] Any such society has interests with a vengeance, and when minds turn toward problems of foreign relations, then those interests must, or should, be kept vividly in mind.

The founding fathers looked toward Europe with a coldly appraising eye. Europeans were the heirs of quarrels, hatreds, and suspicions coming down from a thousand years of dynastic wars, religious conflicts, and political unrest. The United States, on the other hand, was all but starting with a clean slate. Have a care, therefore, said the fathers, how you involve yourselves with endless and bitter wranglings of the old world. And, until the close of the nineteenth century, the government of the United States, absorbed in domestic concerns, was content for the most part "to mind its own business."

But then a change came. Beard described it thus:

The era of universal American jitters over foreign affairs of no vital interest to the United States was opened in full blast about 1890 by four of the most powerful agitators that ever afflicted any nation: Alfred Thayer Mahan, Theodore Roosevelt, Henry Cabot Lodge and Albert J. Beveridge. These were the chief manufacturers of the new doctrine correctly characterized as "imperialism for America," and all of them were primarily phrase-makers, not men of hard economic experience [the proprietor of the Knightstown, Indiana, *Sun* speaking].

The ideology for this adventure was cooked up by the bookish Mahan and was promulgated by politicians. It was "sold" to the country amid the great fright induced by the specter of Bryanism, and amid the din of the wars on Spain and the Filipinos. As the British agent who framed a portion of the

new gospel for John Hay, Secretary of State presumably for the
United States, shrewdly observed, this was one way of smashing
the populist uprising and getting the country in hand. It was
not Woodrow Wilson, the schoolmaster, who first invented the
policy of running out and telling the whole world just the right
thing to do. It was the new men of imperialism.[4]

The internationalists were no better. Imperialists were out
for money and markets, or thought they were. Internationalists
were out to save the world. With stinging sarcasm Beard gibed
at their vague and irresponsible promises, their rhetorical approach to "practical problems." In sharp and acid terms he
described the rise of the internationalist school after the first
Hague Conference in 1899—the Carnegie endowments, the
peace congresses, the subsidizing of lecturers and professorships
on international relations, the mushrooming of "foreign policy
experts" who wanted "understanding." This school was (and
is) intensely moral, and the Presbyterian Woodrow Wilson was
its first and finest flower.

The lines of the Wilsonian creed of world interventionism
and adventurism [said Beard] are in substance: Imperialism is
bad (well, partly) ; every nation must have a nice constitutional
government, more or less like ours; if any government dislikes
the settlement made at Versailles it must put up its guns and
sit down with its well armed neighbors for a "friendly" conference; trade barriers are to be lowered and that will make everybody round the globe prosperous (almost, if not entirely) ;
backward people are to be kept in order but otherwise treated
nicely, as wards; the old history, full of troubles, is to be closed;
brethren and presumably sisters, are to dwell together in unity;
everything in the world is to be managed as decorously as a
Baptist convention presided over by the Honorable Cordell
Hull; if not, we propose to fight disturbers everywhere (well,
nearly everywhere) .[5]

So, with imperialists and internationalists intermittently in
control, the country was embarked upon its career as a "world
power," a career celebrated by the sending of our fleet around
the world to "impress" other nations, celebrated by "Dollar
Diplomacy" in the Caribbean and Latin America, celebrated by
our participation in two World Wars, leaving us with a stupen-

dous debt, a huge and sprawling military establishment with a conscript army, and confronted with a Russian despotism which has its zealous followers in every country on earth, our own included. This, said Beard, is what our imperialist-internationalist adventure has brought us.

But these were Beard's ideas about foreign affairs as he has uttered them in recent years. As a professor at Columbia, Beard supported the First World War. That war was a devastating experience; it forced his resignation from the university. In a biographical sketch of Beard, published in 1939, Hubert Herring quotes him as follows: "And then I slowly awoke to my abysmal ignorance. . . . I learned what war could do. . . . I saw Columbia use the War to suppress men. . . . I saw the freedom of the press trampled by gangs of spies, public and private." When the archives of Central Europe were opened he learned the full measure of his deception. "And then," says Beard, "I returned to American history and, working with Mary Beard, sought to inquire what we can do here to create an American civilization, determined to center my efforts on the promise of America rather than upon the fifty-century old quarrels of Europe."[6]

The progress of the partnership "to create an American civilization" may be seen in all the Beard books and magazine articles that came out in the 1920's. It was the Wall Street crash of 1929 that gave Beard his biggest jolt since the First World War.

Over and over again in his books he had wrestled with the questions of monopolies, the effects of trade restraints, and the concentration of wealth. Some of the founding fathers had thought with dread of the possibility of a few immensely rich Americans at the last confronting millions of propertyless Americans (proprietors who had lost their several stakes). Repeatedly in the history of older nations such conditions had led to conspiracy, insurrection, and general ruin. What guarantee was there that the United States would escape? Beard repeatedly harped upon this theme. In *America in Midpassage* he discussed Madison's views on the question:

Writing in 1829-30, Madison predicted that the population of the United States would probably be . . . one hundred and ninety-two millions in a hundred years, that is by 1930. . . . The future opened before the seer. The majority will be without landed or other property. There will be a "dependence of an increasing number on the wealth of a few." It will spring from the relations between landlords and tenants, between "wealthy capitalists and indigent laborers . . . from the connection between the great capitalists in manufactures and commerce, and the numbers employed by them. Nor will accumulations of capital for a certain time be precluded by our laws of descent and distribution." Still, Madison mused, in the future this tendency to concentration "may be diminished and the permanency defeated by the equalizing of the laws." . . . The challenge will press upon American society in times to come. "To effect these changes [Madison had said] intellectual, moral and social, the institutions and laws of the country must be adapted; and it will require for the task all the wisdom of the wisest patriots."[7]

By chance, it fell to Beard himself to make an assay upon the stupendous question. In 1931 he had suggested to Frederick P. Keppel of the Carnegie Corporation that a study be undertaken to discover what "national interests," words so often employed by politicians and statesmen to justify their conduct, really were. The upshot of his inquiry was that the Social Science Research Council asked Beard to do the job himself. He agreed and, supplied with research assistants and collaborators, Beard set to work in April, 1932. The first of the two principal results of this work was *The Idea of National Interest,* an attempt to "set forth, in systematic form, professions and actions of American statesmen coming under the head of 'national interest.' "[8] The other, published in 1934, was *The Open Door at Home,* being "a trial philosophy of national interest," that is, Beard's own conclusions about what our national interests are and what should be done to advance and protect them. It is, perhaps, the most detailed and systematic statement of Beard's ideas about his own country. It is a positive effort to come to grips with the American political and economic problem. His ideas about foreign policy are an organic part of this book.

Beard's idea was that since the world depression had wrecked economic and social life everywhere, the United States government had a superb opportunity to reorganize all phases of its policy. Opposition was prostrate; let the opportunity be grasped.

The crisis, said Beard, is double; there is a crisis in thought as well as in economy. Science, which had overthrown the domination of religion in the nineteenth century, had now proved as helpless to furnish answers as religion itself. There had long been a "tragic sense of the conflict between the ideal and the real."[9] Industry and science had showed that, as far as material things go, the good life was possible. Yet misery and cruelty and suffering, starvation, chills, and fear flourished on every hand. Come, now, said Beard; traditional ideas and conventions have proven useless in the crash; the artificial character of the barriers of thought are clearly revealed; the spell is broken. There exists the knowledge to do; people are at last free to do it. That is, the way is open for people to act, to dare, to experiment, to try something new. The United States started something new in 1789; the United States, alone among all other nations, is in a position—because of its institutions, geographical position, and enormous wealth—to try something new again.

Recognize the fact, said Beard, "that ethics and esthetics underlie and are essential to the operation of any great society. . . . The three great schemes of thought which have been evolved as solutions of the problem of the periodical crisis and have gained ascendancy in foreign policies—*laissez faire,* imperialism, and communism—are alike in resting their structures on material interests and in either rejecting or minimizing ethical and esthetic considerations."[10] But the United States has unparalleled means and resources, which permit it to *accept* ethical and esthetic considerations in the reorganization of its society.

Under these circumstances, what was the supreme interest of American society? Beard's answer: "The supreme interest of the United States is the creation and maintenance of a high standard of life for all its people and ways of industry conducive to the promotion of individual and social virtues within the frame of national security." "The supreme purpose of such foreign trade as may be carried on is the acquisition of imports deemed requisite to the posited standard of life. . . . The promotion of foreign trade . . . inevitably thrusts American private interests into the heart of other nations, spreads them to all parts of the world, and provokes rivalries and conflicts in widely scattered places."[11] Therefore put a minimum of reliance on foreign trade; import only what is needed to maintain the high living standard.

There are means and techniques available to establish a standard-of-life budget for the nation. Do it. Then determine the potentials of American industry. Now a balance sheet can be struck; then we can tell what commodities the country must import to fill the gaps left by domestic production.

The material conditions for self-sufficiency exist *inside* the United States on a huge scale. *Autonomy is not necessarily desirable, but it is possible.* We don't need a huge international commerce to get rid of our "surpluses." "The so-called surpluses are not inexorable products of nature but are, with some exceptions, the outcome of the system of private property and wealth distribution now prevailing in the United States."[12] Would autonomy lower the standard of living? It might, but not as low as the course now being pursued will eventually lower it.

Then Beard struck at the heart of the industrial jam. "Stubbornly in the way of those who seek an escape from the economic crisis stands the fact of unbalance between plant capacity and buying . . . power. Equally stubborn is the fact that there is an immense concentration of ownership in the United States which brings a large share of the annual wealth into relatively few hands, and forces increasing capital or plant extension for which efficient buying power is lacking." It is necessary to establish "an efficient distribution of wealth within the United

States—an adjustment of production and consumption and continuous control over the processes."[13] Control over the foreign trade necessary to maintain the standard of life fixed may be vested in a Foreign Trade Authority. Defense—the Monroe Doctrine is accepted—means a military establishment strong enough to guard the continental domain.

How shall all this be done? "The task of leadership may appropriately be assumed by the President." Let an Authority be created (1) to fix the standard-of-life budget and (2) to discover how far the resources of the United States will go in providing the wherewithal for that budget. Before the great Report is submitted to the country, let it be presented to the representatives of interests opposed to it and let them be called upon to detail their reasons. "In this open way would be made clearer the measures and practical steps necessary to proceed with the program." Then the Report, in full, condensed, illustrated, and in every other shape would be broadcast to the nation. The Report would be the prime document of policy to which all partial measures would be referred for consideration and testing.

Will the effort to do all this be made? Given the power of private interests to manipulate government, the strength of the military bureaucracy, the ease with which the press and the masses are mobilized for war, it is possible that the United States will repeat old methods, use old ideas, and destroy the basis of civilization itself. But Americans cannot approve of such a course without moral and intellectual stultification.

But with the Report adopted, Congress and the Executive would move and the whole American society would begin to move. To sum up:

By domestic control over all foreign trade, by the relaxation of the capitalistic pressure of the United States on world markets in standardized manufactures and commercial investments, by concentrating national energies on the development of national resources and the efficient distribution of wealth at home, by deliberately withdrawing from the rivalries of imperialist nations, the United States would take its official nose out of a thousand affairs of no vital concern to the people of the United States, would draw back its defense lines upon zones that can be defended with the greatest probability of victory in case of war, and would thus have a minimum dependence on the "strategic products" indispensable to war. And by multiplying many fold its outlays for scientific research in analytic and synthetic chemistry, it could steadily decrease its dependence on world markets for the essentials indispensable to our material civilization in time of peace.

In short, by cultivating its own garden, by setting an example of national self-restraint (which is certainly easier than restraining fifty other nations in an international conference, or beating them in war), by making no commitments that cannot be readily enforced by arms, by adopting toward other nations a policy of fair and open commodity exchange, by refraining from giving them any moral advice on any subject, and by providing a military and naval machine as adequate as possible to the defense of this policy, the United States may realize maximum security, attain minimum dependence upon governments and conditions beyond its control, and develop its own resources to the utmost. Besides offering the most realistic approach to the dilemma and conforming in a high degree to the necessities presented by the posture of nations, it is a more promising way of life for the people of the United States. . . . When the various nations have developed their internal efficiencies, renounced commerce of pressure and violence, and prepared themselves by organization and change of acquisitive spirit for commodity exchange as mutuality of benefit, then the League of Nations can be developed into a cooperative organ for building something approximating "a world order," and facilitating the appropriate international transactions. Until then the United States will have a care for its interests conceived as *security* and *commonweal*.[14]

Under these circumstances, said Beard, "Enthroned between two oceans, with no historic enemies on the north or south, the Republic can be defended against any foes which such a policy might raise up against it."[15]

While this book was in the course of composition the New Deal was roaring along. Beard watched it with the closest attention and—often—with enthusiasm. I know this, for I can well recall some of the arguments and discussions in which he participated at the time. Would Roosevelt have the daring and the wit to keep trying? The President's handling of the bank crisis excited his applause. The torpedoing of the London Economic Conference of 1933 encouraged him to feel that Roosevelt was going to tend to his domestic knitting. Beard was willing to give the NRA a whirl (which John T. Flynn was not) as something new; he welcomed the AAA as an attempt to put agriculture on the same level as industry. He rejoiced that collective bargaining had been made a statute right and welcomed the repudiation of the idea that the misery of the unemployed was a result of their own improvidence.

But by the time *The Open Door at Home* was ready for the press (1934) Beard had begun to get uneasy about our foreign policy. "If, therefore, President Roosevelt has a foreign policy appropriate to the trend of his domestic policy, he has not yet revealed it,"[16] but the policy of the Open Door had been reasserted, there was the old talk about foreign outlets for "surpluses," and the President had already got appropriations for three hundred million and authorizations for a billion dollars more for naval construction. It did not look good.

Then Beard saw the price-control crisis come nearer and nearer and presently became convinced that Roosevelt would turn to foreign war rather than grapple with the domestic Apollyon. In *Scribner's Magazine* for February, 1935, he stated his bitter disillusionment publicly.

"Confronted by the difficulties of a deepening domestic crisis and by the comparative ease of a foreign war, what will President Roosevelt do? Judging by the past history of American politicians," said Beard, "he will choose the latter."[17]

This was a remarkable statement to come as early as 1935 when first enthusiasm was at its height, and everything Beard said about the New Deal thereafter was colored by his dread of the coming conflict.

At the moment, as far as popular interest was concerned, foreign affairs had been pushed aside; there was too much doing at home. War was unthinkable. The Senate had appointed the

Nye Committee to investigate the manufacture and sale of munitions and the beginning of their deliberations was made the more electric by the publication of a series of sensational articles on the armament traffic in *Harper's, Fortune,* the *Living Age,* the *Christian Century,* and other periodicals during the fall and winter of 1933 and 1934. The climax of this chapter in journalism came when the Book of the Month Club circulated the Engelbrecht and Hanighan *Merchants of Death* in April, 1934. All good liberals followed the Nye investigations closely. Every day brought a fresh sensation, and periodicals like the *New Republic,* which were against foreign wars in any way, shape, or form, drew strong conclusions from what Nye and his men dug up. Under the spell of the investigation it seemed as though the American government would go very slowly before it was sucked into another war.

Nevertheless, there was the question of domestic crisis. It wasn't slow in coming and it hit the government in peculiar circumstances. In November, 1936, President Roosevelt had been re-elected by a majority so great that his "mandate" was conceded without argument. He had been stung by the way the Supreme Court had killed the big New Deal laws and now, convinced that "the people are with me," he determined to act. Soon after the election he was engaged with the help of a few confidants in planning what was afterward known as "the Court-Packing Bill." Early in 1937, without any warning, the bill was sent to Congress. The result was astonishing. The President had blundered; somehow he had gored a sacred cow. The opposition, sensing their opportunity, organized to fight him. The President's rage knew no bounds; he could not believe that he could lose. For so adroit a politician, he made one fearful mistake after another. The Court fight lasted for months, and it was not until the summer of 1937 that the President, frustrated, sore, and angry, conceded defeat.

In the meantime, in the spring of 1937, right in the middle of the Court fight, Secretary of the Treasury Morgenthau proposed that the President try to balance the budget. The President was disposed to listen. The business element had long been needling him on his spending policy. Now he was of a mind to shut off the spending; he consented to Morgenthau's suggestion. His consent coincided with the start of a frightening financial crash. This was the so-called recession and it came to the President as a fearful shock. The campaign of the previous year had been waged triumphantly on a "we planned it that way" basis, and now here was ruin looking the Administration in the face.

Loaded down with these troubles, the President decided to go west and look at the country. At this moment Cordell Hull, as he relates in his *Memoirs,* was "becoming increasingly worried over the growth of the isolationist sentiment in the United States." He and Norman Davis went to see Roosevelt in September and suggested that the President make an address "on international cooperation in the course of his journey." Roosevelt agreed and a few days later in Chicago, on October 5, 1937, gave his celebrated "quarantine speech."

"The reaction against the quarantine idea was quick and violent," says Hull. "As I saw it, this had the effect of setting back for at least six months our constant educational campaign intended to create and strengthen public opinion toward international cooperation."[18]

There was no question about the violence of the reaction. The speech was like an alarm bell to many people and the real division of the country over the question of intervention began at that time. Congressmen Hamilton Fish and George Tinkham wanted Roosevelt impeached then and there.[19]

For the time no more was heard from the President on foreign policy. He had a real domestic crisis on his hands. There were anxious and worried conferences about what to do. Joseph Alsop and Robert Kinter in *Men around the President* describe a White House meeting to discuss the situation. Present at this meeting were three New Deal economists—Isador Lubin, Leon Henderson, and Lauchlin Currie. They jointly prefaced their remarks with the question, "Do you wish to save the capitalist system?"[20] By implication they expected an affirmative answer. Henderson himself for months had argued that collusive price agreements were one of the chief sources of the crisis. At all events the President eventually agreed to a big-scale attack on monopoly. More important, he resumed the spending policy and thereafter spent steadily until his death.

This question of monopoly—or rather, the control of production and prices—was old stuff to Beard. To him, if it wasn't the core of the economic problem, it was pretty near it. The New Dealers had already tried "pump priming." Under this policy, said Beard, "controlled industry increased production to take up the primer and, when the money appropriated was exhausted, production dropped again to the levels set by private interests."[21] The New Dealers determined to attack the problem head on. They got from Congress tremendous investigating powers to help them gather facts for the Temporary National Economic Committee; they imported Thurman Arnold from New Haven and put him in the Antitrust Division of the Justice Department to head a great trust-busting campaign. But it was no good; it didn't work.[22]

Into this intellectual vacuum poured the horrendous news from abroad—the torture of the Jews by Hitler, the Moscow trials, the Franco rebellion, and the *Panay* "incident."

Beard spent the winter of 1936-1937 in Washington. He was there when the Court fight started; he was there when the first signs of the recession were seen. At the invitation of Spencer Brodney, the editor of *Events,* he wrote two articles that were published in the July and August issues of that magazine. In the first, called "Will Roosevelt Keep Us Out of War?" Beard said, "The American people may well prepare themselves to see President Roosevelt plunge the country into the European war, when it comes, far more quickly than did President Wilson." In the second article,[23] after referring to the threatening aspect of affairs in Europe, he said: "Beyond the Atlantic is the United States, also arming rapidly, with plans for landing a four-million army 'somewhere' off the American continent. On the whole, President Roosevelt has made no open commitments. But his sympathies are so well known as to need no documentation. There is also a configuration of war sympathies in the United States. It ranges from professional peace advocates who support the Entente's League of Nations, through Conservatives who think that war would be a good thing for the country, to Stalinites who are bent on 'saving Russian democracy.' "[24]

Beard has described in *American Foreign Policy in the Making, 1932-1940,* how Mr. Brodney sent copies of the two articles to Roosevelt, suggesting "that the President would render a great public service if he 'would make a statement to the American people that would set their minds at ease on a matter about which there is doubt and suspicion.' " Stephen Early, Roosevelt's secretary, replied to Brodney, saying that "the President is grateful to you for writing as you did." For the purpose of reply Early enclosed copies of the President's addresses at Chautauqua and San Diego. At San Diego on October 2, 1935, the President had said, "despite what happens in continents overseas, the United States of America shall and must remain, as long ago the Father of our Country prayed that it might remain—unentangled and free." At Chautauqua on August 14, 1936, he said, "We can keep out of war if those who watch and decide have a sufficiently detailed understanding of international affairs to make certain that the small decisions of each day do not lead toward war and if, at the same time, they possess the courage to say 'no' to those who selfishly or unwisely would let us go to war."[25]

Beard was not satisfied with these statements and, as time went on, he became more and more outspoken against the President. What he later thought of his own plans as outlined in *The Open Door At Home* I do not know. Any such operation would have required a tremendous concentration of power. In the early 1930's he had written for the American Historical Association a brief volume called *A Charter for the Social Sciences in the Schools.* The "goals"[26] enumerated in this work implied as much concentration of power as *The Open Door* did. Here Beard, one of the owners and proprietors of the United States, was arguing in effect that his country be turned over to an executive receiver in bankruptcy. Not only this. He argued that, with the endorsement of a plebiscite, an almost overwhelming power of attorney be given to that receiver. Yet at the same time Beard was attacking the Executive because he went ahead and used the power.

The truth was that Beard was caught in a tremendous contradiction. It was a cruel dilemma. Once he made an angry retort to an argument for uniformity in laws among the forty-eight states. "For God's sake," he cried, "this very lack of uniformity may turn out to be the last refuge we have."

What to do? He stalled. For instance, in *The Old Deal and the New*, he said:

No judgment is here ventured on the debatable subject as to whether money and banking should be under private or government control. Many of the issues in such a debate have already been decided by the forces of history, and in favor of government control. But if democracy is to be served and dictatorship avoided, if it is unwise to leave too much discretion over so vital a subject in the hands of one man with a small group of interested advisers, it would be highly advisable for Congress to assume its responsibilities and to reconsider its easy grants of discretionary powers while there is yet time. But if the resumption of responsibility by Congress means a return to the mad and often unscrupulous scramble of pressure groups, which the country has periodically witnessed in the making of tariff laws, little may be gained by such a form of "democratization." The place of Congress in American economy has thus become a public issue.[27]

But one thing he was very clear about was the fact that *the* crisis was *here*. Here, at *home*. And the bitterness of his gall rose as he saw his President, the holding trustee of the Republic of which he, Beard, was one of 130,000,000 proprietors, turn his back upon the crisis and, looking toward the global footlights, "mount the world stage." After that there was nothing for Beard to do but fight, and fight he did. The climax of this particular phase of Beard's opposition to the Roosevelt foreign policy occurred in a long and devastating attack called "Giddy Minds and Foreign Quarrels," which appeared in *Harper's* for September, 1939.

The issue of *Harper's*, published on August 20, came at a time of most acute tension, three days before the announcement of the Nazi-Soviet pact and ten days before the invasion of Poland. The Beard argument was brilliant and savage; its effect on liberal eastern seaboard aid-the-allies circles was instant. They could not bear it and their protests were vehement. I well recall the way this piece of periodical writing was received. I was one of the editors of *Harper's* at that time and had this particular issue of the magazine under my supervision.

The people whom Beard's argument drove to frenzy had been whooping it up for months and their hunger for war as a great moral crusade was plain as day. They talked a lot about saving civilization and western culture, and Beard, with unerring instinct, had picked the cultural barb that would sting and fester under their cultural hides. The lead of his article was as follows:

In the fourth act of "Henry IV" the King on his death-bed gives his son and heir the ancient advice dear to the hearts of rulers in dire straits at home:

> I . . . had a purpose now
> To lead out many to the Holy Land,
> Lest rest and lying still might make them look
> Too near unto my state. Therefore, my Harry,
> Be it thy course, to busy giddy minds
> With foreign quarrels; that action, hence borne out,
> May waste the memory of the former days.

The charge that President Roosevelt, frustrated by the economic dilemma at home, was maneuvering his country into the war was more than intellectuals and crusaders among Roosevelt's followers could endure. Economics bored them and clouded the rapture of their moral zeal. (The President was better at blending the two than they. When, on September 13, 1940, Roosevelt sent the National Defense Advisory Commission's statement on contract letting and labor policy to Congress, he said: "This program can be used in the public interest as a vehicle to reduce unemployment and otherwise strengthen the human fiber of our Nation."[28])

The vituperation poured upon Beard was intense, despite—or perhaps because of—the fact that he spoke aloud the sentiments of thousands of the inarticulate. Camp-follower historians, who subsequently wrote wartime best sellers, moral pamphleteers, and League of Nations zealots sensed at last what had been true for a long time: Beard had kissed the academic shades good-by (actually he had kissed them good-by in 1917 when he quit Columbia over the firing of Dana, Cattell, and Fraser). He was no distinguished scholar, with a suitably distinguished hierarchical position, engaged in a round-table discussion. Learned societies and professional conclaves had been left behind. He was fighting with all the strength he had against a President whom he believed to be untrustworthy and irresponsible.

It seemed as though all the long years of his work as a historian, all the lectures on foreign policy, all the turning over of documents, all the civil liberty fights to keep threatened teachers in their jobs, all the analyzing of men and motives, had only been preparation for this fight against a man who he believed—or I think he believed—was jettisoning the American birthright.

I never heard Beard give a categorical statement of what his own policy would have been. I can only deduce that it would have been something like this: "Put your house in order and see to your defenses. Batten down the hatches and get ready to ride out the storm. Keep your eyes fixed on the domestic crisis; this is far more serious than anything from abroad. This crisis is deeper than Hitler; it is intellectual as well as economic as I said long ago. Save all the pieces of the Republic that you can. We have come nearer to being a free people than any society that has yet been seen; let us keep our Republic that way."

As the attacks upon him grew more bitter, Beard became more intransigent. On February 4, 1941, he appeared before the Senate Committee on Foreign Relations to testify against the Lend-Lease Bill. By this time war was only a few months away and, so overwhelming was the propaganda, opposition was fading. Nevertheless, Beard hewed to the line. His direct challenge to the President was as forthright as Bishop John Fisher's challenge to Henry VIII. After analyzing the bill, Beard said:

"Given the sweeping language of this bill, it seems fitting to suggest that the Title is imprecise. The Title is 'An Act to promote the defense of the United States.' It should read:

All provisions of law and the Constitution to the contrary notwithstanding, an Act to place all the wealth and all the men and women of the United States at the free disposal of the President, to permit him to transfer or carry goods to any foreign government he may be pleased to designate, anywhere in the world, to authorize him to wage undeclared wars for anybody, anywhere in the world, until the affairs of the world are ordered to suit his policies, and for any other purpose he may have in mind now or at any time in the future, which may be remotely related to the contingencies contemplated in the title of this Act.

"In opposing this bill I am not insisting upon negation. A plan for constructive action is possible and desirable. I propose first of all, that Congress reject this bill with such force that no President of the United States will ever dare again, in all our history, to ask it to suspend the Constitution and the laws of this land and to confer upon him limitless dictatorial powers over life and death."[29]

Beard must have known perfectly well that his argument was futile, that he was shouting into the teeth of the storm. Yet he argued on, adamant in his determination that the President should not get away with his evasions unchallenged.

After that, with the war on, Beard devoted himself with tireless energy to two different lines of investigation. One was a re-examination of the position of the American citizen in relation to his society and government. The results of this labor may be seen in *The Republic* and *The Enduring Federalist*. The other task was the excavation of Roosevelt's record in foreign policy. He followed the course of the congressional investigation of Pearl Harbor with an almost microscopic scrutiny. To what the investigation brought forth he added more that he gathered himself and poured out a torrent of memoranda. The possibility that Roosevelt was culpable was the one thing that the Democratic majority could not and would not face. It was the inflamed nerve in the very core of the investigation. The result was that the Majority Report skirted around this core and Beard's memoranda were gratefully received by those who wrote the Minority Report.

For the rest, Beard was responsible for two books: *American Foreign Policy in the Making, 1932-1940* (published in 1946) and *President Roosevelt and the Coming of the War, 1941* (published in 1948). The latter was a ponderous volume in which, with detail and fact piled upon detail and fact until the weight is almost crushing, Beard sought to nail down the proof of Roosevelt's deception so firmly that it could not be got loose.

It often seemed to me that Beard's anger sprang as much from Roosevelt's mendacity as it did from the policy that the President was pursuing. Ironically enough, Beard had scarcely completed the laborious compilation of the second of the two volumes, when the revelations of Roosevelt's aides and associates began rolling from the press. Robert Sherwood, for example, in his *Roosevelt and Hopkins,* confesses that it was he, Sherwood, who suggested the reiteration of the famous words "again and again and again" in the lines spoken in Boston by Roosevelt during the third-term campaign in 1940: "I have said this before, but I shall say it again and again and again: Your boys are not going to be sent into any foreign wars." Says Sherwood, "Unfortunately for my own conscience, I happened at this time to be one of those who urged him to go the limit on this, feeling as I did that any risk of future embarrassment was negligible as compared with the risk of losing the election."[30]

Surely this phenomenon of Roosevelt's long deception is remarkable. Beard contends that whatever the reasons for the actions may have been, the sum total of the Roosevelt actions has been completely to undermine constitutional government and set the stage for a Caesar. Perhaps it is an ominous sense of some future caesarism that impels the Roosevelt idolators to justify themselves. Already there is growing up a literature—an example is Thomas A. Bailey's *The Man in the Street*—that admits the presidential mendacity and then with painful elaboration seeks to gloss it. If there were overriding circumstances, if the President saw more clearly than his countrymen what must be done, if war was inescapable, why are not Roosevelt's apologists content with the manifest facts and consequences—if they are manifest? Why are they not satisfied to let the man stand on his glowing record? After all, he bossed the greatest war in history. But they are not satisfied; some impulse ceaselessly drives them on in their task of lustration.

About this last work on foreign policy there was much of the quality of the work on the Constitution. The two were alike in their method, in their attack on the conventional view, in their suggestiveness of the need for further research, in the wrath they aroused. As with the earlier work, only time can determine whether Beard or his critics will be justified.

MERLE CURTI

Beard as Historical Critic

APPRAISALS OF Charles A. Beard's work thus far contain little
or no reference, oddly enough, to his contributions as an historical critic. Channing reviewed almost no historical works,
and Turner's contributions in this field were relatively few, but
Beard began affixing his signature to critical notices at the
threshold of his career and continued almost to his death. The
number of such reviews in the professional and popular journals is indeed impressive: It runs to well over 150. Even this
mass of critical writing does not exhaust the theme, for Beard's
critical talents found further expression in his capacity as editor
and particularly in the careful and thoughtful comments he
made on the manuscripts that his friends asked him to read.
Beyond all this he occasionally discussed in his more formal
writing the historical literature of the period with which he was
concerned.

When Beard's biography is written, his reviews will provide
welcome clues to the development of his thought. Thus, for instance, he tells us that it was not until he reached manhood that

he discovered any American tradition other than the Federalist-Whig-Republican frame in which he was nurtured.[1] And it is good to have his testimony that about 1896 he read *The Psychic Factors of Civilization* by Lester Frank Ward and always regarded himself as fortunate that he early met the remarkable social scientist who impressed him "as a monolith of living granite."[2]

A careful reading in chronological sequence of Beard's reviews illuminates many controversial questions about his intellectual development. Here we find his early reactions to the writings of the Marxist and Fabian socialists. His reviews permit us to see the natural history of his thought on economic forces in the historical process. They also document his interest in historical theory, in science, in humanistic democracy, in social planning, in the idea of civilization. Long before World War II his reviews clearly indicated his opposition to war, imperialism, and fascism. The record is worth reading in view of certain unfair allegations his critics later made—including the charge that he was profascist. Overarching all these issues, the reviews, chronologically read, go far to answer the question: Did Beard change his essential ideas in the later years of his life?

The reviews not only help us understand Beard's thought, and, as I shall show, provide us with a body of critical material indispensable to any adequate evaluation of historical scholarship in America during the first half of the twentieth century; they also provide extraordinarily faithful portraits of his personality. Here are no barren husks. The reviews are full of life and freshness and nourishment. In them we see Beard's complex and rich personality as it is difficult or impossible to see it in his more formal writings. To read the reviews is, for one who knew him, like sitting down again and listening to his sharp and pungent comments, enjoying once more his wit and brilliance and originality. It is not possible within the space at hand to quote from the reviews sufficiently to give even a rough index of what is in store for anyone who will spend several hours discovering them for himself. But two or three representative samples may be given as an invitation to exploration.

Beard combined satire on a good deal of academic scholarship with lofty patriotism in his ebullient acclaim of Parrington's *Main Currents of American Thought*. "Now it appears," he impishly wrote, "that Mr. Parrington is about to start an upheaval in American literary criticism. He has yanked Miss Beautiful Letters out of the sphere of the higher verbal Hokum and fairly set her in the way that leads to contact with pulsating reality—that source and inspiration of all magnificent literature. No doubt, the magpies, busy with the accidence of Horace, the classical allusions of Thoreau, and the use of the adverb by Emerson, will make a big outcry, but plain citizens who believe that the American eagle could soar with unblinking eyes against the full-orbed noonday sun if he had half a chance will clap their hands with joy and make the hills ring with gladness."[3] In commending Allan Nevins' abridged edition of John Quincy Adams' diary he wrote: "It will be an experience next summer to sit in an old New England graveyard, under dark firs surrounded by moss-covered stones, and sip Mr. Nevins' distillation of crab-apple juice."

Still, it is not just Beard with plenty of salt, pepper, and vinegar that you will discover. You will also find a man with genuine appreciation of others and great intellectual humility. Even in the review of a book that he felt called on to judge most severely, he almost invariably indicated that notwithstanding all the limitations of the book, it still had some value and one could still learn something from it. Unfavorable criticisms were generally couched in contingent terms. Thus in speaking about Victor Bérard's *La France et Guillaume II* Beard wrote, "If brilliant hypothesis, carefully selected statistics, and ardent hopes were conclusive, this would be an impressive book. Whether its thesis is a prophecy or a delusion, the future alone can decide." After pointing out what appeared to be some of the limitations of Gabriel's *The Course of American Democratic Thought* Beard paid respects to the pioneer character of the undertaking, to its suggestiveness, and its "intellectual sparks." He concluded by warning, "Let him who thinks that he can draw the arrow to the head take up Mr. Gabriel's bow and test his strength and skill." Or, to cite one more example of modesty and humility, Beard launched an impressive criticism of the early volumes of Toynbee's *A Study of History* with these words: "If, at this stage of Mr. Toynbee's exploration and exposition, criticism were ventured by a reviewer of painfully limited knowledge it would be somewhat as follows."[4]

The catholicity of Beard's interests is abundantly illustrated in the range of books he reviewed. These included the works of American, British, and Continental scholars. In the decade and a half before the First World War he wrote many critiques of books on English history—an early professional interest.[5] But French, German, and Italian history or current politics also came within his scope.[6] The reviews included both basic scholarly contributions and books of a more ephemeral, topical interest. The focus of my analysis is on his evaluations of historical scholarship. Yet in view of Beard's conviction that history and politics and economy cannot properly be separated in airtight compartments, it would be unwarrantable to discuss only his concern with historical literature in the narrower sense. I shall, however, make no effort to analyze the many notices of books dealing with municipal affairs, government administration, and economic planning.[7] His role as a critic in these fields must await more competent hands.

We may now turn to Beard's general approach to the evaluation of historical scholarship. Many of his early reviews, and a few of the later ones, merely summarized the contents of the book under consideration.[8] The summaries are clear, succinct, and fair. In the great majority of cases, however, Beard was not content with mere summarizing, though he never failed to make clear just what the book was about. Naturally the character of the documentation provided a point of departure. If a book depended largely on secondary materials, due notice of the fact was given.[9] The reader of the review learned whether the book was largely based on readily available primary materials or whether it also rested on newly discovered, out of the way manuscripts or hitherto overlooked documents.[10] But Beard saw no magic in the mere use of new materials. Thus, in his *Great Britain and the American Civil War* Ephraim D. Adams, after a minute analysis of manuscripts relevant to Anglo-American relations during the Civil War, "left the conclusions of the older writers on this subject . . . firmly intact." Again, Beard carefully scrutinized the footnote citations in Allan Nevins' *John D. Rockefeller* and noted that the new materials made available to the author by the family possessed little relevance to the author's justification of Rockefeller's activities. On the other hand, when new materials compelled a revision of established views, as in the case of Tyler Dennett's *Theodore Roosevelt and the Russo-Japanese War,* Beard could write, "Thanks, many thanks, Mr. Dennett; you deserve the crown of wild olive" for a "priceless book."

Beard was concerned with the originality of a book, not only in terms of its materials, but in the sense of its organization and interpretation of the materials, familiar and unfamiliar. He hit hard at products that were mere collections of data and information—especially at Ph.D. dissertations or studies in imitation of the conventional doctoral thesis—although he admitted that even these had their usefulness.[11] If the author did not place the theme he had chosen in a larger frame of relationships, Beard almost invariably supplied the frame.[12] The insight and skill with which this was done often made the review a genuine contribution to knowledge and understanding. It is not too much to say that in this way Beard helped to remake prevailing syntheses, especially of American history.

Now and again he called attention to omissions and indicated the possibility of further research. In discussing Haynes' *Third Party Movements since the Civil War,* for example, he noted that the author had failed to study the social and economic condition of residents in the sections chiefly affected by third party radicalism and suggested that farm mortgages, crop failures, and foreclosures invited statistical enumeration and analysis. And in reviewing the *Political History of England* series before the relatively recent interest in social and intellectual history—in

the first decade of the present century, to be exact—Beard
spelled out the limitations imposed on an understanding of political development by the omission of social, economic, and intellectual factors.[13] Was there a twinkle in his eye when he
called attention to the overlooking of womankind in Woodrow
Wilson's frequent references to "your sons" in *The New Freedom?* In any case, repeated notations of the exclusion of women,
together with the good example the Beards themselves set,
helped in the growing tendency of historians to include women
in their discussions. Or, again, in 1907 in the review of De Alva
Alexander's *Political History of the State of New York* the
seminal remark was made that the controversy over neutral
rights could not alone explain the War of 1812. And it may be,
too, that the incisive way in which Beard spoke of the neglect
of the legislative branch by writers on American politics was
wholesome, for in time this gap was in part filled.

Beard was of course concerned even more with what was done
and the way in which it was done than he was with omissions.
Let no one think that he was lacking in appreciation of what he
once called "the troublesome and research-demanding details,"
for he was as quick to note the shortcomings of scholarship in
this respect as he was to acknowledge their relevance when he
found them.[14] Relevance, however, was the key, for Beard was
sensitive to the selection of evidence with the purpose of proving a point and to the discarding of countervailing testimony.
Thus when McLaughlin set out to prove that American judicial
supremacy was a mere borrowing from England, Beard took
him to task for not inquiring why this idea did not develop in
other English-speaking lands. "Above all," Beard continued,
"he leaves out of account the undoubted legislative supremacy
exercised under the early state constitutions—a supremacy that
was everywhere threatening property and minority rights and
was, in Madison's opinion, largely influential in bringing about
the Convention." In spite of McLaughlin's contention Beard
argued that support as powerful as that arrayed by McLaughlin
might be found for the idea that judicial control was a really

"new and radical departure of the closing years of the eighteenth century which did not spring from Anglo-Saxon ideas but from the practical necessity of creating a foil for the rights of property against belligerent democracy governing through majorities in substantially omnipotent legislatures."[15]

Nor was Beard's concern for definition of terms and their precise use a result of the later popularity of semantics. It was in 1906, for instance, that he pointed out the identification of the ruling class with the nation—an identification common to Hodgkin, Stubbs, Freeman, and Green.[16] And in the same year, in commenting on George B. Adams' *Political History of England,* Beard argued for leaving aside in historical expositions "all modern theory and terminology" and for emphasizing rather "concrete relationships and practices." Furthermore, at the beginning of his professional career Beard disparaged the use of adjectives and adverbs that implied praise or blame on the score that the true function of the scholar is to describe and explain. In 1907 he condemned Broderick and Frothingham for the use of vehement expressions and loose characterizations in their *History of England 1801-1837.*[17] In the same way he pointed out in 1941 that although Allan Nevins was properly scrupulous in refraining from using derogatory adjectives in writing about John D. Rockefeller, he frequently used "unprecise language" and "derogatory characterizations" in speaking of the great oil magnate's critics.

Beard's concern about the use of words grew with the years. In appraising Siegfried's *America Comes of Age* he remarked with wonted playfulness that the emphasis on our materialism was an ancient song repeated so many times that any sophomore in historical studies could "sing it to a saxophone." But what was meant by "materialism"? A definite term in the history of philosophy, it was utterly meaningless in its common journalistic use. "The present reviewer," Beard wrote, "flatly denies that America is more materialist than any European country, in the sense that, considering the opportunities, no larger proportion of the total energy in this country is devoted to acquiring material goods than in any European country." Or, later, in reviewing Gabriel's *The Course of American Democratic Thought,* he put emphasis on the great need, especially in the study of intellectual history, for rigid definitions and discriminations. Since language and thought are intimately related, Beard was particularly wary of the use of metaphors, especially when these involved the writer in "imaginative metaphysics"— as seemed to be true in Toynbee's use of such figures as "social atoms" in describing human beings and relationships.[18]

An author's general style, no less than the occasional loose use of words, met with frequent comment. Even before Beard left Columbia in 1917 he did not conceal his disdain for academic drabness and dullness in historical writing. In describing Schlesinger's *Colonial Merchants and the American Revolution* as "the most significant contribution that has ever been made to the history of the American Revolution" he added: "Lest it be suspected as a doctor's dissertation, it should be said at once that it is written in a style that many a seasoned historian may well envy." Or, again, in commending *The Spirit of '76 and Other Essays* by Carl L. Becker, William E. Dodd, and John M. Clark, he rejoiced: "Judging from these essays, the adding-machine discipline to which American universities subject doctors of philosophy cannot destroy supple minds. . . . Nominally, the studies are historical in form, but they escape altogether the severe limits set by Clio's academic votaries, in that they are suffused by warm thought, melting stubborn facts into a philosophic view of man and nature."[19]

Beard was precise, too, in discussing historical style. If Channing did not write like Macaulay, if he did not lay on his colors so furiously, he wrote in a clear and dignified manner, with a touch of dry humor here and there.[20] Samuel Eliot Morison's *Maritime History of Massachusetts* seemed especially noteworthy for demonstrating that research and accuracy could be combined with literary finish. Even economic enterprise could be set forth, not in the dull fashion of most academicians, but with caviar so delightful as to command general appreciation.

And there was praise for the "muscular English" of Edward Meade Earle's introduction to *The Federalist*. In fact, in the 1940's in honoring the clear and incisive style of the essays dedicated to Charles E. Merriam, Beard was able to say that the writing of the younger generation marked a decided advance on most of the books written by members of the older generation.[21] In connection with this discussion of Beard's interest in style I must note that dignified and austere writing with an air of impartiality did not necessarily insure in his eyes the "objectivity" commonly associated with it.

You will be wondering when I am going to talk about the frame of reference concept. I have called attention to the fact that as early as 1906 in reviewing volumes in *The Political History of England* Beard indicated that the governing concept of an exclusively political history militated against an understanding of political development—inasmuch as this was not in actuality divorced from social, economic, and intellectual factors. Here Beard was thinking, at least by implication, in terms of the frame of reference. So likewise in pointing out the prevailingly narrow conception of constitutional history, which ignored the fact that law is an embodiment of interest, Beard had his finger on the idea he was later to make explicit.[22] It was in his mind, though the term itself was not used, in the 1906 review of Jaurès' *Histoire socialiste*. "The avowed purpose of the Socialists to force a disintegration of the intellectual synthesis upon which the present order rests will compel them, in time," Beard wrote, "to reopen the whole question of historical interpretation and construction." The story as told, Beard found, was "remarkably impartial; indeed, there is no reason why an intelligent socialist should not be as impartial as a tory or whig. One who dissents from the views of both tory and liberal may write as scientifically as one who maintains either side."[23] A decade later Beard found that in the hands of Robert Michels the materialist interpretation of history became the instrument of the enemies of the socialists, the instrument, so to speak, of the *status quo* champions of the Hohenzollerns.[24]

The implications in these statements became explicit in the discussion in 1927 of Siegfried's *America Comes of Age*. The French scholar indicted American civilization for its materialism. What one saw, Beard said in effect, depended on the observer's assumptions and on the angle of vision from which he viewed the object. "If it would not be showing a crass materialistic spirit, the present reviewer, with due reverence for France, the mother of civilization, might point out that M. Gandhi would probably have some difficulty in discovering a profound spiritual difference between M. Poincaré and Mr. Coolidge, between the use of Annamese troops to preserve French loot in China and the use of American Marines in the interest of 'law and order' in Haiti . . . between the Paris banker and the New York stock broker, between the editor of *Le Temps* and the editor of *The Times*." From this point on Beard seldom reviewed a book without making clear the author's frame of reference. In his trenchant piece on *Recent Social Trends in the United States* (1933) he commented on President Hoover's announcement that the report rested on "all the facts." Obviously, Beard wrote, an impossibility. The obtrusive facts, perhaps? If so, obtrusive by whose vision? Or maybe the important facts? Important to whom and to what ends?[25]

It was an easy step to the larger consideration of the issue of objectivity in historical writing. The points that Beard made so eloquently in his controversial address as president of the American Historical Association and in other writings in the early 1930's now found application in his reviews. Thus he looked beneath the surface of the austere and apparently impartial *Constitutional History of the United States* of Andrew McLaughlin and detected assumptions and preferences conforming to the Federalist-Whig-Republican tradition, with a touch of Cleveland Democracy. "This is not to say that Mr. McLaughlin is crassly or subtly partisan, but that he has not applied the clarifying Socratic elenchus to his own conceptions." The point was then illustrated by noting omissions or minimizations in the McLaughlin discussion of the powers conferred by the Constitution on the federal government. Actually, Beard held, McLaughlin had written, not a constitutional history of the United States, but a selection of materials and comments down to about 1876, calculated not to encourage the average citizen to apply any criticism to constitutional issues but to confirm him in those "easy conceptions which run current in that comfortable portion of American society which imagines itself to be all of society."

Democrat though Beard was in a genuine sense, he did not suppose that one frame of reference was the equal of any other. He did not go all the way with some younger historians who discovered in the anthropological or cultural approach to history a transcending of all frames of reference. Admittedly, however, the cultural emphasis on all "primary" manifestations of society in an interrelated development promised a fuller, more precise, and more usable understanding of history than many others. At times Beard seemed to be uncertain himself on this point. For example, in maintaining that in *The Rise of the City* Schlesinger's "eclectic impressionism" was actually an interpretation, Beard conceded that the Harvard scholar might be justified in assuming that this was the only resort of contemporary scholarship. The main point Beard did make was that this too carried profound philosophical implications.

One more example must suffice to illustrate the point that, in promoting the frame of reference concept as an analytical key to historical literature, Beard did not believe that this approach gave the author who chose a particular frame immunity from all criticism, as some writers have supposed any relativist must assume. On the contrary. In discussing Edward C. Kirkland's *History of American Economic Life,* the wit and freshness of which he liked, Beard maintained that in separating economics from politics the author had left out of the account "vital, fundamental, and often conditional factors in the economic life of the country—the theme of the book." If Kirkland protested that it was not his intention to include political factors, still he could not escape "the intellectual consequences of the work he has done." Beard held that the general reader or the young student would get a one-sided and erroneous impression as a result of the frame of reference of the book. It would also confirm certain economists "in the fiction that wealth is distributed by 'the natural process' of economic life, whereas in truth that is only one phase of the complicated business." In other words, Beard adopted an instrumentalist criterion in evaluating the effect of a given frame of reference.

These illustrations merely open the doors to an understanding of the rich and varied ways in which Beard used the frame of reference concept in his historical criticism. They fail even more markedly to present anything like an adequate view of the more theoretical aspects of the concept. The interested reader must himself turn to Beard's reviews of Robert S. Lynd's *Knowledge for What?*, Nevins' *Gateway to History*, and Maurice Mandelbaum's *The Problem of Historical Knowledge*. Of the last book, an attack on historical relativism, Beard bluntly declared "Mr. Mandelbaum has missed the whole point of the business." He documented his indictment by making it clear that he had never written the things Mandelbaum attributed to him. With brilliant questions Beard then largely demolished Mandelbaum's particular indictment.

Beard's critical approach to historical writing did not undergo any revolutionary shift at any time during his career. It is nevertheless possible to indicate certain periods, broadly defined and subject to many qualifications, into which his historical criticism falls.

In the first period, roughly from about 1902 to the First World War, Beard joined Frederick Jackson Turner and Edward Channing in attacking a still widely held idea—the Anglo-Saxon interpretation of institutional development in England and the United States. This curious fantasy explained Anglo-American institutions in terms of their alleged origin in the forests of primitive Germany.

Beard attacked the thesis on several flanks. Drawing upon his own studies of English medieval history and his knowledge of

later constitutional development, he shattered the thesis by
indicating the great debt of English constitutionalism not only
to the Norman and Tudor periods but above all to the concrete struggles of competing interests.[26] As early as 1907 he
challenged the assumption of Julius Hatschek that the limitations upon powers of the state in England resulted from the
persistence of Teutonic institutions and declared that before
the issue could be cleared up "anthropology must come to our
aid."[27] On other occasions Beard varied his attack. He conceded to Vinogradoff a right to carry township representation
back to the Anglo-Saxon period; but he insisted that here, as
in Vinogradoff's refusal to see any sharp line between inquest
and compurgation, it was a question of determining the "limits
of legitimate historical constructive imagination."[28] Again, why
were the Webbs in their *English Local Government from the
Revolution to the Municipal Corporations Act* unable to trace
the subsequent history of the county court of Henry II's day?
Beard laid the blame at the door of "the curious mental aberra-
tion which led scholars to go to the German forests for the beginnings of liberty" and thereby to neglect the really great period of local English institutions.

In this period Beard also attacked formalism in English and
American constitutional history. In speaking of some "monumental treatises of the prodigiously industrious German savants" Beard wrote that "each of the volumes under review is
dry and legal; each wears an aspect of remoteness from politics—
the very warp on which constitutional law is woven. The written constitution has lulled each author, with the possible exception of André Lebon, into a false sense of security."[29] It is worth
noting that this was in 1910, three years before *An Economic
Interpretation of the Constitution* appeared. Beard was talking
not about American constitutionalism, but about the unfortunate tendency in German and English scholarship to divorce
constitutional documents from their context. Again, in writing
about Walter F. Dodd's *Modern Constitutions,* Beard could say
in 1909 that "without some real understanding of history and

the economic forces of a nation, an examination of the bare text of a constitution is more likely to be misleading than illuminating."

One further example. Beard pulled no punches in advancing this point of view in his discussion of Frederic J. Stimson's *American Constitution.* We see him in 1908 dipping into his precise knowledge of English and American constitutional history and at the same time invoking the pragmatic or instrumentalist approach to ideas as functional instruments in actual struggles. English radicals, Beard claimed, in their long struggle for democratic government evolved the notion that the ideal political system they sought was but a return to precedents. The institutions implied in the rights of man philosophy were given "a historical reality in the tribal-feudal arrangements of the Anglo-Saxon period." "Beyond the 'red thread of the Norman conquest,'" Beard insisted, "were found representative government, popular local administration, and stalwart individualism of the Spencerian type. Thus history was used with scientific zeal to serve the instant need of politics." Then Beard listed errors in the book and identified them, not only with a faulty concept of history, but with an "anarchical jurisprudence."[30] In short, long before he wrote his own economic interpretation of the American Constitution, Beard was sensitive to the inadequacy of the formalistic type of English constitutional studies, which divorced institutions from conflicts of interest, and to the shortcomings of comparable American emphases.

But Beard was not always negative in the contribution he made through reviews to a three-dimensional conception of constitutional history. Thus in evaluating Schlesinger's *Colonial Merchants* he emphasized the point that it disposed of "those fiction writers who make the American Revolution a quarrel over legal theories and also of those amusing persons who speak of it as an uprising of the American people, in the name of law and order, against a German usurper on the British throne. Thus do the economic aspects of history come into clearer perspective as science advances into the domain of mythology."

This period also defined Beard's lifelong interest in the problem of power. We glimpse it in his hard, tough criticisms of metaphysical and romantic discussions of appearance divorced from reality, of ideas unrelated to interests. In his review of Arthur F. Bentley's *Process of Government* (1908) Beard noted the effective use Bentley made of the idea of group interests as distinguished from class interests in the Marxian sense.[31] Beard's concern with the problem of power provided a sharp needle for puncturing the histories of economic thought that located utopia in the Middle Ages.[32] But he was no more gentle with socialist interpretations that placed utopia in the future without coming to grips with the problem of power.[33] The reviews of three of Harold Laski's books in the early 1920's best illustrate Beard's distinction between appearance and reality—his conception of the basic importance of taking into due account the locus and functions of power. To his mind both *Political Thought from Locke to Bentham* and *The Foundations of Sovereignty* were fatally weak in their neglect of economics. To discuss political ideas without reference to the struggles for power of such interest groups as Whigs and Tories seemed comparable to clinging to the Miltonic account of creation in the post-Darwinian era. When Laski praised Burke for his "hatred of oppression" Beard asked, "Whose oppression? Where? All oppression?" "Consider the state of England and France in the eighteenth century," Beard went on, "and then answer whether Burke did not head the greatest conspiracy in defense of oppression ever formed."[34] On the other hand, Beard was full of praise for *The Grammar of Politics,* which he reviewed in 1925. For here Laski in taking into full account the realities of economics in relation to politics adopted a method certain to make "the leaves rustle in the academic grove." Beard was to return to this theme again and again in the reviews written in later years.[35] And he gave classic expression to his analysis of the problem in his critical essay on Brooks and Henry Adams.[36]

Throughout his career Beard welcomed scholarly efforts to illuminate contemporary history, but in his second period, from the First World War to the middle 1930's, he was especially concerned with this. He turned from other tasks to notice the revisionist writing on this First World War.[37] He insisted on the importance of the multiarchival approach and on a consideration of what lay behind the diplomatic papers. He also warned the revisionists against merely shifting exclusive guilt for the war from the Central Powers to the Allies. In his review of Barnes' *Genesis of the World War,* Beard cautioned, "If there is peril in the attempt to enforce the Versailles theory of responsible and punitive damages, there is equal danger in the attempt to whitewash the German Kaiser, the Crown Prince, the war party, the super-patriots of the Fatherland. . . . Merely to shift heroes and villains will only confuse the issue."[38] And, instrumentalist that Beard was, we find growing evidence of his disillusion with the events that followed the war and seemed in some way to be related to it.[39]

Beard's skepticism was evident when he wrote about matters and values close to his heart. This was true in the case of the New History, which, along with James Harvey Robinson and Carl Becker, he had done so much to inaugurate. Becker expressed, in one of his books that came to Beard for review, the hope that education might become emancipated from "the pressure of economic and social tendencies" that caused it to bog down. Beard also set store by education, as his labor in the instruction of young and old demonstrates. Yet what passed for education in many quarters made him wonder whether Becker, skeptical though he was for all his idealism, might not be expecting too much of it. At the time when he read the Becker book he also included in the same review his reflections on the textbook in recent history of the United States written by an historian whom he described as "a scholar of understanding and discernment." The text seemed to Beard conventional in its respectability, superficial in its platitudes, and philistine in its deference to the *status quo.* Beard concluded that, in view of the status of the author of the book and its probable wide use in the colleges, the elder statesmen did indeed have a stultifying hold on college instruction.[40]

Even in the complacent 1920's, however, Beard found much
to cheer him—the appearance for example of J. Franklin
Jameson's *American Revolution Considered as a Social Movement*. Here one of the first scholars of America, an elder
statesman at that, definitively closed the romantic and Ban-
croftian discussion of the American Revolution. He did it by
showing that the lineup of forces was essentially economic, that
metaphysical abstractions added up to little indeed, and that
with sufficient hard work the intricate and illusive connections
between economic and cultural forces might yield to study.
Here was impressive testimony from the dean of American
historians that no phase of American civilization could be sat-
isfactorily considered apart from the others. "A truly notable
book . . . cut with a diamond point to the finish."

In other reviews of major American historians Beard demonstrated his mature powers. Especially notable was his bold and
skilful use of the related social sciences and of new currents of
social thought. Thus in analyzing historical writing he employed the sociology of knowledge and the doctrine of historical
relativity. He was too much the empirical realist to close his
eyes to the relevancies of the current scene that might throw
light on historical interpretations of the past. These and other
criteria that he brought to bear in reviewing outstanding works
on the national history in this period can be illustrated in his
critical discussion of the contributions of Edward Channing and
Frederick Jackson Turner.

Paying tribute to Channing's wide and deep researches, to
his laborious days well spent, and to his "firm and weighty
judgments on controversial points," Beard also called attention
to the "respectability, in the finest sense of that word" that characterized every page of the Harvard historian. But his respect
for "a mind of great natural powers" did not blind him to what
seemed to him to be shortcomings in Channing's *History of the
United States*. In reviewing the fourth volume he dissented
from the view that the Federalist-Republican schism grew
out of differing ideas about the nature of the new government.
He disagreed with the judgment that economic factors merely

accentuated cleavages created by ideas. Did the ideas, Beard asked, spring out of thin air, or were they innately present in the human mind. Though he disavowed belief in the economic man, as he had done earlier and was to do again, Beard claimed that the time had come to lay the old ghosts of nationalism and state rights divorced from economic content. "Nowhere, in these massive six hundred pages," he wrote of the fourth volume, "is there any departure from the canons of the American historical guild." It seemed not only certain but altogether fitting that the mantle of respectability should be laid on this volume as it had been on its predecessors, for it was essentially the old story: "Nothing unpleasant is laid before the mind"— not even in the discussion of American behavior that made the War with Mexico inevitable. New social material there was, but that, too, was used to create only a mosaic, not a new interpretation. For Channing was "as silent as the grave as to whence and whither" and left unanswered some of the most important questions, which Beard proceeded to list.

His comments on the fifth and sixth volumes were even more critical. In writing of the sixth and last volume, Beard remarked that here was to be found what the Ph.D.'s in history thought. It seemed impossible to discover what notion of worth and worthiness governed the selection of materials—why there was no space given to the social and literary movements of the period, inasmuch as these had been considered in the preceding volume. Although Channing found the Civil War at bottom a clash of rival economic systems, he proceeded to tell the traditional tale. "The reviewer surrenders" was the final dart in this notice of Channing's concluding volume.

Beard's discussion of Frederick Jackson Turner provides an even more important example of his historical criticism at its best. The *New Republic* asked him in 1921 to review the collected essays of the great exponent of the frontier in American history, and on at least two other occasions Beard wrote at length about Turner and his work.[41] On one occasion he paid him high tribute indeed. The influence of Turner, he wrote, was "immense and salutary" in bringing fresh air into the realm of the provincialism and mythology of the Teutonic school and that of the New Englanders. His enthusiasm for the neglected history of the West was altogether commendable. And his emphasis on the importance of free land in American development carried economic implications at a time when most historians dealt with "shadow politics." Although he did not say so, Beard in expressing approval of Turner for thinking of American history "mainly in terms of economic group conflicts" may well have been thinking of his own emphasis on such conflicts and of the realistic work of Arthur F. Bentley in political science, which he had favorably reviewed in 1908.[42] In any case he was as convinced in 1939 as he had been in 1921 that Turner's life was "an ornament to American scholarship and to the republic from which it sprang." Especially, he went on, when one looked at the setting of American historical scholarship in 1893 Turner's magnitude was unquestionable, for, despite the anticipations of his frontier thesis, it was truly unique in conception and technique. Beard added that, in emphasizing individualism as a frontier phenomenon as strongly as he did, Turner must for the moment have bypassed the community spirit it bred—a spirit he later celebrated when the influence of Spencer and Darwin was less overweening. Beard gave high praise to Turner in saying that as the historian of the agricultural era he was not only the outstanding historian of his generation but almost "the only one who did not devote himself to rehashing hash."[43]

Beard was ready to agree with Turner up to a point—to the point, namely, that the era of free land did give a special quality to American democracy. But in the 1921 critique and in the later evaluations he made it clear that he regarded as too sweeping Turner's statement that American development is explained by free land. As Beard saw it, the agrarian West, slavocracy, labor, and capital did largely explain American development up to 1893 "but certainly free land and the westward advance of settlement alone do not."[44] Nor were the data at hand for proving or disproving Turner's contention that the frontier was the line of most effective Americanization—this was but an impression. Nor could Beard in 1921 agree that the legislative powers of the national government sprang chiefly from the frontier, for at most such legislation was influenced, not conditioned, as Turner had it. That the loose construction of the Constitution became more marked in the chronological period of westward advance was true, but the influence of Hamilton and the economic interests he represented was, Beard insisted, in considerable degree at least, the explanation.

As for democracy, it came to England as well as to America and in fact it was on the march in the United States even before new states made their appearance west of the Alleghenies. Beard did note that in his essays Turner recognized the importance of industrial forces, though he said little in print of the conflicts of capitalists and organized workers. In fact, Beard wondered why historians were so slow in recognizing the importance of the rise of labor. Could it be the spell exercised by the Turner thesis? Furthermore, Beard believed that the frontier thesis failed to offer an adequate explanation not only of American political and economic development but also of the more comprehensive development of American civilization itself. The Constitution, after all, was framed chiefly by lawyers, not by farmers. It was chiefly commercial interests that interpreted it. And men of distinction in art, literature, and the sciences sprang for the most part from urban rather than from rural milieus. At the same time Beard made it clear in 1939 that in his opinion the idea was well established that the elbowroom of the frontier, the rich treasures it offered, the freehold agriculture it encouraged, had "given to expressions of human nature in the United States some of the distinctive features we call American."[45] I believe that the consensus in the historical profession today largely supports Beard's evaluation of Turner's limitations and contributions.

There is no sharp break between what I have called the second and third periods in Beard's career as an historical critic.

His concern with American foreign policy in his later years was well rooted in World War I and its aftermath. In the 1920's, as I have indicated, he supported the revisionist school. This support was in part an expression of his determination to distinguish between appearances and official theses on the one hand and realities and actualities on the other. In part Beard's position rested on his concern over the setback the war gave to civil liberties and his uneasiness about the vast increase of the war powers of the presidency and the implications of this for democracy. In reviews of books on our Caribbean policy he challenged the use of the Monroe Doctrine as a cloak to cover up our economic imperialism.[46]

In taking issue with writers of the 1920's who maintained the inevitability of war, Beard was expressing his opposition to the idea of inevitability in the historical process. And now, in the later years he likewise refused to accept the thesis that the choice in foreign policy was limited to one last chance to lend military aid to the nations resisting fascist aggression. In reviewing Albert Carr's *America's Last Chance* (1941) Beard put his position simply and clearly. "It is possible of course, that the United States will have similar chances in the future (if the past is any guide) and that this is not the last chance. It is possible also that the Government of the United States, which seems about to embark on Mr. Carr's total war, will be surprised by the results of 'taking the last chance.' "

In view of the charge that Beard's position on foreign policies made him in effect, if not straightout, a sympathizer with fascism, it may be well to take account of certain reviews of books on that phenomenon. In writing in 1929 about Herbert W. Schneider's *Making of the Fascist State* Beard noted that there was nothing really new in the fascist condemnation of democracy and that Mussolini was not all of Italy. The doctrine of action reminded him of Theodore Roosevelt and "the strenuous life." That something might be learned from the experimental attempt to reconcile individualism and socialism, politics and technology, he had little doubt. But there was no approval of fascism, only approval of Schneider's "realistic and highly important survey," which got beneath the verbiage and political forms "without rancor and with the saving sense of humor."[47] Later, in reviewing Megaro's *Mussolini in the Making* Beard shot one of his characteristic barbs when he remarked that inasmuch as the Duce had proved himself "sound" on property he had become respectable in foreign eyes.[48]

In discussing the development of the frame of reference concept in Beard's critical arsenal we have seen that it was well formulated before the mid-thirties. It is merely necessary to add at this point that the larger doctrine of historical relativism of which it was a part reached its full fruition in the last decade and a half of Beard's life. Not only in talking about his own work, but in writing about that of his friends who shared his own relativistic views he showed himself fully aware of the limitations of this theory. Thus in reviewing Carl Becker's *The Heavenly City of the Eighteenth Century Philosophers* Beard concluded: "Such is the dilemma to which the relativity of the modern historical school inevitably leads. . . . Until the knot-cutter has arrived, Professor Becker's statement of the problem will remain a classic, a beautifully finished literary product." Skeptical as Beard was of neat formulae and of efforts to allocate "causes" with mathematical precision, he quite naturally showed this skepticism in various reviews. In place of the older idea of a chain of causes determined throughout, Beard argued for the indeterminacy principle, that is, for the assumption that the historian can, at least for the time, merely discover "conditioning realities which make possible what happens without causally determining it in detail."[49] Into this theory Beard thought the evolution not only of war but of capitalism must be fitted; and so thinking, he was among the first to sound a note of caution when historians gave signs of becoming apologists for the big business men of recent American history.[50]

Biography was virtually the only historical form that Beard never attempted—a fact one may regret in view of his warm human sympathies and understanding of human nature. It is clear, however, from his reviews of biographies what criteria he held for good craftsmanship in this field. As he pointed out in his review of Samuel Eliot Morison's *The Life and Letters of Harrison Gray Otis,* the biography of a man of little importance personally might be "a significant contribution to the history of American economics and politics, destined sometime to be written."[51] He realized the difficulties of writing about figures within the memory of living men and illustrated these in his comments on Samuel W. McCall's *Life of Thomas Reed.* Nor did he have much respect for what he called the old-fashioned biography, which assumed the uniqueness of the hero. Such a biography was the one W. D. Puleston wrote of Captain Alfred Thayer Mahan. Beard thought the biographer should also have considered those qualities that made Mahan "typical of a class and a period." Beard proceeded to relate the great navalist to his world-imperialist setting, to the web of bureaucracies, and to the interests he represented—not sparing the inconsistencies of Mahan that his biographer failed to reveal, I must also call attention to the perceptive review Beard wrote of Carl Sandburg's *Lincoln: The Prairie Years.* He did not condemn the informal, unorganized diary-like character of the text, based as it was on wide study and much brooding. When specialists had finally ceased dissecting the flaws of the book, Beard suspected it would stand up as a "noble monument of American literature" by reason of the beautiful way in which Sandburg showed how in a time of crisis the folk wisdom Lincoln embodied served a people better than great philosophies and systems of thought. It was, in other words, the essentially human element in Lincoln and the relation of this to his milieu that appealed to Beard. But his conception of biography, as well as his critical approach, can best be illustrated concretely by reference to his correspondence with a friend, Albert J. Beveridge, whose second major contribution to American historiography was a study of Abraham Lincoln.

Indeed, a few words should now be said about the contributions made to historical criticism through Beard's reading of the manuscripts of colleagues and friends. The exchange of letters with Beveridge illustrates the pertinent and helpful suggestions Beard must have given in many instances to friends at work on historical projects. Beard was one of several scholars who read the manuscript of *The Life of John Marshall*.[52] The warm praise he bestowed on the last two volumes must have cheered Beveridge. "I have read them with growing satisfaction," Beard wrote, "and am more than proud to be associated in even the smallest way in your great enterprise. You have been far too generous in acknowledging help. Everybody knows that the big job is all yours. That is one sure thing. And it will be read long after the Senator from Indiana or even Indiana is forgotten. You have the kind of immortality that the great Greeks won."[53]

Beard read the early manuscript chapters of *Lincoln* "with the deepest interest and the most profound pleasure." His marginal comments dealt with details to which he took exception. His first major suggestion was that Beveridge take the manuscript "and write straight away a new moving draft without any footnotes and then insert the notes afterward. That will give," Beard continued, "your truly moving spirit a free swing and thus improve the style of the book and at the same time give you the precision which is required by science."[54] Beveridge took the hint. In later correspondence Beard urged the biographer to go through the manuscript "with an eagle eye and substitute *Saxon* for Roman words, thinking of Bunyan rather than Milton, and then let the steel cut portrait stand, trivial, pathetic and foreshadowing as it is."[55] In the end Beard had high praise for the style. "The text is splendid, Homeric in directness and matter-of-factness. It is so new and so well put together that all people will marvel at your achievement. . . . If you go on at this rate you will beat wonderful John Marshall."[56]

Meantime Beard made several concrete criticisms that did not fall on indifferent ears. Beveridge had begun the biography with a reference to Napoleon—a dramatic contrast to

Lincoln. Beard felt this was a bit farfetched and offered an alternative start: "When Abe Lincoln was born Jefferson was just about to leave the presidency. Hamilton was five years in his untimely grave. Lincoln was to fuse the democracy of the one with the vigorous government of the other." Beveridge took to the suggestion and made a fresh start.[57]

Beard also thought that Beveridge had oversimplified the politics of the 1830's. More important, in his opinion Beveridge did not do justice to the Mexican side in discussing the war with our southern neighbor. In the first place Beveridge used only American sources. "Would you take an English explanation of European diplomacy between 1870 and 1914 as the last word? Now, honest?"[58] Making clear that he himself did not share the old Whig view that looked on the war as a simple conspiracy of the slavocracy, Beard nevertheless contended that the American diplomacy was no better than the Mexican. In fact, he added, it was worse in view of the fact that the Mexicans, unlike the Americans, had no real government. To buttress the point he mentioned the dubious activities of such Americans as Poinsett and Jones. Beveridge wanted to know what was wrong with these two distinguished figures. Well, Beard replied, Poinsett had mixed into Mexican politics with a view of getting the group he favored into power. "What would you say," he asked, "if the Mexican minister in Washington had tried by intrigue in American politics to fasten Woodrow Wilson on this country for a third term?"[59] In regard to the conduct of Commodore Jones at Monterey Beard asked: "Did a Mexican officer ever try to seize an American city—Mobile or New Orleans by mistake? What would have happened if he did? Oh boy!" Beard spared no pains to make his point. "I am only asking you to try to see that show through Mexican eyes, for a moment," Beard admonished, "just to even up the balance. I repeat, the Mexicans were bad enough, but they were not a nation and had no government."[60] To put it differently, the big thing was to get the essential facts as they were, not to make a "righteous case" for our diplomacy. In doing so and in placing

Lincoln against that background, he was opening the way for savage, and justified, criticism.[61] Beard went on to say that there was no point in trying to whitewash Jackson, Tyler, Polk, or anyone else. "Why not stick to biology? We were going to have that land, and we got it."[62] Six weeks later Beard urged again, "Above all, don't get righteous; that is a game that two can play!"[63] To strengthen his case, Beard sent on specific references to materials, including Mexican accounts.[64] Despite his show of resistance, Beveridge saw the force of some part of Beard's position and revised accordingly.

Nor was the Mexican War the only issue on which the two men at first did not see eye to eye. "I think," Beard wrote, "you play up the savage side of the abolitionists—for whose biological processes I make no apology—and give much too much, far too mvch space to Southern defenses. . . . In your laudable desire to do justice you damn the abolitionist (by implication) and make out the best possible case for the slave owners. . . . I should sum up the abolition case and methods—sum up the slave case and methods—and then integrate Lincoln's views with the two sides."[65] And later: "Whether slavery would have been abolished without the abolitionists—peacefully—is at best highly speculative. After all the way that was chosen was the way that was chosen."[66]

Similarly, Beard pointed to the danger of accepting at face value the worst stories about John Brown in Kansas. Beveridge ought at least to cite Villard's work. Beard also believed that in following Charles Warren in the chapter on the Dred Scott decision Beveridge had been too one-sided; he called attention to the discussion of Haines on "Lincoln and the Supreme Court."[67] In each case Beveridge took these suggestions into account.

Beard also questioned Beveridge's tendency to devote a great deal of detail to events and personalities that were only peripheral to Lincoln. The canvas, he thought, was often too crowded and the illustrations too trivial—the account of Douglas' marriage "to the most beautiful thing that ever lived, for example."[68] But he always offered his criticisms humbly and at the same time spoke most warmly about the merits of what Beveridge was doing. In turn Beveridge appreciatively wrote of the great value of Beard's marginal notes. "I shall make use of them in one of the many rewritings." Agreeing with Beard on the matter of excessive detail on Douglas, he wanted to know how one was to get rid of it! Nevertheless, he found a way.[89]

These illustrations suggest the nature of Beard's critical contributions to the historical undertakings of his friends. I can myself testify to the careful, thoughtful, and provocative criticisms, in detail and in the large, that he generously gave to one of my own manuscripts.

The theme of Beard as historical critic is in no sense exhausted by a consideration of the reviews he wrote and the help he gave to friends and colleagues. His occasional contributions to discussions at professional gatherings illuminated the subject in hand, and anyone who attended the meetings of the American Historical Association's Commission on the Social Studies will testify to his cogent and eloquent historical criticism. Nor should the student of this phase of Beard's career overlook the long, thoughtful introduction to the edition of Brooks Adams' *The Law of Civilization and Decay* that appeared in 1943. Here Beard meticulously compared the texts of the American, English, French, and German editions, straightened out the tangled question of the intellectual relations of Brooks Adams and Henry Adams, and evaluated the critical reception of the book. In combining detailed, precise analysis with a large view of the place of the essay in the history of thought Beard displayed his versatile powers to advantage.

Finally, one should also call attention to the more or less formal discussions of American historical writing and thought in the books in which the Beards collaborated. Here the gift for judicious appraisal, for incisive allocation of a book to its proper category, for a perception of the larger meaning were tellingly revealed. The concluding sentence of the discussion in *America in Midpassage* is worth pondering: "If historians working in the scientific spirit, seeking emancipation from the tyranny of old assumptions, persisted in the effort to bring all schemes of selection into some kind of articulation and stronger consensus, and could perform this function in historiography, even to a limited extent, then all divisions of contemporary thought and all formulations of public policy were bound to receive a higher and wider illumination."[70]

In summary, it is clear that Beard's warm and appreciative spirit, his wit and brilliance, his incisiveness and his gift for phrase, all suffused his critical writing. It is also apparent that his reviews often anticipated his own books. At the same time his contributions in this field reflected his conviction that history is a seamless web, that any effort to divorce politics or constitutional developments or intellectual abstractions from the whole of human experience is bound to be misleading rather than enlightening. It is also clear that Beard's historical thinking did not undergo any abrupt or radical shifts. It is equally clear that it was anything but static. His contributions to historical thinking can be symbolized in the words he wrote in *The Economic Basis of Politics:* "Long the victim of material forces man had, by taking thought, made himself the master of wind and wave and storm. May he not, by taking thought . . . make himself master of his social destiny? Perhaps not; but as the human mind is greater than the waterfall which it compels or the lightning's flash which it confines, so the control of human destiny is a nobler object than the search for material power. Even though every door be slammed in our faces, still must we knock."[71]

ARTHUR W. MACMAHON

Charles Beard, the Teacher

IN 1909 WHEN Columbia's veteran college dean, John Howard Van Amringe, was about to retire, the campus paper polled the students on his successor.[1] Charles Beard was the overwhelming preference. He had been teaching hardly more than four years; his own pioneer courses in politics had begun in 1907. Though always accessible, he cared as little as any man about academic management. His easy ways belied how fiercely intent he was on research, writing, and practical service. Yet students, graduate and undergraduate alike, turned to this man as to the light. The warmth about the mouth complementing the glint of the eagle eyes, the spare simplicity, the unstudied attitude of proud and equal deference to all human beings of whatever age and position, all radiated beyond his own classes. As I think back on the magic of it, I recall that when I was a junior I found myself suddenly thinking one day—unbidden by any personal situation—that if I did not have a father and were free to choose one in all the world, he would be Charles Beard. I had not been in his courses, nor indeed did I take work in his department until I was a graduate student and already an instructor, but I had enjoyed something like substitute contacts as a member of debating teams to which he gave much time as an adviser. The impressive thing about the idea I mention is that at the time it seemed to me natural and obvious; I took it for granted that many if not all students felt exactly the same way.

Charles Beard's influence as a teacher was not confined to the dozen years he was a professor at Columbia. A country journalist even before he entered college, he carried into graduate work and scholarship the communicative zest that made him a builder in the movement for adult education. Though his contribution to the founding of Ruskin Hall while he was a student at Oxford in 1899 was made in the upswing of labor politics, it was characteristic of Beard to wish to link workers' education to the resources of the great university tradition. Later, even before Beard left Columbia, he was associated with the pioneer training school for the public service established in 1911 under the New York Bureau of Municipal Research and, as head of the Bureau's Training School for Public Service after 1917 and later of the Bureau itself, he gave much of his time to such training. In the same period, too, he lectured at the New School for Social Research and conducted a course for the School of Social Work. While at Columbia, as well as later, he gave sustained series of lectures which were not only the source of published works but also the occasion of close contact with two college communities.[2] In the late thirties, he returned for a semester to the old department at Columbia, which in a real sense he had never left, so substantial had been the projection of his presence. Beard's unflagging zest as a teacher was likewise shown in a year of full-time residence at the Johns Hopkins in 1940-1941. There his crowded seminar overflowed in endless conferences of a singularly vital and warming kind, and he became the busy architect of a plan for the study of American cultural history.

Through the long years in which Beard had no permanent connection with any institution, he was in fact an advisory member of countless departments of government and history. His influence was not merely as a writer of texts and treatises. It was not merely as the faithful participant in conventions and other gatherings of teachers in the fields of the social studies. In addition, as V. O. Key said in introducing Beard to the American Political Science Association in 1947, no one will ever know how many individual scholars without shred of institutional claim sought and received help from one who was ostensibly fully occupied as a professional writer and always acutely aware how scanty are the working hours in the racing years, but who was too instinctively a teacher to disregard requests for counsel. Not least important was the time Beard spared for comment on the basic problems of research and instruction. The Educational Policies Commission of the National Education Association in its report in 1937 on *The Unique Function of Education in American Democracy* stated that "when approaching the problem, the Commission decided to seek assistance from the man best qualified for the task by scholarship, social insight, and devotion to democratic institutions. The Commission thereupon voted without difficulty and with complete unanimity that Dr. Beard was especially fitted for this task."[3] The assignment was not the only call of the sort; undertakings of this kind were especially suited to a man who had exhibited a lifelong brooding concern about what goes on in the discussion of public affairs.

Beard's influence as a teacher, then, was multiple and continuous. The constant factor was a fusion of personality and viewpoints. It is with this complex during the period of his full-time teaching that I am mainly concerned.

Many qualities enter in varying combinations to make a good teacher; nor is there one type of great teacher. The strength of one ingredient may offset the absence of others. Two elements, however, are usually present in outstanding teachers; their interaction helps to make the teacher as distinguished from other craftsmen of thought and expression. One element is curiosity about truth amounting to passion. The other is concern for the fulfillment of individuals. The emphasis varies with the type of teacher. Sometimes the latter trait is dominant. In that sense, as George Herbert Palmer put it, the aptitudes of the successful teacher include vicariousness and a readiness to be forgotten.[4] On the other hand, in many great teachers—perhaps the greatest—it is love of the subject for the sake of comprehending it that is paramount. The gift of communication there must be, of course; sometimes the special force of effective transmission lies in sheer lucidity, sometimes in the excitement of suffused eloquence. In great teachers, probably, both love of subject and concern for students are aspects of the underlying zest to see things as they are, attended by a thrill of discovery that prevents rest until not only the result but also the method of discovery itself is shared with others.

One gropes vainly for words that explain why and how seekers reach out and share with others. Charles Warren in an essay in 1912 on notable Harvard teachers, commenting on men like Agassiz, Shaler, Norton, and Peirce, found it no curious coincidence that all who had been "great not merely because of their learning, but because of the lasting impress they made on their students," should have had in common the characteristic of "human sympathy."[5] The phrase describes rather than explains an Agassiz, for example, chary of abstraction, hot on bringing others into "the light of the world's concrete fullness," as William James said of him.[6] Agassiz's method was the much challenged device of the lecture. Yet Henry Adams recalled that during his own student years at Harvard "the only teaching that appealed to his imagination was a course of lectures by Louis Agassiz on the Glacial Period and Palaeontology which had more influence on his curiosity than the rest of the college instruction together."[7]

Personality cannot be separated from outlook. To seek to promote great teaching by prescribing "great personalities" has well been called a counsel of futility. Consequently, before passing to Charles Beard's characteristics of person and of speech and his methods of instruction, it is appropriate to consider attitudes that were fundamental in his power as a teacher.

Much of Beard's influence as a teacher was a result of the awareness of time and change that he always conveyed, along with a confidence in the future that flooded upward through even the most astringent mordancy. Speaking as president of the American Political Science Association in 1926 to those who were peculiarly his fellows and successors in classroom instruction, Beard asked: "Can those of us who teach and write to-day honestly avoid the challenging fact that their students must work in the substance of the approaching years, not the ashes of the yesterday?"[8] The title of this presidential address was clue and challenge in itself: "Time, Technology, and the Creative Spirit in Political Science." In his class lectures as in his writing, references to "becoming reality," the "becoming future," and "constantly becoming situations" were as frequent as allusions to "the Socratic elenchus." Two of his favorite turns of speech were joined in a sentence in a mid-career discussion of the methods of political science that Beard contributed to a symposium on research: "The Socratic elenchus is the prime instrument for training intelligence; and the only tolerable goal of our labors must be an artistically perfect adjustment of our conduct and ideas to the noblest imagined potentialities of the constantly becoming situations, thus uniting the word and the deed which were not asunder in the beginning and will not be at the end."[9]

In Charles Beard something that was almost ambivalent flowed from the fact that his idea of progress associated vast cumulative forces and a creative morality. Illustrations may fittingly be drawn from the stage of his active teaching. In a published lecture on *Politics* contributed in 1908 to a series by various departmental spokesmen, he declared his faith that "society has come from crude and formless associations beginning in a dim and dateless past and moves outward into an illimitable future, which many of us believe will not be hideous

and mean, but beautiful and magnificent." The sentence that
followed hinted at the source of the ambivalence while affirm-
ing a larger unity. "In this dynamic society, the citizen becomes
co-worker in that great and indivisible natural process which
draws down granite hills and upbuilds great nations."[10] An
essay in 1910 on the study and teaching of politics was an en-
thusiastic prospectus of the many opportunities and attractions
offered by the new field of study. There was place, he wrote,
for the scholar's detachment while serving "the practical interests of humanity in its great struggle to secure the highest economies of collective effort in combination with the largest fruit-
fulness for the individual life."[11] Possible roots for the ambivalence I have mentioned were evident in another remark in the
same paper. "Master publicists," Beard exclaimed, "are made
largely by time and circumstance; and it is given to few men
to write the moral philosophy for the political passion of a
great age, or to clothe a powerful social interest in the form of
an inexorable and compelling logic."

I leave it to others to consider Beard's resolution of a universal problem. Any viable philosophy, however open-ended
and however normative, must concede that life abounds in determined sequences, if not inevitable choices and fixed ends.
Suffice it here to deal with the way in which the problem reacted
on Beard's teaching. One effect was an ever-present sense of
largeness as well as movement. A further outcome was a rapid
and at times unpredictable alternation of Beard's moods of emphasis. Sometimes, with almost acid irony, the stress was upon
the mighty processes in which men's efforts contribute to results
better than their own motives or are bent to different or even
opposite ultimate ends. Then, swiftly as the changing sky,
Beard's outlook and manner might become those of the ardent
or indignant idealist. Part of the excitement of his teaching lay
in this almost gusty shift of viewpoint and change of pace.

Nevertheless the decisive quality in Beard's impact as a
teacher was consistency rather than alternation. The dominant
and lasting chords were always humanity, standards, judgment,

responsibility, hope. Perhaps the effect was religious in the sense in which Alfred North Whitehead used the word in saying that the essence of education is the inculcation of duty and reverence—duty arising "from our potential control over the course of events" and reverence from the perception "that the present holds within itself the complete sum of existence, backwards and forwards, that whole amplitude of time, which is eternity."[12] In Beard's case the positive net effect was partly due to sheer vitality. As he himself said in a lecture (if a student's notes reported him rightly), "Pessimism isn't a matter of philosophy but of temperament." The basis lay even more directly, however, in his view of the world.

The outlook that Beard brought to teaching was shown in his first and almost forgotten book, *The Industrial Revolution*, published in England in January, 1901, and reprinted nine times. It was written to sell for a shilling. In his preface to the 1902 printing Beard commented on its reissuance without a thorough revision, saying: "I believe it will continue to serve my original purpose, which was to supply a concise and inexpensive outline of the Industrial Revolution as a guide to students seeking for the first time the historical basis of modern social and economic problems." The book was intended primarily for adult education in the labor and co-operative movements. In 1902 Beard himself did not doubt "that the reorganization of industrial society upon a democratic basis will be brought about by a political and social movement depending for its numerical strength upon the working classes." F. York Powell, Regius Professor of Modern History at Oxford, whom Beard and his fellow American, Walter Vrooman, had secured as presiding officer at the inaugural meeting of Ruskin Hall on February 22, 1899, contributed an introduction on Beard's request because, as he wrote to another, "He is an old pupil of mine, and the nicest American I ever knew."[13] Powell's own anxious concern was for the enlightenment of working people on the threshold of great political power. Yet he was downright about the past when he wrote in the introduction to Beard's book: "The English people, never by any plague, or famine, or war, suffered such a deadly blow at its vitality as by the establishment of the factory system without the proper safeguards."

As for Beard, it was full of meaning that the name Ruskin was given to the building founded in 1899 as a residence center for workers within sound of Oxford's bells. And it was to those who appraised the economic order in terms of beauty, kindness, decency, and the high esthetic of function and style that Beard appealed in his first book. "The Political Economists who regarded society as composed of a group of independent and warring units did not long occupy the fortress of knowledge unassailed," he wrote. "Owen, Carlyle, Maurice, Kingsley, Ruskin—the humanitarians—impeached in eloquent, if not always logical, English the old assumptions."[14] Beard himself had none of the traces of condescension not always absent in the humanitarians, even Ruskin and York Powell. What he shared was their classless sense of usefulness and distributive justice. Before Beard came to Columbia for the completion of his graduate work he had lived and lectured in England's Black Country. He returned to the United States angry at squalor and waste. Essentially, however, the book he had already written was a plea to take advantage of the opportunities opened by the Industrial Revolution. Along with indignation there was confidence in a possible future that would be "beautiful and magnificent."[15]

In Beard's teaching his innate respect for human beings, his sense of movement, and his confidence in the becoming future always triumphed in their combined effort over irony, over sarcasm, over even occasional bitterness and innuendo. I think he was cautious about the rising schools of psychology in the study of politics not so much because they stressed factors that challenged the environmental interpretation of events but more because the new explanations—as Ernest Barker phrased the matter in a notable inaugural address—threatened to deny "the unity secured to the mind by a pervading and freely moving reason."[16] Indeed, Beard's later views on certain foreign policies (with the postulates and conclusions of which I could not agree) showed how little of determinism there was in his thinking. For at the core of his anger then was the belief that opportunities had been missed by wrong decisions.

In Beard's transforming presence as a teacher, students sensed understanding even in condemnation. He practiced what he mentioned in commenting later on a former instructor, the historian George Lincoln Burr. "I do remember one thing that I heard him say in his seminar during the fall term of 1899, when I was a student at Cornell. . . . The saying was: 'It is only through sympathy, never through hatred, that we can understand an age or a people.' . . . It struck fire in my mind then, and has burned there for more than forty years."[17]

I think my memory does not trick me in recalling an incident that throws light on the attitude and atmosphere that Charles Beard brought to teaching. Promethean may be exactly the word. We were in his office between classes. Did I know what he considered the greatest lines in English poetry? It was more than a guess when I named at once the closing lines of Shelley's *Prometheus Unbound*. I was right. At least I was right for that hour, and I was right also, I think, in terms of a deep and durable resilience in the man; whatever he said, his bearing and voice and the spirit behind them implied that love does not repent and that hope can create from its own wrecks the thing it contemplates. Even if my memory errs about this incident—an electric moment still in my retrospect—the fact that I could conceive it at all is a commentary on the qualities that Beard communicated to the men about him.

Beard's classroom methods were uneven, apart from the alternation of viewpoint that I have mentioned earlier. Graduate students, for example, remember marches of logical exposition—sometimes level, oftener mounting—and the timbre of an eloquence that seemed almost imperious. On the other hand, I am interested to note that Irwin Edman, who took politics as a freshman, has written of Beard the teacher as a "lanky figure leaning against the wall, drawling wittily with half-closed eyes." Edman wrote that, under "his easy, drawling manner, we sensed a passionate concern for an understanding of the realities of government, the economic forces and the interested persons involved in it, and the ideal of government: the liberation of the energies of men." But Edman, when recounting his galaxy of great Columbia teachers, could identify no special technique that accounted for Beard's influence. "He was clear, he was suggestive, he was witty. But none of these things could quite account for the hold he had on the smug and the rebels alike, on both the pre-lawyers and the pre-poets." Edman added his own estimate: "I suspect it was a certain combination of poetry, philosophy, and honesty in the man himself, a sense he communicated that politics mattered far beyond the realm commonly called political, and an insight he conveyed into the life that forms of government furthered or betrayed."[18]

Beard's unevenness of method made him at times seem perfunctory as well as unpremeditating. None the less, even on these occasions, he usually added significance as well as gusto. Thus in 1909, the year of the appearance of his own *Readings* on politics, he wrote in the *History Teacher's Magazine* with almost naive enthusiasm about the use of source material. "I always take Ash's edition of the charter of New York City—a portly volume of about a thousand pages—into my classroom and perform before the eyes of the students the experiment of running through the chief titles." This remark might be a travesty on descriptive political science in its heyday when facts were free and equal. Under Beard's casual touch, however, the operation would doubtless be an *experiment* in which municipal functions would begin to mean something in their relations and involvements. Another procedure that risked being perfunctory was to summarize some writer—Aristotle, for example—taking his ideas just as they came, chapter by chapter. Here Beard's genius showed itself in the offhand running comments and perhaps a few words at the end.

When one describes Beard's teaching as often casual he remembers as apt what Confucius (in the rendering of Lin Yutang) said of the ideal teacher: "His words are concise but expressive, casual but full of hidden meaning, and he is good at drawing ingenious examples to make people understand him."[19] The oblique method is in line with what Sidney Hook has said about how to convey the vision indispensable in great teaching. "Its presence should be inferrible from the spirit with which the instruction is carried on," he has pointed out, adding that "it should operate in such a way as to lift up the students' hearts and minds beyond matters of immediate concern and enable them to see the importance of a point of view."[20]

Still, as I have said, much of Beard's power and impact in graduate teaching was by lectures. Although soliloquy is not always instruction, the method of the lecture, at its best and in many forms, can recapture the condition of nascence, thus approximating a series of mental experiments in which ideas are born or at least lived through again in such a natural order and with such vitality that the hearers seem to be present at the first birth of the ideas themselves. Sometimes this precious quality goes with a tentative, testing, even halting advance from one point to the next. Beard's usual manner was more sweeping and assured but it contrived, aided by the kindling face and the edged voice, to share the sense of discovery. On occasion it was his habit—perhaps encouraged by early training in logical argumentation at DePauw—to direct the march of thought to a conclusion in the manner of the *Federalist Papers*. A story was almost always at hand to be told with considerable power of mimicry, which was not less appreciated because in this art Beard was seldom able to get wholly outside his own character. Personal anecdotes were few; there was none of the improvised autobiography that has well been called the nadir of teaching.

The shock method as such was not characteristic of Beard's teaching. It was not that he did not preach the need for the eternally challenging question: is it true; is it true for my age; is it true for me; isn't exactly the opposite true? He consciously practiced simplification and emphasis. "A good teacher must exaggerate," a student's notes report his saying to a class in 1918, and he quoted Ruskin. This quality was personal and an aspect of his art. It has been present in most of his creative writing; its relative absence in his textbooks on politics somewhat dulled their edge while doubtless widening their usefulness as texts. To his own students Beard's presence implied so rich a background of understanding, tolerance, and unspoken qualification that the selectivity and stress of his teaching technique were never dogmatic.

Beard's reading and memory made it easy for him to point his lectures and conversation not only with historical anecdotes but also with exact quotations. Students were especially charmed, I think, by a few that constantly recurred. But the range of allusion was wide and surprising. Still there was in Beard no trace of the code that assimilates scholarship to good manners, making aptness in elegant quotation seem one with knowing the right people and where in Paris to have shirts made. This observation leads me to add that, although Beard never paraded iconoclasm and often spoke of the decent respect that is due to the opinions of mankind, one of the qualities that galvanized students was a vague yet real sense of Beard's indifference to academic punctilio, convention, and prestige. It is more than a play on words to say that Beard was earnest rather than serious; certainly he was not solemn, although it was not in a man with so much feeling to maintain the constantly light touch. Ten years after he left Columbia Beard wrote of university life in general: "Perhaps it needs a little laughter, more than it does changes in administration and curriculum." Humor was not the whole of his prescription. Without disparaging the opportunties that universities afford, he found in them "too much routine, not enough peace; too much calm, not enough passion; . . . too many theories, not enough theory; too many books, not enough strife of experience; too many students, not enough seekers."[21]

In his attitude toward the run of students, Beard's humanity dominated his realism. His standards of excellence led him, as a matter of cold insight privately expressed, to see in few students minds and interests that properly warranted much trouble on the college teacher's part. Beard did not dissemble, however, when he utterly failed to show this attitude in class or conference. He treated all with respect and genuine liking. Doubtless this trait was deepened by the perspective, pity, and modesty that edge and underlie irony. Beard never engaged in sarcasm at the expense of his hearers. I remember only one instance of rage. It was when an untidy student allowed his lolling hand to finger the necklace of the girl next to him in a graduate lecture. Even then Beard's disgust did not explode until afterward. It was the anger of his whole nature against something unfitting, blowsy, soft.

Perhaps a combination of tolerance and realism led Beard to be too easy as a critic and guide of students' work. His characteristics in this respect might have been a handicap if he had remained long in graduate instruction. Certainly he could be a ruthless as well as a driving editor as he showed in reviewing papers written at the Bureau and elsewhere. Mainly Beard evoked by warmth and example. The method of leadership natural to him was suggestiveness; he tended to assume that others would be artists too or must find their own level. "I urge you," he said to a class, "to have a dislike for books when they are not inspired; when you read one just wonder how much better you could write it yourself—and try it."

Beard's influence as a teacher included the effect of his personal example and his textbooks in shaping bodies of subject matter for instruction. His own graduate work at Columbia, following a year at Oxford and a half year at Cornell and two more years abroad, involved work in public law under John W. Burgess, Frank J. Goodnow, John Bassett Moore, and others. It was the closing period of the golden age of the Columbia Faculty of Political Science, a leader in the still small circle of places in the United States for advanced social studies. Beard began his actual teaching in history and did his first sustained writing in that field, although years before as a young journalist he had dealt with politics firsthand. Soon a deep and inveterate concern with public policy, together with the temper of the time, led him to conceive a program of instruction oriented to active citizenship and trained administration in the modern state. In 1907 Beard launched what was virtually a separate college department of politics, linked to the existing graduate Department of Public Law and Jurisprudence. His new beginning course became the matrix of the textbook on *American Government and Politics* published three years later. This text was almost unique when issued; for a time it dominated a field it helped largely to create. Its omnibus and relatively impersonal character increased while it diluted Beard's consolidating influence upon the subject. The combined effect of man and book helped to standardize the introductory course in American colleges as a careful description of the structure and methods of American government on its several levels. The acceptance of this pattern was reflected in the 1913 report of a committee of the American Political Science Association, which recommended "the advisability of selecting American government as the basic course because it is convinced that there is an imperative need for a more thorough study of American institutions, because the opportunity for this study is not now afforded in any but a few of the best secondary schools, and because it is exceedingly important that the attention of an undergraduate be directed early in his course to a vital personal interest in his own government, national, state and local."[22]

In contributing to the trend, Beard's influence was important rather than strictly novel. James Bryce's descriptive volume had been available for nearly two decades. Edmund J. James at Pennsylvania and Albert Bushnell Hart and A. Lawrence Lowell at Harvard, among others, had been teaching American government fairly realistically. Beard himself, in an ebullient essay on the study and teaching of politics in the year in which his text appeared, observed that "within the last quarter of a century . . . the stress and content in the study of politics and government have been revolutionized." It was no longer confined, he wrote, to "commentaries on Aristotle, the Constitution, and the waywardness of politicians," although the field should not lose "its charm for the scholar of philosophic bent, occupied with large and important theories as to the origin, tendencies, and destiny of mankind politically organized."[23]

The trend in a sense, and certainly as Beard conceived it, was a return to the study of government from the standpoint of statecraft. Such had been the early ideal of the subject shared by lawyers whose interests were political as well as legal. But the impulse had remained largely unrealized. "On the whole," Luther L. Bernard has pointed out in a survey of the development of social thought and institutions in the United States, "the historical and public law aspects of politics won out in spite of the manifest wishes of Franklin, Washington, Jefferson and Madison, due to the more strategic position and greater influence of history and law in the colleges."[24] Even at Columbia, where the term "political science" has been used in the title of the graduate faculty founded in 1880 to cover history, economics, and later sociology as well as public law, the teaching tradition was heavily historical and legal. The original outgoing purpose of preparation for public affairs, moreover, had tended to turn in upon itself. In the colleges generally at the time when Beard returned from England, the condition described by Henry Seidel Canby was not untypical: "Sociology and economics were under way. Only government lagged, for we Americans still felt that the founding fathers had handed down from Sinai all we needed to know about government."[25]

When the change came, however, it was motivated too often by an uncritical faith that a detailed description of the organs of government would automatically quicken not only intelligence in using them but also and especially the will to do so. The effect for many students was to divert attention from formal political theory and from subjects like administrative law without giving them a new grasp of the ends of man's organized efforts and the dynamics of his political life. Beard himself could take for granted a superb background of reading in political philosophy and public law; not everyone who sought to follow in his steps was alert to what this background implied.

From the outset, of course, Beard intended that description should be directed to the moving forces. In his keynote lectures on politics in 1908 he spoke of the quest for responsibility and declared his belief "that the party in general and particular, as a center of power and a working institution, offers the richest field of investigation now open to the student of politics, and the results of really scientific investigation would have the highest theoretical and practical value."[26] Beard also helped to direct the attention of observers of government to what became known as the politics of pressure groups. His interest and influence were signalized by his early and characteristically generous recognition of the significance of Arthur F. Bentley's *The Process of Government* on its appearance in 1908. It was no fault of Beard that as the vogue of this approach spread and monographs on pressure politics multiplied, realism at times seemed to be standing in its own light, obscuring, on the one hand, the diffused sources and accretion of the ideas of a people and, on the other, the distinctive role of party.

Soon after he took up the teaching of politics, and for a time with especially direct and informing influence, Beard was a leader and organizer, though not exactly a pathfinder, in the rising branch of study called public administration. He had been a student and colleague of Frank J. Goodnow, of whom he wrote much later, "It may be safely said that Mr. Goodnow was the first scholar in the United States to recognize the immense importance of administration in modern society and to sketch the outlines of the field."[27] Still Beard's concern with social problems and policy led him to react from Goodnow's legal approach to city government; he launched a graduate course on municipal activities and dashed off a textbook on the subject. The Beard of those years had the zeal to compile the reform charters of cities in printed, loose-leaf style. He worked closely with the New York Bureau of Municipal Research, which since 1906 had become a center of influence upon every level of government. The bulletin written by Beard for the Bureau in preparation for the New York state constitutional convention of 1915 is pronounced by Dwight Waldo in his survey of half a century of writing on public administration to be "an important document in the history of American political thought." "For this 'new *Federalist*,'" as Waldo calls the bulletin in his estimate, "is a conscious statement of fundamental philosophy and a summary and synthesis of the political thought of the previous decades." Although some of it is outmoded, "for the most part American political science and public administration have been content to work within its framework."[28]

In later years Beard was whimsically skeptical about some of the proverbs of the early public administration movement. None the less, he was long an influential enthusiast and never really an apostate about the existence of "an enormous body of exact and usable knowledge in the domain of administration" and about its teachability. "Anything that is known can be communicated, can be imparted to youth," he said in a reminiscent talk on "the philosophy, science, and art of public administration" before the annual conference of the Governmental Research Association in 1939; "it can be taught, learned, and used." He added: "If universities have a warm and living interest in the future of our government and civilization they will teach it, and public officials and politicians will take note of it, profit by it, and improve the public services as a result of it."[29]

Beard himself while an active teacher was increasingly intent upon a type of subject matter that had been overlaid by descriptive political science, although in Beard's own case an awareness of it had never been absent in his personal conduct of even the most elementary course. By the time he left Columbia his main teaching interest was a discussion of what he called principles. In speculating one day about the scope of politics, he referred to Aristotle's analysis and read the list of that writer's main headings, exclaiming: "Is not that a magnificent array of topics compared with Beard's 'Government and Politics,' for example, or any other treatise from the United States?" But his approach remained chary of formal categories. He told a class in the principles of politics at the Bureau in 1918: "I have little patience with attempts to classify forms of government. After all, when you get down to the brass tacks of government, what do you have? You do not have any state at all; there is no such thing. What you have in government is concrete acts of power. . . . The only way we can know the state is through concrete manifestation of power. The only way to find the manifestation is to discover its historical circumstance."

Political science in the United States, Beard believed, had been impoverished and trivialized by denying the structure of society. In seeking to lift and rescue the subject, he remained skeptical of the value of thinking in abstractions apart from content and context. Events are indispensable prompters in framing fundamental issues and seeking relevant answers. "On the whole," ran his double complaint when discussing research in 1929, "our political thinking has not kept up with our factual evolution; it lags behind the march of affairs; it has been concerned with minutiae, not great causes and ideas."[30] The body of academic theory he sought to encourage was the sort of systematic thinking about ends and means that should be characteristic of constructive statesmen.

Charles Beard was always much more than a teacher; he never ceased to be one. Doubtless much was gained for the schools as well as the public when he became a member-at-large of all faculties and was spared for thinking and writing. Still something was lost by the circumstances that limited the direct impress of his presence and of the accommodating play of his mind upon several generations of students. How much was lost we shall never know, so mysteriously ramified is the transmission of such a personality. As Henry Adams said, "A parent gives life, but as parent, gives no more. . . . A teacher affects eternity; he can never tell where his influence stops."[31]

GEORGE S. COUNTS

Charles Beard, the Public Man

CHARLES A. BEARD was one of the foremost scholars of his time. He was a master of knowledge and thought in the broad field of the social sciences, particularly in history, government, and politics. Indeed it can be said truly of him that nothing human was alien to his interests. He enjoyed the unique distinction of having been chosen by his peers to the presidency of each of two great learned societies in which he labored—the American Political Science Association and the American Historical Association. He bore easily both his scholarship and his honors.

His broad scholarly interests were joined with a concern for mankind. Although he was entirely at home in the academy, his mind was not academic. For him scholarship was not a realm remote from farm, factory, market, and legislative chamber; it was no refuge to which he might retire and escape the rigors, the disappointments, and the tragedies of life. He never sought the cloistered security of the ivory tower. On the contrary, he carried scholarship into the world of men and things, and carried the affairs of that world into the domain of scholarship. He viewed the academy as a social institution that could justify its existence only by lighting the way and making easier the road to the future. He always saw knowledge and thought in relation to life and sustained to the end the faith that the development of the social sciences in the modern age might enable men to escape the catastrophes that have overtaken the great civilizations of the past. Even in his last days, as the shadows lengthened, he shared personally in the fears and hopes of his fellow human beings. To him history was a record of the interaction of ideas and interests.

During the middle thirties Beard and I were contrasting the contemporary period with the period of the founding fathers. I asked him in what fundamental respects the two periods differed in terms of quality of leadership. He replied that in proportion to the population the earlier period was blessed with a larger number of "public men." He of course was referring not to officeholders or politicians, but rather to private citizens who were deeply concerned about the general welfare and the future of the Republic. In this sense Beard was himself one of the most distinguished public men of the age in which he lived. He was at the same time a great statesman working in the realm of scholarship and a great scholar working in the realm of statesmanship.

It is not easy to determine the deepest values and purposes of any man. To do so for the rich and many-sided personality of Charles A. Beard would appear unusually difficult. Yet anyone who came to know him discovered in him a certain simplicity and artlessness that quickly revealed his inner spirit. He was incapable of concealing either his feelings or his ideas. He was an outgoing and outgiving person. Certainly to his friends he was a man without guile. And his adversaries, of whom there were many, experienced little difficulty in discovering where he stood on any question. The record, moreover, of his writings and public acts clearly reveals the man. Though a great scholar, he belonged fully to that rare company of the "pure in heart" that embraces both the simple and the wise. In his last years he possessed the curiosity and openness of a little child.

Above all, Beard was humane in his outlook and in his relations with people. To him the basic value of the Christian tradition and the democratic ethic, the dignity of the individual human being, was a guiding principle. Injustice and tyranny outraged him. "When I was in secondary school," he once told a group of friends, "I became aware of the injustices in the world around me and resolved to do what I could to remove them." This statement provides a key for understanding the great scholar. Throughout his life he devoted his talents to the amelioration of the lot of the people.

Beard labored and battled to the end of his days for the maintenance of the great tradition of human liberty and American democracy—the great tradition of English rationalism and the French enlightenment—the great tradition of Jefferson and Lincoln. In response to a query in 1935 about who among the founding fathers was the greatest he replied without hesitation: "Jefferson was the greatest. Jefferson combined in his person the best of both the Old World and the New." He could have said as truly as this great leader of the early Republic that he had "sworn upon the altar of God, eternal hostility against every form of tyranny over the mind of man." In order to distinguish his position clearly from that of "totalitarian democrats" he often qualified his conception of democracy with the word "humanistic." He could support no body of social doctrine, however appealingly presented, that repudiated the liberal and humanistic heritage of mankind.

This broad universal loyalty was closely linked with pride in and love of his own country. He was as American in speech and manners as were the Indiana farmers among whom he grew to manhood and whom he could imitate to perfection with boyish glee. One of the finest things that can be said about America is that Charles A. Beard could have been produced in no other country of the world. This is not to say that he defended her faults as well as her virtues. On the contrary, as a loyal son he expected much from her and was deeply pained when she or her representatives violated her essential traditions of liberty and democracy. Criticism of American faults, shortcomings, and betrayals he regarded as the most profound expression of loyalty.

Though some of Beard's contemporaries greeted his *An Economic Interpretation of the Constitution* as an irreverent attack on the founders of the Republic, Beard himself regarded the study as a contribution to the understanding of a company of .peerless statesmen. He never tired of comparing the *Federalist* favorably with the best social and political thought of Europe. Also he often remarked that the men who carried through a successful revolution and launched a new nation on the North American continent blazed a bold and promising trail in the political history of mankind. They broke through the tragic cycle of despotism, revolutionary violence, and despotism, and built a new state on the foundations of political liberty and constitutional government.

Beard resented the affectation of superiority that he encountered in various representatives of European civilization. And he resented it because he was convinced that it had no solid basis in fact. He loved to relate with a characteristic chuckle an incident that took place in Belgrade in the winter of 1927. While in Yugoslavia studying its government, he was asked to address the English-speaking community on the subject of American political institutions. At the conclusion of his address an Englishman arose in the audience, felicitated the speaker, and asked him if he would say a few words "about that thing they call gräft in America." Beard responded gladly and said that it could easily be understood in terms of three factors or conditions: "In the first place, America was settled preponderantly by Englishmen; in the second place, America was a fabulously rich land; and in the third place, these transplanted Englishmen took full advantage of the opportunity." The incident illustrates at once his sense of humor—for the man was the British minister—and his deep irritation at a certain snobbishness often found in the English upper classes and at any pretentious "bearers of the white man's burden." Yet on occasion he characterized the English people as the most civilized of nations.

As a student of history and the contemporary world, Beard abhorred Europe's interminable wars, long-cherished hatreds, and colonial adventures. On his return from Yugoslavia in 1928 he spoke of the whole of Europe as just a "big Balkans" and often referred to that motherland of America as a madhouse. His hope that the United States could keep away from Europe and her quarrels was the fundamental source of his conception of "continentalism" and his opposition to American participation in the Second World War. Though bitterly and irreconcilably hostile to Hitler and to fascism in all of its forms, he was convinced that if America participated in the war, even allied victory would leave his country in a worse condition after than before the war.

In July, 1945, I sent him a copy of a manuscript I had prepared on "Recent Changes in Soviet Education." He responded immediately on July 13 with a letter that concluded as follows: "The sky is clear and ominous: only two mighty armed powers are on the horizon. What impends and with what portents? Day and night I wonder and tremble for the future of my country and mankind." In his last book he referred to Russia as "one of the most ruthless Leviathans in the long history of military empires."[1] One may still argue that Beard was mistaken and that America pursued the better course in joining the struggle to crush the Axis powers, but that line of reasoning becomes less obvious or convincing as the passing years reveal evidence supporting his prophetic vision of the nature of the postwar world.

Beard maintained throughout his life a profound and abiding interest in the people who do the work of the nation and the world. He always regarded himself as a man of the people and never lost a sense of kinship with them.   Although as a boy he had known hard manual labor on his father's farm in Indiana, this concern had much deeper roots.   It grew out of his basic humane and democratic loyalties and out of his intellectual comprehension of the realities of industrial society.   By working people he did not mean the "proletariat according to Marx" or the industrial working class, but rather all who work by hand or brain.   To be sure, in his more serious and revealing moments he would often speak of the "obligation to toilers in mine, field, and factory," but this was not because he thought that all virtue resides in people engaged in manual labor.   He believed rather that at the present time in history they had a larger claim on his attention.

He did exhibit, particularly in his earlier years as a scholar, an exceptional interest in the organized labor movement.   As a young man in England he was much impressed with the vitality, the outlook, the intellectual quality, and the growing power of British labor and labor leaders.   He saw in this movement of the people a great force battling for human rights.   Also at this time he probed deeply into the thought of international revolutionary socialism and was profoundly influenced by it.   Though never a Marxian, after rereading Marx and Engels in the middle thirties in the German edition of their collected works, he remarked that their total achievement stands over all other comparable efforts in history as a "mountain stands over the surrounding foothills."   Yet he noted that Marx had said a class war might end in the destruction of all.   On returning to America and assuming his teaching duties at Columbia in 1904 he gave generously of his time and talents to the American labor movement.   He brought the struggle of labor and capital into his writings.   Also he sought actively to interest others in the fortunes of labor and engaged in the heartbreaking work of collecting funds for the support of the labor movement.

In the course of the years Beard suffered some disillusionment.   He found that all labor leaders are not idealists and that narrow personal interest plays its part in trade unions.   On the afternoon of December 1, 1911, he and Mrs. Beard were out ringing doorbells in a campaign to raise money to defend the McNamara brothers against a "capitalist frameup." The brothers were being tried on a charge of dynamiting the Los Angeles *Times* building, killing twenty-one persons and wounding many others. As the Beards turned their feet homeward after collecting considerable sums from friend and stranger, they picked up an afternoon paper. The headlines proclaimed in two-inch letters that the McNamaras had confessed to the crime! But this experience, and others like it, failed to shake Beard's devotion to improving the conditions of life and labor of the working people. To be sure, in later years he sometimes advised his younger friends not to waste their "precious time and energies" in doing some of the things that he had done with such gusto in his youth.

Like many other democratic-minded people throughout the world Beard followed the early course of the Russian Revolution with interest and hope. Unlike most of them, however, he was always skeptical and perceived in the twenties the tendencies toward absolutism inherent in the Soviet system. In the latter part of July, 1948, shortly before he went to the hospital, he expressed the view that he had been mistaken in his general interpretation of Marxist socialism. He had believed, he said, that this movement was a continuation of the English, American, and French revolutions and a fulfillment of their ideas in the industrial age. The developments in Russia led him before his death to abandon this view completely.

He hated aristocracy in all of its manifestations and was always prepared to break a lance with the defenders of caste and special privilege. He hated snobs and snobbery, stuffed shirts and pretentiousness, wherever they appeared, and particularly in the realm of scholarship. He feared the concentration of wealth as the foundation of a new aristocracy in America. And in the battle to halt this threat to democracy in his lifetime he was ever ready to place his time, his energy, and his scholarship at the disposal of the people, through both private organizations and government officials and agencies. By 1947 he seemed to think that victory in this struggle against the power of a plutocracy was in sight. At any rate, in the summer of that year he said that in his judgment the day of great fortunes in America was drawing to a close by way of income and estate taxes.

Illustrative of Beard's practice of identifying himself with the people in their struggles was his work with the dairy farmers of Connecticut in the middle thirties. At that time the milk industry, like most industries, was in difficult straits, and the producers went on strike. A dairy farmer himself and well known among the farmers of the state, Beard was asked by Governor Wilbur L. Cross to serve as an impartial chairman to explore the entire situation and endeavor to settle the strike. In this Beard was successful, not by acting as a protagonist of a single interest, but by conducting a statistical study of the entire milk business. Through this approach to a strike situation with the methods of scholarship, he strove to keep the discussion on a basis of fact and thus lower the temperature that at times was near the boiling point. Even as it was, in one all-day session in his own home, with all the factors represented, violence was prevented only with great difficulty. He took advantage of the situation to encourage the farmers to organize more effectively, to study their problems objectively, to gain greater facility in the art of public speaking, to learn how to present their case to the people and the state authorities.

Another side of Beard as a public man is revealed in his successful struggle in 1935 with the financial interests controlling the Missouri Pacific Railway Company. Owning a few bonds and convinced that the general welfare and the interests of the small holders were being violated, he proceeded to organize a "bond-holders' committee" and to challenge the might of the Van Sweringens and J. P. Morgan and Company. He desired to test his faith that under American democratic institutions the little fellow can appeal to his government against an industrial giant and obtain justice. Under his chairmanship the committee called on the United States Senate to investigate the situa-

tion. "Without such an investigation," he said in the name of
the committee, "there is every danger that the huge Van Sweringen empire will continue in the midst of our Republic, and
so long as that empire . . . continues so long are great interests
in constant danger." He asserted further that "until we get rid
of the stranglehold of the Van Sweringen bankers and of the
Van Sweringens themselves on this vast aggregation of large
railway systems, investors will be without safety, government
agencies will be harassed and invaded, and the democratic processes and representative government will be flouted."[2] Because of the action of Beard's committee and the ensuing
investigation, the bankruptcy act of 1933 was modified in the
direction Beard desired. Beard never hesitated to defend the
rights of the people, as he understood them, against the en-
croachments of the most powerful groups and forces in America.

Closely related to Beard's direct interest in the working people was his dedication to popular enlightenment. He saw this
as indispensable to the "perdurance," as he would say, of democratic institutions. He once reported a conversation on this
subject with a German scholar after Hitler's rise to power.
According to this scholar, the destruction of the Weimar Republic was due in part to a failure of German historiography. In
spite of their brilliant contributions to world scholarship the
German historians, he said, had never been interested in writing a history of the German people for the German people. In
concurring in this judgment Beard revealed one of the central
concerns of his life.

In the spring of 1944 I visited Beard in the Commodore
Hotel where he was stopping on his way from North Carolina
to New Milford. I found him reading proof on the *Basic History of the United States,* in which Mary Beard had collaborated. When asked what he was doing he replied with deep feeling: "This is our last will and testament to the American
people." One may say that all of his studies, articles, and books,
including particularly his textbooks for schools and colleges,

were directed toward the goal of popular enlightenment. A basic article of his faith was that the people could be trusted, if they possessed the knowledge relevant to their interests and purposes. The basis of his opposition to Franklin D. Roosevelt during the prewar and war years was the conviction that the President was not taking the people fully into his confidence on matters of foreign policy, that he was in fact concealing his intentions and engaging in the manipulation of public opinion. It is interesting to note that in spite of his severe criticism of foreign policy in later years, Beard had expressed the thought in private conversation in 1937 that Roosevelt might become the greatest of the presidents.

From the years of early manhood Beard engaged tirelessly in launching and supporting ventures dedicated to the spread of enlightenment among the people. Curiously enough, the first of these ventures was not in the United States but abroad, in England. While at Oxford he met Walter Vrooman, "bursting with idealism and eloquent of speech," but lacking the practical talents essential to carry his ideas into execution. Mrs. Vrooman, born Amne Grafflin of Baltimore, possessed considerable funds in her own right, which she was prepared to devote to some project for popular enlightment. Working together, the three founded a school for workers' education at Oxford. Because of Ruskin's interest in creative labor, his connection with the great university, and his social philosophy as expressed in *Unto This Last,* they gave to the new school the name of "Ruskin Hall." Beard organized the project, made contact with the vigorous co-operative movement, aroused the interest of trade union leaders, and addressed many meetings of working people in the cities of England and particularly in the Manchester industrial region. This enterprise was one of the earliest in the workers' education movement, which has played a central and crucial role in the life of the English people during the present century. In 1947 the Rationalist Press Association of England founded an annual lectureship for a period of seven years at Ruskin Hall in honor of "the distinguished American social historian, who was one of the co-founders of the College and was on the staff from 1899 to 1902."

Back in his native land Beard continued his active interest in workers' education. In 1921 he played a leading part in the establishment of the Workers Education Bureau of America, whose central purpose was the co-ordination of the diverse activities and agencies that had developed in this field during the years. From the first his relation to the Bureau was marked by a sense of personal responsibility, as with everything he espoused. He disliked intensely a perfunctory or honorary connection with any undertaking with which his name was associated. As chairman of the "citizens' group" that helped to raise the first funds for the Bureau he contributed two thousand dollars from his own pocket. As member of the Executive Board and chairman of the Editorial Board of the "Workers' Bookshelf" he gave freely of his time and energies to launch the Bureau on its career. Spencer Miller, Jr., one of his students and director of the Bureau for a quarter of a century, characterizes Beard as one of the "real founders" of the institution and always its "adviser, counsellor, and friend."

Beard's interest in popular enlightment, however, was by no means limited to the field of "workers' education." He maintained down through the years an interest in adult education broadly conceived. In 1918, shortly after his resignation from Columbia, he associated himself with his old friends John Dewey and James Harvey Robinson in founding the New School for Social Research, and was soon joined there by Thorstein Veblen. Although the name of the institution suggests concern with advanced scholarship, its purpose was to foster learning, disseminate knowledge, and stimulate thought on the part of the adult citizens of New York without regard for academic traditions and requirements.

Although he devoted much of his life to the enlightenment of the older generation, he always recognized the importance of the education of the young. This interest is shown in his text-books and also in his service on and for various educational commissions. Among the latter the Commission on the Social Studies of the American Historical Association is perhaps most notable. He served actively on this Commission throughout its career, from 1929 to 1934, giving his talents without stint to its work. He wrote the first and most basic of the sixteen volumes comprising the report of the Commission—*A Charter for the Social Sciences;* he was a member of the editorial committee of three that prepared the final volume on *Conclusions and Recommendations;* and he participated as an elder statesman in the deliberations of the Commission from the first meeting to the last. In addition he was consulted regularly by almost every scholar who worked on any one of the many assignments that the Commission authorized. His counsel was sought partly because of his helpful spirit but also because of his unique command of knowledge.

From the beginning of his life as a scholar down to the day of his death Beard was a valiant champion of the freedom of the mind. He recognized such freedom as the source of popular enlightenment, the living spirit of the democratic process, and the only dependable bulwark against the return of despotism. In the course of his life, therefore, he often defended rebels against authority even though he did not always share their views.

In his own work he lived by this principle. He pursued his inquiries fearlessly into realms that had been practically closed to critical scholarship. Yet, at the same time, he was something of a realist and was not above resort to strategy. He once told me that early in his career as teacher and student he concluded that there are three dangerous fields, which the inquirer enters at his peril: sex, politics, and theology. He concluded further from the record that a university professor might be radical in any one of these three fields and hold his post, that if he were radical in two he would be in danger of dismissal, and that if he were radical in all three he would be sure to go. He decided therefore to confine his labors to what he considered the most important of the three, politics, and leave the other two strictly alone.

Beard's decision to resign his post at Columbia University was made in defense of intellectual freedom. Certain little known details of the celebrated case throw unusual light on his character. In the spring of 1916 Beard had been called before a committee of the Board of Trustees and in the presence of President Butler had been "grilled" for half an hour concerning his views and teachings. He had then been ordered to warn all other men in his department against teachings "likely to inculcate disrespect for American institutions." About the same time two social science colleagues had been similarly summoned before the trustees and reprimanded for criticizing before a student group the Plattsburg military training program. In March, 1917, the trustees voted a general doctrinal inquisition but, in the face of vigorous faculty protest, in which Beard played a leading role, abandoned their investigation and agreed to abide by recommendations of a faculty committee set up to pass upon views of faculty members. Then in violation of this agreement and contrary to the recommendation of the faculty committee, the trustees dismissed Professor Harry W. L. Dana and J. Mc-Keen Cattell in the fall of 1917 for associating during the summer with people charged but not proved to be disloyal. President Butler prevented, too, the promotion of another professor because he had spoken disrespectfully of the Supreme Court. Beard became increasingly concerned over what he regarded as an effort to "humiliate or terrorize every man who held progressive, liberal, or controversial views."[3]

But the incident that determined Beard to act was the Fraser dismissal. Before we thought of entering the war, President Butler had become greatly interested in a young man who was active in the movement for the establishment of an international organization to keep the peace. Leon Fraser was employed by the Association for International Co-operation that Butler dominated, and his job was to travel about the country disseminating peace propaganda. The president suggested to Beard that this man be appointed to his staff in the department of politics. Unimpressed with the qualifications of the candidate Beard refused to make the recommendation requested. The president then appointed Fraser on his own authority over Beard's head. Soon thereafter America entered the war. The young man, now on the Columbia staff, continued to make public speeches of the sort Butler had paid him to make before Butler changed his views about war. Butler was offended by this behavior and dismissed his recent protégé. Beard vigorously supported our entry into the war and disagreed entirely with the views of Dana, Cattell, and Fraser. Intellectual freedom was, however, more important to him than any particular set of views and he could no longer stomach the arbitrary actions of Butler and his trustees. His resignation, then, was primarily provoked by the president's arbitrary dismissal of a man in his own department with whom he thoroughly disagreed and who had been arbitrarily appointed over his protest by the president who now dismissed him.* He believed it fundamental to the existence of free society "that teachers should not be expelled without a full and fair hearing by their peers, surrounded by all of the safeguards of judicial process."[4]

His resignation was a powerful blow struck in the name of intellectual freedom in the American democracy—a blow whose effect is felt to this day. A few sentences from his letter of resignation on October 8, 1917, reveal his courage and purpose:

Having observed closely the inner life at Columbia for many years, I have been driven to the conclusion that the university is really under the control of a small and active group of trustees, who have no standing in the world of education, who are reactionary and visionless in politics, narrow and mediaeval in religion. , . .

---

* EDITOR'S NOTE: Leon Fraser thus dropped from Columbia was director and vice-president, 1930-1933, and chairman of the board and president, 1933-1935, of the Bank of International Settlements, and vice-president, 1935-1937, and president, after 1937, of the First National Bank of New York.

As I think of . . . [my colleagues'] scholarship and their worldwide reputation and compare them with the few obscure and wilfull trustees who now dominate the university and terrorize the young instructors, I cannot repress my astonishment that America, of all countries, has made the status of the professor lower than that of the manual laborer, who through his union, has at least some voice in the terms and conditions of his employment.

Holding his position literally by the day, the professor is liable to dismissal without a hearing, without the judgment of his colleagues who are his real peers. I am sure that when the people understand the true state of affairs in our universities they will speedily enact legislation which will strip boards of trustees of their absolute power over the intellectual life of the institutions under their management.[5]

From this time on American teachers regarded Beard as an unqualified champion of freedom in schools, colleges, and universities. They turned to him, as to no other man, for counsel and support in the defense of their rights and liberties. And so when in 1934 William Randolph Hearst with his powerful chain of newspapers and magazines launched an attack on the teaching profession of the country in the name of his peculiar brand of "Americanism," the *Social Frontier* invited Beard to address a meeting of teachers at Atlantic City on February 24, 1935. With the following statement he brought an audience of nine hundred to its feet:

In the course of the past fifty years I have talked with Presidents of the United States, Senators, Justices of the Supreme Court, Members of the House of Representatives, Governors, Mayors, bankers, editors, college presidents (including Charles W. Eliot), leading men of science, Nobel Prize winners in science and letters, and I have never found one single person who for talents and character commands the respect of the American people, who has not agreed with me that William Randolph Hearst has pandered to depraved tastes and has been an enemy of everything that is noblest and best in the American tradition. Alfred Smith—a true friend of public education—added to his many deserved laurels when before a cheering multitude in

New York City he defied Mr. Hearst. The answer of the people of New York was final and conclusive. There is not a cesspool of vice and crime which Hearst has not raked and exploited for money-making purposes. No person with intellectual honesty or moral integrity will touch him with a ten foot pole for any purpose or to gain any end. Unless those who represent American scholarship, science, and the right of a free people to discuss public questions freely, stand together against his insidious influence he will assassinate them individually by every method known to his yellow press. Only cowards can be intimidated by Hearst.[6]

The influence of this just indictment was felt throughout the country and in diverse segments of the population. Teachers gained courage, and the Hearst campaign against the schools crumpled and withered away. Many years later Beard joyously reported seeing a worker in Hollywood, on strike against some Hearst enterprise, carrying a placard with these words: "Professor Beard says that no honest person will touch Hearst with a ten foot pole."

A fourth characteristic that qualified Beard for his career as a public man was his interest in the realities of life and society. He revolted against pedantry, scholasticism, and what he sometimes called the "academic treadmill." He had little faith in degrees and the traditional trappings of college and university. He turned down an honorary degree at the University of North Carolina's sesquicentennial because he did not believe in honorary degrees. He often remarked on the "good sense" of his father in sending him abroad for a couple of years so that he might see something of the world.

On his return to America he once said that he felt a bit ashamed of his own country. Its history, as he put it, seemed a "little thin." But he soon discovered, as he began to burrow into the past and become familiar with the realities of the present, that it was not American history but the American historian that was a "little thin." Wherever he turned he found a great wealth of exciting material. If American historical writing is beginning to reflect the richness and variety of the past, it is due in some measure to the breadth of interest and tireless activity of Charles Beard.

He emphasized sources, old documents and new documents, facts and statistics bearing on many aspects of American life. Although he did not hesitate to make broad generalizations, he endeavored to relate them closely to the data and always treated them with a measure of skepticism. He was fully aware of the frailties and limitations of the human mind. He was easily irritated by the "systems" of European thinkers who seek to box the universe and eternity. Although he admired the work of Marx for the depth, the breadth, and the realism of his scholarship, he refused to accept him as an infallible guide through the long future. He believed that the scholar, like Antaeus, derives his strength from maintaining close contact with mother earth.

In his research and teaching Beard strove to cultivate neglected areas and call them to public attention. He was deeply interested in the great driving forces and conditioning factors of the contemporary age—capitalism and socialism, science and technology, labor and management. In his researches on the writing of the Federal Constitution he said that he was amazed to find the imprint of economic interests on practically every page of the Madison Papers. The disclosure of this particular reality of course outraged the academic guardians of a sacred myth. At the same time, through his realistic treatment of the founding fathers, he broadened the base of popular understanding and enriched the field of scholarship. His interest in technology and its impact on social institutions bore a similar fruit. Following the report of the dropping of the atomic bomb on Hiroshima he remarked with a touch of pride on August 12, 1945: "I wrote my first book on *The Industrial Revolution.*"

He early recognized the importance of efficiency in government and saw that democracy, if it is to survive as a political system, must become more efficient in its operations. This led to his emphasis on administration, which he came to regard as one of the greatest and most essential of the practical arts. He brought the study of this art into his courses on government and introduced it into his books. It was this concern over efficient administration that led him in 1915 to associate himself with the Bureau of Municipal Research in New York City and in 1917 to organize the Training School for Public Service, and to serve as its Director for the next five years. It was this interest, too, and his knowledge of the practical side of government that brought the invitation from the Mayor of Tokyo to make a study of municipal administration in the capital city of Japan. His belief that sound local government was a bulwark of democracy led him to accept the invitation in 1922 and to remain approximately a year, during which he stimulated the founding of an Institute of Municipal Research there. This same concern led him to return to Tokyo on invitation in 1923 to give advice on the reconstruction of the vast city area damaged by the earthquake of September of that year. In 1927 the American Yugoslav Society persuaded him to go to Belgrade and, with this interest in efficient government in mind, to make a study of the government of Yugoslavia. Later events proved the conclusions presented in his report, *The Balkan Pivot,* to be prophetic of "things to come."

Beard possessed all those qualities of character essential to the public man, if not the qualities necessary for election to public office, which he never sought. His unqualified and uncompromising devotion to the public interest as he saw it, and he did see it with the eyes of a prophet, marked and guided his activity as teacher, scholar, and writer.

He was richly endowed with the basic human virtues. His courage, as demonstrated again and again, was sublime. When he decided to resign from Columbia in 1917, he did not know just how he would make a living for his wife and two young children. Before taking the fateful step he and Mrs. Beard considered the matter realistically and prepared themselves for the worst, including the possibility of physical hardship. In honesty and integrity he had few peers, as the entire record of his life demonstrates. He was generous in terms of time, energy, and money to every cause with which he identified himself. If a man leaves this world holding in his hands only that which he has given away, he took with himself on September 1, 1948, a great abundance of all the good things of the spirit. He could be generous to those who had treated him badly. In the middle thirties he remarked to me that after all President Butler was the greatest university president among the living. Butler, he said, was a civilized person, at home in both the world of scholarship and the world of affairs. He too was a "public man" even though his social orientation differed profoundly from that of his old critic.

One of Beard's most useful traits as a public man was his independent spirit. His devotion to the people did not mean at all that he believed the "voice of the people" to be the "voice of God." He could criticize his beloved labor movement and his closest friends unsparingly if in his opinion the occasion called for it. He could also be stubborn and a little cantankerous at times. Though ready to take criticism himself, as we shall see in a moment, he had a good deal of confidence in his own judgments and disliked wasting his time listening to fruitless discussion. At the close of a morning meeting of the Commission on Social Studies of the American Historical Association I asked him what he thought of the deliberations. "Oh!" he said, "I listened only for the first half-hour, concluded that they were going round in circles, and so turned off my instrument." He often observed that his deafness was sometimes a blessing in disguise. His "instrument" was much easier to manage than Herbert Spencer's legendary earmuffs.

Associated with his independence was also an unaffected humility. He had little pride of opinion as such and was quite ready to change his mind in the light of the evidence. After severe criticism of a manuscript he had prepared for a commission, he could throw it into the wastebasket as a "piece of cheese" and begin all over again. He would thus accept criticism at times from people far less qualified than he to deal with the matter under consideration. He seemed to enjoy poking fun at his own "sacred document" or "inspired word." He once took delight in showing me a facsimile of a single page of Marx's original manuscript for *Das Kapital*. It was badly mutilated with words and sentences crossed out and new words and sentences added. "How do the 'Marx boys' explain this?" he asked. "For obviously Marx didn't believe his first version to be divinely inspired. And if he had taken another look at his manuscript before sending it to the press, only God himself could know what he would have done to it." When Beard was asked in 1941 whether he was satisfied with his *Economic Interpretation* he replied at once in the negative. He said that it had been written without sufficient attention to historical perspective. Had he been rewriting it he probably would have emphasized not so much that the framers were not democrats as that they *were* republicans in a world where republicanism was forward-looking.

The great scholar possessed an extraordinary and inexhaustible sense of humor. He seemed always to be on the lookout for the humorous side of any subject, no matter how serious. If he had ever been called upon to face a firing squad, he would have done so with a joke and a smile. He loved to play pranks on the mighty of this world and to puncture balloons of self-righteousness and vaunted superiority. At a convention of the American Political Science Association he wandered into a sectional meeting where the participants were discussing the contribution of psychoanalysis to the problems of government. After some time the chairman, noting his presence in a back row, called upon the onetime president of the Association for a few words. Beard rose and said that what he had just heard reminded him of an incident. It seems that the miners' beloved "Mother Jones" was on her deathbed. She had lost consciousness, the room was decked with cut flowers in great profusion, and friends were standing about the bed in tears of sadness. At the very moment when she was expected to breathe her last she regained consciousness, opened her eyes, looked at the flowers and the assembled mourners, and in tones of surprise said: "What the hell is going on around here?" Beard then sat down amid delighted applause, and the meeting disbanded.

He was an incomparable companion. Whatever the subject, he always had something relevant and original to say. He was a natural mimic and would have made a great actor. In spite of his "physical infirmity," as he called his deafness, and in spite of his devotion to his work, he seemed always to enjoy and have time for his friends. Every letter from him was an exciting event. It was sure to contain salty remarks and humorous touches, even if it was only an acceptance of an invitation to meet at the Grand Central Station. In letters to his younger friends, to whom he was always willing to give his time and attention, he would sometimes sign "Uncle Charlie, X, his mark." He was a unique and entirely lovable personality, a true son in every respect both of his native Indiana and of the great world, which he ever sought to comprehend and civilize.

In his outlook as scholar and as statesman Beard reflected the optimism characteristic of his countrymen. This outlook is clearly evident in an incident that took place in the autumn of 1931. He and I were motoring over the hills of Connecticut in the vicinity of New Milford. Having been profoundly impressed by the vast range of his knowledge and thought, a range that seemed to embrace the entire human record from ancient times, I asked how long it would take him to tell all he had learned from his lifetime study of history. After contemplating the question a few moments he replied that he "thought" he could do it in "about a week." We drove on a short distance in silence. Whereupon he said he could probably do it in a day. After another brief pause, he reduced the time to half an hour. Finally, bringing his hand down on his knee, he said: "I can tell you all I have learned in a lifetime of study in just three laws of history. And here they are:

"First, whom the gods would destroy they first make mad.

"Second, the mills of the gods grind slowly, yet they grind exceedingly small.

"Third, the bee fertilizes the flower that it robs."

About ten days later we took a stroll along Riverside Drive in New York City. Evidently he had been giving further thought to my question. At any rate, he said he would like to add a fourth law to his laws of history:

"When it gets dark enough you can see the stars."

As he viewed the rise and spread of totalitarian systems in the Old World in the thirties his optimism respecting the human future was shaken. On one occasion he comforted himself with the thought that, however great the catastrophe, "the human spirit" and "the people" are indestructible. But as the skies darkened he began to wonder whether the liberal and humanistic outlook of the modern period might not be merely an accident due to the discovery of the New World, a brief interlude between despotisms that he began to fear were the natural state of man. The news of the atomic bomb led him to write me on August 12, 1945: "You and I had better get together soon, gather up the fragments of 'our little systems', and take new observations from the stars (if there are any)." In the autumn of 1947, when he was in a pessimistic mood, I asked him if he thought the human race would survive the release of nuclear energy. "Of course it will," he replied. "Don't worry about that. The human race is tough. It has traveled a long and hard road. It will survive." When I expressed some surprise at his optimism he responded in words that were scarcely reassuring: "Don't misunderstand me. I am not saying that mankind may not suffer a catastrophe that will set it back two thousand years. But it will survive." Apparently the stars may be seen but dimly, and the mills of the gods may grind slowly indeed.

Beard's last years were not happy. From deep conviction he found himself critical of the policies and the popular leaders of his country. Many of his old friends avoided him. Others attacked him and imputed base motives. Although his proud spirit refused to bend before the gales of passion, he could not wholly conceal his innermost feelings. He who had always loved companionship often experienced a sense of loneliness. In the spring of 1944 he called my attention to a picture of himself in *Life,* which, he said, pleased him greatly. It was the picture of an old man with a cane walking alone amid the leafless trees of a North Carolina hillside toward the setting of an autumn sun.[7] After recovering from a severe illness the next winter he told me a bit wistfully that he had been so near the great divide that "death seemed a little sweet." Yet to the last Beard was a fighter, and in the thick of the fight he found a release from loneliness. Within a month of his death he wrote the preface for a biography of Mr. Justice Black praising his service to the people. Discouraged though he was in those last days, Beard was still pursuing his quest of truth, outlining further studies of history, and planning new battles for the fulfillment of the promise of American democracy. These unfinished tasks were on his mind when on an evening in late July, 1948, a few days before he was to start on his last journey to the hospital, he said to me as I bade him farewell: "Tell my former friends in New York that the old man looks as if he might live ten years longer."

HOWARD K. BEALE

Beard's Historical Writings

IN SPITE OF his time-conɹuming public activities, his earlier
teaching and his later educational endeavors, his vast periodical
writings, and his impressive output in the field of political science, Beard turned out a series of histories that in breadth of
scope and sheer mass is overwhelming.* His early interest lay
in European history. His *Industrial Revolution,* published in
England in 1901, appeared before he had completed his graduate work and went through ten printings.[1] As a doctoral dissertation at Columbia, he published in 1904 *The Office of Justice of the Peace in England in Its Origin and Development.*
Charles Gross reviewed the book savagely, charging Beard with
superficial and careless work, with ignorance of certain pertinent materials, and with failure to present "new general conclusions of much importance,"[2] but Edward P. Cheney called
the study a "valuable contribution" to historiography.[3] Next
came in 1906 *An Introduction to the English Historians.* Here
Beard presented samplings of varying interpretations of English history under broad divisions such as "The Foundations

* These figures on Beard's publications were compiled in April, 1949.

of England," "Feudalism and Nationalism," "Mediaeval Institutions," "The Stuart Constitutional Conflict," and "The Empire in the Nineteenth Century." These he subdivided into
topics like "Two Theories of the Anglo-Saxon Conquest," "The
True Nature of Magna Carta," "Motives for Colonization,"
and "The Cabinet System," to each of which he wrote a brief
introduction. Beard's first recorded appearance before the
American Historical Association was an assignment to discuss
a paper in European history presented by Ralph C. H. Catterall
of Cornell at the Madison, Wisconsin, meeting in December, 1907.[4]

During the years 1908-1909 appeared *The Development of
Modern Europe* and the *Readings in Modern European History.* Each was in two volumes. Each was written in collaboration with James Harvey Robinson. Here the principles of the
"new history" advocated by each man were put into practice.
The history was "new" in the emphasis, announced in the subtitle, that the authors placed upon contemporary history, in
the reduction of space devoted to military and political history,
and in its full treatment of economic and social forces, the industrial revolution, imperialism, movements like socialism, the
development of science, and the history of ideas. To give scientists, philosophers, businessmen, even workers and economic
forces a place equal to that allotted generals and politicians was
revolutionary indeed to those brought up on history as hitherto
conceived. So, too, was Robinson and Beard's pointing of history toward contemporary problems. Another youthful historian, later to become like both the authors, president of the
American Historical Association, reviewed the volumes enthusiastically in the *American Historical Review.*[5]

After many years of writing in American history and political
science, Beard returned to the European field to produce one
more volume. In June, 1922, Harry Elmer Barnes, soon to
become an outspoken revisionist, had published only demands
that the current interpretation of the causes of World War I
be revised.[6] Hayes and other leading historians were still cir-

culating versions of those causes that had been written without benefit of sources released after the war. A year later Hazen was to reissue his *Europe since 1815* in nearly double its original length without revising his wartime treatment of the causes of the war conceived in 1916 in a spirit worthy of Britain's wartime propaganda agencies. Only Fay among Americans had written revisionist history.[7] Beard was again pioneering, then, when in June, 1922, he delivered a series of lectures at Dartmouth, published as *Cross Currents in Europe To-day,* in which he joined Fay, who had already published several articles, as an early sponsor of revisionism concerning World War I. Besides the three revisionist lectures on "Diplomatic Revelations" Beard included in this interesting and too often neglected collection critical but not unsympathetic treatments of the Russian revolution, of the rise of "new peasant democracies," and of socialism in the history of the European labor movement. When Fay's revisionist *Origins of the World War* was published in 1928 Beard greeted it enthusiastically with what Fay remembers as "the first, best, and most influential review" of it that appeared.[8]

In American history Beard's first work was *The Supreme Court and the Constitution* (1912), in which he supported the view that the framers had intended the Supreme Court to declare laws of Congress unconstitutional. Then came his famous trio, *An Economic Interpretation of the Constitution* (1913), *Contemporary American History, 1877-1913* (1914), and *Economic Origins of Jeffersonian Democracy* (1915). The first and the third of these became important landmarks in American historiography; the second, emphasizing the importance of recent history in the time of Theodore Roosevelt, was little noticed by historians or the public. Next Beard did a series of lectures on *The Economic Basis of Politics,* originally delivered at Amherst College in 1916 but published only in 1922. In 1927 appeared the initial portion of the monumental history of the United States done in five volumes in collaboration with his wife, Mary R. Beard. The total work is officially titled,

rather confusingly, *The Rise of American Civilization* in four
volumes. Actually the historical world thinks of the first two
volumes, which appeared together in 1927, subtitled *The Agri-
tultural Era* and *The Industrial Era* as *The Rise of American
Civilization.* The third volume, published in 1939, which itself
was published as two volumes, is known under its subtitle
America in Midpassage. The fourth, *The American Spirit: A
Study of the Idea of Civilization in the United States* (1942), is
also usually considered as a separate book. In the first two volumes the Beards trace America's development down to the middle twenties. In *America in Midpassage* they carry the tale to
1938. They not only paint the political and economic picture
of the lush prosperity of the late twenties and describe the New
Deal of the middle thirties but treat foreign policy exhaustively.
This volume, too, attains a high level as social and intellectual
history. Less successful than most of Beard's writings is *The
American Spirit.* As its subtitle indicates, the Beards here venture further into intellectual history and seek to study one
central theme in American history. Finding in "the idea of
civilization" such a unifying force, they trace this idea from
eighteenth century France through colonial times to the New
Deal. The final collaboration of the Beards was *A Basic History
of the United States,* published in 1944. In this book the
authors sought to compress into brief compass the essence of
their lifelong study of American history. In the meantime
Beard alone had added to his earlier contributions in constitutional history *The American Party Battle* (1928), a new introduction to the 1935 edition of *An Economic Interpretation of
the Constitution,* an essay titled "Historiography and the Constitution" (1937),[9] a new edition of *The Supreme Court
and the Constitution* (1938) particularly pertinent because of
Roosevelt's attack on the Supreme Court, *The Republic* (1943),
and a new chapter called "Economics and Politics in Our Revolutionary Age" in a 1945 republication of his *Economic Basis
of Politics.* He had also written in 1935 a brief biographical
series, *The Presidents in American History.*

Throughout the thirties Beard's interest turned more and more to the historical background of American foreign policy. In collaboration with George H. E. Smith, Beard published in 1934 a pair of books, *The Idea of National Interest* and *The Open Door at Home*. They constitute not only a history of foreign policy, but a superb example of the history of ideas. In the first volume Beard sought to "present theories and facts without criticism" in an effort to describe what Americans had thought and done about "the idea of national interest." In the second volume he subjected to critical analysis the facts revealed about the various historic schools of thought and their activities and endeavored to glean from history a workable American "philosophy of national interest." The result was a combination, in domestic policy, of protection for individual civil liberties and extensive economic planning for abundance and, in foreign policy, what Beard called enlightened "continentalism." There followed *The Devil Theory of War* in 1936, *Giddy Minds and Foreign Quarrels* in 1939, and *A Foreign Policy for America* in 1940. In the first, provoked by the revelations of the Nye Committee's investigations of munitions makers, Beard analyzed the reasons for our entry into World War I and concluded that no devil in the form of bankers, munitions makers, or politicians, nor yet any impersonal economic forces had led us into that war. Beard concluded rather that peace-loving American citizens, following peacetime pursuits where their interests seemed to lead, were themselves responsible for our entry into war. In the other two books, issued just as war broke upon Europe, Beard sought to apply his knowledge of history first to a criticism of America's current foreign policy and then to the formulation of what he regarded as a wise foreign policy.

Finally came *American Foreign Policy in the Making, 1932-1940* in 1946 and *President Roosevelt and the Coming of the War, 1941* in 1948. In writing the first Beard was handicapped by the fact that the sources were mostly controlled by a government unwilling to make them available to any but the military and such scholars as were willing to write official history on government pay for government purposes. The book in consequence is necessarily written largely from messages, speeches, and published documents and from magazines and newspapers; and it has the limitations imposed by Beard's exclusion from more revealing sources. The second volume is similarly handicapped. It is much less handicapped, however, because popular interest in the emotion-charged question of responsibility for what had happened at Pearl Harbor forced a congressional investigation of responsibility for the disaster. The congressional committee called forth from secret archives some of the material from which scholars are rigidly excluded and published much otherwise carefully guarded evidence. Hence Beard had access to rich sources that, except for the congressional investigation, would long have remained closed to all who were not certain to write the kind of history responsible people in government were willing to have produced. One of Beard's last public appearances—that before the Political Science Association's meeting in December, 1947—he used to protest, in the name of the democracy endangered thereby, against the policy of excluding all but carefully selected official historians from the important records of democratic government's conduct of foreign relations.[10] And in a popular article only eleven months before his death, he voiced the same protest.[11]

Not only in his larger works but in many smaller items did Beard publish his reflections on the subject of a philosophy of history. Important among these were his presidential address to the American Historical Association in 1933,[12] his article titled "That Noble Dream," a reply to Theodore C. Smith's attack on his school of history,[13] his essay in collaboration with Alfred Vagts on "Currents of Thought in Historiography,"[14] his introduction to the 1932 edition of John B. Bury's *Idea of Progress,* his introductory essay for a 1943 edition of Brooks Adams's *Law of Civilization and Decay,* and his "Grounds for a Reconsideration of Historiography" and "Note on the Need for Greater Precision in the Use of Historical Terms" in

Theory and Practice in Historical Study. He wrote extensively also on the purposes and meaning of the social sciences, including history. His conception of history cannot be understood without knowledge of these writings. Early he had published an essay on *Politics* (1908). Later he played a major role in the drafting of *A Charter for the Social Sciences in the Schools* (1932) and *Conclusions and Recommendations* (1934) of the Commission on Social Studies created by the American Historical Association. He also wrote for the Commission a volume on *The Nature of the Social Sciences in Relation to Objectives of Instruction* (1934), important to an understanding of his views on history. *The Discussion of Human Affairs* (1936) and his "Neglected Aspects of Political Science" in the *American Political Science Review* (1948) deal further with the problems of the social studies.

Finally, Beard wrote a number of textbooks,[15] all of those in the historical field in collaboration with someone else. With William C. Bagley he wrote an *Elementary World History* (1932), *A First Book in American History* (1920), which appeared in three editions, *The History of the American People* (1918), which ran through seven editions, *The History of the American People, for Grammar Grades and Junior High Schools* (1918), *A Manual to Accompany the History of the American People* (1919), and *Our Old World Background* (1922), which was issued in two editions. Roy F. Nichols joined Beard and Bagley in coauthoring *America Today* and *America Yesterday,* both of which appeared in 1938. Charles Beard joined his wife Mary Beard in writing a *History of the United States: A Study in American Civilization* (1921), which appeared in five editions, and *The Making of American Civilization* (1937), issued in two editions. In 1935 Beard ventured into educational history and published, with William G. Carr, *Schools in the Story of Culture.* Besides their *Development of Modern Europe* and their *Readings,* already discussed, Beard and James Harvey Robinson produced in collaboration a *History of Europe, Our Own Times* (1921), which ultimately passed through five editions. With Robinson and James H. Breasted, Beard published *Outlines of European History* in 1912, 1914, and 1918, and with Robinson, Breasted, Emma P. Smith, and Donnal V. Smith a *History of Civilization* (1937).

Exclusive of his textbooks Beard's writings in European history number eight volumes totaling 3,510 pages, in American history twenty-one volumes totaling 8,443 pages, and in the two fields together twenty-nine volumes totaling 11,953 pages. If the above-mentioned books on the social studies are included, the total is thirty-four volumes containing 12,611 pages. The textbooks number fifteen volumes and 8,448 pages. Thus in the field of history and its problems Beard authored forty-nine volumes comprising 21,059 pages in addition to numerous scattered periodical writings, speeches, prefaces, reviews, pamphlets, and articles in collections of essays.

The circulation figures on Beard's histories, too, are impressive. These figures of course do not take into account the wide influence that resulted from Beard's broad personal contacts and the public activities in which he sought to apply the teachings of history, but the figures do provide a measure of one source of his influence. In all, 270,097 copies of his European histories, 5,500,782 copies of his American histories not counting texts, 24,177 copies of his books on the social sciences, and 5,557,107 copies of his history textbooks were sold.[16] These figures do not include the circulation for one book for which statistics are not available, the Japanese edition of two books, an Austrian German edition of one book, the German edition of one book, Braille books and recordings circulated by libraries for the blind, and probably other foreign editions that the editor has failed to find. But, excluding these, 11,352,163 copies of Beard's books dealing with history found their way into the public's hands.[17]

Yet it is not the quantity but the quality of Beard's writing that gives it importance. His *Industrial Revolution* was one of the first books on that important phenomenon. His and Robinson's writings on European history, in which Beard was responsible for most of the economic element, pioneered in "the new history" that emphasized social and economic forces and ideas. *An Economic Interpretation of the Constitution,* his *Economic Origins of Jeffersonian Democracy,* and his *Economic Basis of Politics* profoundly affected American historiography. The first of these and his last two books on foreign policy have excited more controversy and more denunciation than any other history of the half century. His *Economic Origins of Jeffersonian Democracy,* parts of *The Rise of American Civilization, The Idea of National Interest,* and *The Open Door at Home* rank among the small number of great American books that deal with the history of ideas. His and Mary Beard's *America in Midpassage* is a great example of a successful synthesis, which is overshadowed by the even better *Rise of American Civilization,* one of the most highly praised books of the century and probably the most successful large-scale synthesis in American historical writing.

JACK FROOMAN

EDMUND DAVID CRONON

Bibliography of Beard's Writings

THIS BIBLIOGRAPHY includes all available printed items of which Charles A. Beard was the author, with revisions and later editions noted. For the sake of brevity, however, certain bibliographical niceties have not been observed. Place of publication (if other than New York) and publisher are given for the first edition of each title, but for later editions only new publishers are noted. Reprintings, reissues, and "editions" that are changes only in form, binding, or illustration are not listed. Most of Beard's major books have appeared in American, British, and Canadian editions published by agents of the original publishers; these editions are not listed since they represent no change of content. The existence of foreign language editions and of Braille and "talking book" editions for the blind is noted.

BOOKS AND PAMPHLETS BY BEARD ALONE:

The Administration and Politics of Tokyo: A Survey and Opinions. Macmillan, 1923. (Two Japanese eds., one a summary)
American City Government: A Survey of Newer Tendencies. Century, 1912.
American Foreign Policy in the Making, 1932-1940: A Study in Responsibilities. New Haven, Yale University Press, 1946.
American Government and Politics. Macmillan, 1910. New and rev. ed., 1914. 3d ed., 1920. 4th ed., thoroughly rev., 1924. 5th ed., 1928. 6th ed., 1931. 7th ed., 1935. 8th ed., with William Beard, 1939. 9th ed., with William Beard and Wilfred E. Binkley, 1944. 10th ed., with William Beard, 1949.
The American Party Battle. Macmillan, 1928. Repr., Workers Education Bureau Press, 19—?
A Charter for the Social Sciences in the Schools. Scribners, 1932.
A Collection of Lectures (in Japanese). Tokyo, Shisei Chosa-kai, 1923.
Contemporary American History, 1877-1913. Macmillan, 1914.
Cross Currents in Europe To-day. Boston, Marshall Jones, 1922.
Cumulative Annual Guide to American Government and Politics. Macmillan, 1935-1938.
The Devil Theory of War: An Inquiry into the Nature of History and the Possibility of Keeping out of War. Vanguard, 1936.
The Discussion of Human Affairs: An Inquiry into the Nature of the Statements, Assertions, Allegations, Claims, Heats, Tempers, Distempers, Dogmas, and Con-

tentions Which Appear When Human Affairs Are Discussed and into the Possibility of Putting Some Rhyme and Reason into Processes of Discussion. Macmillan, 1936.

The Economic Basis of Politics. Knopf, 1922. New ed., 1934. (German, Japanese, and Mexican eds.)

The Economic Basis of Politics. 3d rev. ed., 1945, with a new Chapter 5 titled "Economics and Politics in Our Revolutionary Age."

An Economic Interpretation of the Constitution of the United States. Macmillan, 1913. Repr., with new introduction, 1935.

Economic Origins of Jeffersonian Democracy. Macmillan, 1915.

European Sobriety in the Presence of the Balkan Crisis. Association for International Conciliation, 1908.

A Foreign Policy for America. Knopf, 1940.

Giddy Minds and Foreign Quarrels: An Estimate of American Foreign Policy. Macmillan, 1939. Excerpts in *Harper's Magazine,* CLXXIX (September, 1939), 337-351.

Government Research, Past, Present and Future. Municipal Administration Service, 1926.

Hitlerism and Our Liberties: Text of Address Given at the New School for Social Research, Tuesday, April 10, 1934. New York? 1934?

How American Citizens Govern Themselves. Educational Bureau, National War Work Council of Young Men's Christian Associations, 1919.

The Industrial Revolution. London, Sonnenschein, 1901. Corr. ed., 1902. Repr., London, Allen and Unwin, 1927.

An Introduction to the English Historians. Macmillan, 1906.

Issues of Domestic Policy. Chicago, University of Chicago Press, 1932.

Jefferson, Corporations and the Constitution. Washington, National Home Library Foundation, 1936. Orig. as four articles: "The Constitution and States' Rights," *Virginia Quarterly Review,* XI (October, 1935), 481-495; "Corporations and Natural Rights," *ibid.,* XII (July, 1936), 337-353; "Jefferson in America Now," *Yale Review,* n.s. XXV (December, 1935), 241-257; "Little Alice Looks at the Constitution," *New Republic,* LXXXVII (July 22, 1936), 315-317.

My Views Regarding the Reconstruction of Tokyo (in Japanese). Tokyo, Shisei Chosa-kai, 1924.

The Myth of Rugged American Individualism. Day, 1932. Orig. in *Harper's Magazine,* CLXIV (December, 1931), 13-22; repr. in *The People, Politics, and the Politician,* A. N. Christensen and E. M. Kirkpatrick, eds., Holt, 1941.

The Nature of the Social Sciences in Relation to Objectives of Instruction. Scribners, 1934.

The Navy: Defense or Portent? Harper, 1932.

The Office of Justice of the Peace in England, in Its Origin and Development. Columbia University Press, 1904.

Philosophy, Science and Art of Public Administration: Address Delivered before the Annual Conference of the Governmental Research Association, Princeton, New Jersey, September Eighth, 1939. Princeton? 1939.

Politics: A Lecture Delivered at Columbia University in the Series on Science, Philosophy, and Art, February 12, 1908. Columbia University Press, 1908. Repr. in *Columbia University Lectures on Science, Philosophy, and Art, 1907-1908,* Columbia University Press, 1908.

President Roosevelt and the Coming of the War, 1941: A Study in Appearances and Realities. New Haven, Yale University Press, 1948.

The Presidents in American History. Messner, 1935. New ed., rev., 1941. Rev. ed., 1946.

Public Policy and the General Welfare. Farrar and Rinehart, 1941.

Public Service in America. Philadelphia, Municipal Court, 1919.

The Republic: Conversations on Fundamentals. Viking, 1943. Excerpts in *Life,* January 17–March 20, 1944; talking book ed.; Brazilian, two Japanese eds.

Six Years' Experience with the Direct Primary in New Jersey. New York, 1917?
The Supreme Court and the Constitution. Macmillan, 1912. Repr., Facsimile Library, 1938.
The Traction Crisis in New York. Bureau of Municipal Research, 1919.
The Unique Function of Education in American Democracy. Washington, Educational Policies Commission, National Education Association, and the Department of Superintendence, 1937.

BOOKS IN COLLABORATION WITH OTHERS:

[WITH WILLIAM C. BAGLEY]
Elementary World History: A Revised and Simplified Edition of Our Old World Background. Macmillan, 1932.
A First Book in American History. Macmillan, 1920. Rev. ed., 1924. 2d rev. ed., 1934. (Braille ed.)
The History of the American People. Special ed. for Army Educational Commission, American Expeditionary Forces, Macmillan, 1918. Regular ed., 1920. Repr., Sacramento, California State Printing Department, 1920. Rev. ed., Macmillan, 1923. 2d rev. ed., 1928. 2d rev. ed. with correction, with Maximo M. Kalaw, 1932. (Braille ed.)
The History of the American People, for Grammar Grades and Junior High Schools. Macmillan, 1918.
A Manual to Accompany The History of the American People. Macmillan, 1919.
Our Old World Background. Macmillan, 1922. Rev. ed., 1925.

[WITH BAGLEY AND ROY F. NICHOLS]
America Today. Macmillan, 1938.
America Yesterday. Macmillan, 1938.
America Yesterday and Today. Macmillan, 1938. (Brazilian ed.)

[WITH MARY·RITTER BEARD]
America in Midpassage. 2 vols., Macmillan, 1939. (Two German eds.)
American Citizenship. Macmillan, 1914.
The American Spirit: A Study of the Idea of Civilization in the United States. Macmillan, 1942. (Braille ed.)
A Basic History of the United States. Doubleday, 1944. (Braille, talking book eds.; Austrian, Japanese, Swiss eds.)
History of the United States. Macmillan, 1921. (Later eds. have subtitle: *A Study in American Civilization*) Rev. ed., 1929. 2d rev. ed., 1932. 3d rev. ed., 1934.
The Making of American Civilization. Macmillan, 1937. Repr. with additional material, 1939.
The Rise of American Civilization. 2 vols., Macmillan, 1927. College ed., 1930. New ed., rev. and enl., 1933. (Braille, talking book eds.)

[WITH WILLIAM BEARD] *The American Leviathan: The Republic in the Machine Age.* Macmillan, 1930.

[WITH WILLIAM G. CARR] *Schools in the Story of Culture.* Washington, National Education Association, 1935. Orig. as seven articles: "Before Schools Began," "Schools of Greece and Rome," "Schools of Cloister and Castle," "Colonial Schooldays," "The Battle for Free Schools," "The Schools Accept New Jobs," "The Schools Weathering a Storm," in *National Education Association Journal,* XXIII (November-December, 1934), 201-203, 230-232; XXIV (January-May, 1935), 7-10, 41-44, 77-80, 117-120, 149-152.

[WITH THE COMMISSION ON SOCIAL STUDIES IN THE SCHOOLS] *Conclusions and Recommendations of the Commission.* Scribners, 1934.

[WITH THE EDUCATIONAL POLICIES COMMISSION OF THE NATIONAL EDUCATION ASSOCIATION] *The Unique Function of Education in Democracy.* Washington, D. C., N.E.A., 1937 (abr. in *Education Digest,* III [June, 1937], 1-6).

[WITH ROBERT MOSES AND OTHERS] *Report of Reconstruction Commission to Governor Alfred E. Smith on Retrenchment and Reorganization in the State Government, October 10, 1919.* Albany, J. B. Lyon Company, 1919.

[WITH FREDERIC A. OGG] *National Governments and the World War.* Macmillan, 1919.

[WITH GEORGE RADIN] *The Balkan Pivot: Yugoslavia; a Study in Government and Administration.* Macmillan, 1929.

[WITH JAMES HARVEY ROBINSON]

The Development of Modern Europe: An Introduction to the Study of Current History. 2 vols., Boston, Ginn, 1907-1908. Completely rev. and enl. ed., 1929-1930.

History of Europe, Our Own Times: The Eighteenth and Nineteenth Centuries, the Opening of the Twentieth Century, and the World War. Boston, Ginn, 1921. (Later eds. have altered subtitle: *The Opening of the Twentieth Century, the World War, and Recent Events*) Rev. ed., 1927. Repr. with additional material, 1932.

Readings in Modern European History: A Collection of Extracts from the Sources Chosen with the Purpose of Illustrating Some of the Chief Phases of the Development of Europe during the Last Two Hundred Years. 2 vols., Boston, Ginn, 1908-1909.

[WITH ROBINSON AND JAMES HENRY BREASTED] *Outlines of European History.* 2 vols., Boston, Ginn, 1912-1914. Rev. ed., 1918. Enl. and rev. ed., 1927.

[WITH ROBINSON, DONNAL V. SMITH, AND EMMA PETERS SMITH] *Our Own Age.* (Vol. II of *A History of Civilization*) Boston, Ginn, 1937. Enl. ed., 1952.

[WITH BIRL E. SHULTZ] *Documents on the State-Wide Initiative, Referendum, and Recall.* Macmillan, 1912.

[WITH GEORGE H. E. SMITH]

Current Problems of Public Policy: A Collection of Materials. Macmillan, 1936.
The Future Comes: A Study of the New Deal. Macmillan, 1933. Repr., Workers Educational Bureau, 19—?
The Idea of National Interest: An Analytical Study in American Foreign Policy. Macmillan, 1934.
The Old Deal and the New. Macmillan, 1940.
The Open Door at Home: A Trial Philosophy of National Interest. Macmillan, 1934.
The Recovery Program (1933-1934): A Study of the Depression and the Fight to Overcome It. Macmillan, 1934.

BOOKS EDITED BY BEARD:

America Faces the Future. Boston, Houghton Mifflin, 1932.
A Century of Progress. Exposition ed., Chicago, Harper, 1932. Regular ed., New York, Harper, 1933.
The Enduring Federalist. Garden City, Doubleday, 1948.
Loose Leaf Digest of Short Ballot Charters: A Documentary History of the Commission Form of Municipal Government. Short Ballot Organization, 1911.
Readings in American Government and Politics. Macmillan, 1909.
Toward Civilization. Longmans, Green, 1930.
Whither Mankind: A Panorama of Modern Civilization. Longmans, Green, 1928. Repr., Blue Ribbon Books, 1934.

ARTICLES BY BEARD:

American Association of University Women Journal, XXVIII (June, 1935), 195-198: "Creating the Good Life for America."

American City, XIII (October, 1915), 310-311: "Training the Commercial Organization Secretary"; XLIX (October, 1934), 47: "The Crisis in Local Government and the Task Ahead."

American Federationist, XXIX (July, 1922), 500-502: "The Potency of Labor Education."

American Historical Review, XIX (January, 1914), 282-298: "Some Economic Origins of Jeffersonian Democracy"; XXXIX (January, 1934), 219-231: "Written History as an Act of Faith"; XLI (October, 1935), 74-87: "That Noble Dream"; XLII (April, 1937), 460-483: "Currents of Thought in Historiography" (with Alfred Vagts).

American Mercury, I (April, 1924), 394-396: "What Is a Statesman?" (repr. in *The American Mercury Reader,* Lawrence E. Spivak and Charles Angoff, eds., Philadelphia, Blakiston, 1944); XI (July, 1927), 283-287: "A Bankruptcy Fire-Sale"; XXXVII (February, 1936), 190-196: "Minority Rule in America"; XLVI (April, 1939), 388-399: "We're Blundering into War"; LV (November, 1942), 529-535: "In Defense of Congress."

American Political Science Review, XX (May, 1926), 273-283: "Some Aspects of Regional Planning"; XXI (February, 1927), 1-11: "Time, Technology, and the Creative Spirit in Political Science"; XXIV (February, 1930), supplement, 25-32: "Conditions Favorable to Creative Work in Political Science"; XXVI (February, 1932), 28-44: "The Teutonic Origins of Representative Government"; XXVI (April, 1932), 223-240: "Representative Government in Evolution" (with J. D. Lewis); XXVIII (February, 1934), 11-15: "Historical Approach to the New Deal"; XXXIV (April, 1940), 232-235: "Administration, a Foundation of Government"; XLII (April, 1948), 211-222: "Neglected Aspects of Political Science."

American Teacher, XXIII (May, 1939), 27-28: "Next Step for the Progressives" (with Robert H. Jackson and Frank Murphy).

Annals of the American Academy of Political and Social Science, LXII (November, 1915), 64-68: "The Budgetary Provisions of the New York Constitution"; LXIV (March, 1916), 215-226: "Training for Efficient Public Service"; CLXXXV (May, 1936), 29-34: "The Living Constitution" (abr. in *Vital Speeches,* II [July 1, 1936], 631-632).

Annual Report of the American Historical Association, 1916, I, 271-274: "Report of a Conference Held in Cincinnati, Dec. 27, 1916, on the Organization of a University Center for Higher Studies in Washington" (with others); 1921, I, 74-82: "Final Report of Committee on a University Center for Research in Washington" (with others).

Asia, XXXV (January, 1935), 4-9: "What Is This Sea Power?"

Atlantic Monthly, CXL (December, 1927), 831-836: "The Fiction of Majority Rule"; CLXXI (April, 1943), 87-93: "Historians at Work: Brooks and Henry Adams."

Bulletin of the University of Georgia: Institute of Public Affairs and International Relations, XXX (November, 1929), 70-78, 79-81, 82-84: "The Contest between Rural and Urban Economy," "Danger Spots in Europe," and "Forces Making for Peace."

Canadian Historical Review, XIV (March, 1933), 1-8: "The Historian and Society [Papers read at the 47th annual meeting of the American Historical Association, 1932]" (with George M. Wrong).

Columbia University Quarterly, XII (June, 1910), 268-274: "The Study and Teaching of Politics."

Congressional Digest, XIV (October, 1935), 245-246: "Should Congress Enact a Federal Sedition Law?"; XIV (December, 1935), 317, 319-320: "Should Congress Be Empowered to Override Supreme Court Decisions?"; XVII (March, 1938), 90-92: "Speech before the House Committee on Naval Affairs Urging Congress to Disregard the President's Recommendations."

Consumer's Cooperation, XXII (October, 1936), 150-153: "What Do We Mean by Democracy?"

Current History, XXIV (August, 1926), 730-735: "Heroes and Villains of the World War"; XXIX (October, 1928), 82-84: "The Last Years of Stephen Raditch"; XXXIII (March, 1931), 801-806: "Justice Oliver Wendell Holmes"; XL (September, 1934), 641-650: "America: A Month's Record"; XLI (October, 1934), 77-83: "The Politics of Our Depression"; XLI (November, 1934), 203-209: "Emerging Issues in America"; XLI (December, 1934), 333-339: "Confusion Rules in Washington"; XLI (January, 1935), 459-466: "America Twists and Turns"; XLI (February, 1935), 586-592: "Our Foreign and Domestic Policies"; XLII (April, 1935), 64-71: "The President Loses Prestige"; XLII (June, 1935), 290-300: "America Debates War Plans"; XLII (July, 1935), 345-352: "Social Change v. the Constitution"; XLII (August, 1935), 513-521: "Looking Forward to 1936"; XLII (September, 1935), 625-632: "The New Deal's Rough Road"; XLIII (October, 1935), 64-73: "The Labors of Congress"; XLIII (November, 1935), 182-190: "American Business Is Better"; XLIII (December, 1935), 290-298: "Keeping America out of War"; XLIII (January, 1936), 399-406: "Industry's Attack on the New Deal"; XLIII (February, 1936), 513-520: "Challenge to the New Deal"; XLIII (March, 1936), 625-632: "On Keeping out of War"; XLIV (April, 1936), 66-72: "In Defense of Civil Liberties."

Dial, LXIV (April 11, 1918), 335-337: "The University and Democracy"; LXVI (June 14, 1919), 598-599: "Propaganda in Schools."

English Journal, XXV (June, 1936), 496-498: "Savants Select Most Influential Volumes" (with John Dewey and Edward Weeks).

Events, I (January, 1937), 9-12: "Going Ahead with Roosevelt"; I (March, 1937), 161-165: "Our Choice in Foreign Policy"; I (April, 1937), 241-245: "Roosevelt and the Judges"; I (May, 1937), 341-346: "The Supreme Court Controversy"; I (June, 1937), 407-411: "Court and Constitution"; II (July, 1937), 1-6: "Will Roosevelt Keep Us out of War?"; II (August, 1937), 81-86: "War—If, How, and When?"; II (September, 1937), 163-164, 165-169: "'Will Roosevelt Keep Us out of War?' Dr. Beard's Rejoinder," and "On the Diplomatic Front"; II (October, 1937), 257-262: "Those Old-World Quarrels"; II (November, 1937), 327-331: "America's 'Duty' to England"; II (December, 1937), 441-446: "The Interpretation of Events"; III (January, 1938), 23-26: "The World-Revolution Begins" (repr. in *Scholastic,* XXXII [February 19, 1938], 6+); III (February, 1938), 81-86: "Roosevelt's Place in History"; III (March, 1938), 161-164: "Shooting It Out in Russia"; III (April, 1938), 275-277: "The Supreme Issue for America"; IV (November, 1938), 383-387: "Monopoly in Fact and Fiction"; V (June, 1939), 401-404: "Looking Forward to 1940"; VI (September, 1939), 161-164: "Neutrality Deadlock"; VIII (November, 1940), 321-323: "War with Japan?"

Far Eastern Review, XIX (April, 1923), 263-266: "For a Greater Tokyo"; XXI (June, 1925), 252-256: "Memorandum Relative to the Reconstruction of Tokyo."

Foreign Affairs, XIV (April, 1936), 437-452: "Education under the Nazis" (excerpts in *Bulletin of the Department of Secondary-School Principals,* XX [May, 1936], 46-49).

Forum, LXXXVI (July, 1931), 1-11: "A 'Five-Year Plan' for America"; XCI (June, 1934), 332-334: "The World As I Want It"; XCVII (February, 1937), 89-95: "How to Stay out of War" (with others).

Good Government, XXXVI (January, 1919), 11-18: "Government Employment Policy."

Harper's Magazine, CXXXVII (October, 1918), 655-656: "A Call upon Every Citizen"; CLVII (August, 1928), 265-273: "Is Western Civilization in Peril?"; CLVII (November, 1928), 680-691: "Democracy Holds Its Ground: A European Survey"; CLVIII (January, 1929), 133-143: "Bigger and Better Armaments"; CLVIII (February, 1929), 320-330: "Prospects for Peace"; CLVIII (March,

1929), 470-479: "The American Invasion of Europe"; CLX (January, 1930), 144-152: "Whom Does Congress Represent? The Problem behind the Lobbies" (repr. in *The People, Politics, and the Politician*, Asher N. Christensen and Evron M. Kirkpatrick, eds. [Holt, 1941], 338-349); CLX (February, 1930), 281-291: "The Dear Old Constitution" (repr. in *Contemporary Problems in the United States*, Horace Taylor, ed. [Harcourt, Brace, 1935], 73-81); CLXI (July, 1930), 147-153: "Squirt-Gun Politics"; CLXIV (February, 1932), 257-267: "Our Confusion over National Defense: Shall We Listen to the Pacifists or the Admirals?"; CLXIV (May, 1932), [800-804?]: Reply to the Secretary of the Navy C. F. Adams; CLXXXV (November, 1942), 607: "Talking into the Wind."

Historical Outlook, XX (December, 1929), 369-372: "The Trend in Social Studies."

History Teacher's Magazine, I (November, 1909), 49-50: "The Use of Sources in Instruction in Government and Politics."

In Review, Governmental Research Association, 1948: "It Is Not True."

Journal of Adult Education, II (January, 1930), 5-7: "The Electric Fire of Thought"; III (January, 1931), 8-11: "The Dislocated Soldier of Industry" (repr. in *Unemployment and Adult Education*, Morse A. Cartwright, ed. [American Association for Adult Education, 1931], 9-12); V (January, 1933), 5-10: "The Need for Direction: What Is the Adult's Goal in the Social Sciences?"; VII (January, 1935), 5-9: "Practice and Culture"; VIII (June, 1936), 247-249: "James Harvey Robinson"; IX (April, 1937), 121-125: "Ideas: An Inquiry" (abr. in *Education Digest*, II [May, 1937], 10-12).

Journal of Higher Education, III (December, 1932), 464-469: "The Quest for Academic Power" (repr. in *Bulletin of the American Association of University Professors*, XIX [January, 1933], 16-22).

Journal of Social Forces, III (March, 1925), 495-497: "Municipal Research Abroad and at Home."

Journal of Social Philosophy, V (October, 1939), 7-15: "A Memorandum on Social Philosophy."

Living Age, CCCLVII (January, 1940), 410-417: "Twilight of Social Systems."

Menorah Journal, XIV (January, 1928), 21-28: "Is Babbitt's Case Hopeless?"

Mississippi Valley Historical Review, XXX (September, 1943), 159-170: "Thomas Jefferson: A Civilized Man."

Nation, CVI (April 25, 1918), 502-504: "Human Nature and Administration"; CXX (March 25, 1925), 311-313: "War with Japan: What Shall We Get out of It?"; CXX (April 1, 1925), 347-348: "Count Karolyi and America"; CXXIII (July 7, 1926), 7-8: "The Great American Tradition"; CXXV (August 17, 1927), 150-151: "Agriculture in the Nation's Economy"; CXXXIII (July 22, October 7, 1931), 82-84, 364-365: "Presidential Appointments"; CXLII (April 1, 1936), 405-406: "What about the Constitution?"

National Education Association Department of Superintendence Official Report (1935), 290-291: "The Nation Seeks Security."

National Education Association Journal, XXI (November, 1932), 271: "The Future of America"; XXIII (March, 1934), 94: "The Future Comes" (with George H. E. Smith). See also *Schools in the Story of Culture* (with William G. Carr).

National Elementary Principal, XVII (February, 1938), 104-106: "Education Enriched by Living" (repr. in *National Education Association Journal*, XXVII [November, 1938], 227-228).

National Municipal Review, I (July, 1912), 431-435: "Recent Activities of City Clubs"; IV (October, 1915), 637-645: "The New York Constitutional Convention"; VI (March, 1917), 201-206: "Political Parties in City Government: A Reconsideration of Old Viewpoints"; VII (September, 1918), 449-467: "The Bolshevik Session of the National Municipal League Annual Conference"; VIII (January, 1919), 26-33: "Public Employment"; IX (April, 1920), 222-225: "For the McCormick Bill"; X (November, 1921), 541-542: "Suggested Economy for Congress"; XII (September, 1923), 520-523: "Municipal Research in Japan"; XIV (January, 1925), 1-2, 7-11: "A World Bureau of Municipal Research" and

"American Influence on Municipal Government in the Orient"; XXII (December, 1933), 581-583: "A Sign of the Times"; XXXIII (November, 1944), 503-510: "The League and the Future."

National Parent-Teacher, XXX (September, 1935), 18-19, 33: "Books for Building Stones."

New Republic, I (November 14, 1914), 18-19: "Jefferson and the New Freedom"; III (May 15, 1915), 35-37: "In Justice to Judge Lindsey"; IV (August 21, 1915), supplement, 1-16: "Reconstructing State Government"; IV (October 9, 1915), supplement, 1-3: "Historical Woman Suffrage"; VII (July 29, 1916), 329-331: "The Woman's Party"; X (February 17, 1917), 66-67: "What a Budget Should Be"; XIII (November 17, 1917), supplement, 3-4: "Political Science in the Crucible"; XXV (December 1, 1920), 15-17: "On Puritans"; XXVII (August 24, 1921), 350-351: "On the Advantages of Censorship and Espionage"; LII (November 16, 1927), 348-350: "History in the Public Schools"; LXIII (June 18, 1930), 115-120: "Government by Technologists"; LXIII (July 30, 1930), 305-307: "Money in Federal Politics" (repr. in *The People, Politics, and the Politician,* Asher N. Christensen and Evron M. Kirkpatrick, eds., Holt, 1941); LXVIII (August 19, 1931), 7-11: "Conservatism Hits Bottom"; LXVIII (October 14, 1931), 223-226: "Making a Bigger and Better Navy"; LXIX (January 20–February 3, 1932), 258-262, 287-291, 314-318: "Big Navy Boys"; LXXII (November 2, 1932), 318-319: "The Tariff in the Campaign"; LXXIII (November 30, 1932), 66-67: "Planning and Chain Stores"; LXXVII (December 6, 1933), 97-98: "Spooks: Made in Germany"; LXXX (October 24, 1934), 299-300: "Germany up to Her Old Tricks"; LXXXI (December 26, 1934), 188-190: "Blessed Profit System"; LXXXI (February 6, 1935), 350-352: "That Promise of American Life"; LXXXV (November 27, 1935), 71-72: "Queries from the Hills"; LXXXVI (February 12, 1936), 8-9: "Heat and Light on Neutrality"; LXXXVI (March 4–March 18, 1936), 100-102, 127-129, 156-159: "Peace for America"; LXXXVII (August 5, 1936), 370-372: "Ruskin and the Babble of Tongues"; LXXXVIII (September 2, 1936), 92-94: "Rendezvous with the Supreme Court"; LXXXVIII (October 7, 1936), 247-248: "Five Pages from Newton D. Baker"; LXXXIX (November 18, 1936), 86-92: "Report of an Investigation on the Case of Jerome Davis" (with others); LXXXIX (January 20, 1937), 350-353: "New Morgan Thesis"; XC (March 10, 1937), 127-129: "Why Did We Go to War?"; XCI (May 12, 1937), 13-14: "The Future of Democracy"; XCIII (January 19, 1938), 306: "Mine Eyes May Behold"; XCIII (February 2, 1938), 356-359: "Collective Security"; XCIV (March 9, 1938), 123-124: "Big Railway Smash"; XCIV (March 30, 1938), 210: "Rough Seas for the Super-Navy"; XCVI (September 21, 1938), 182-184: "Anti-Trust Racket"; XCVII (January 18, 1939), 307-308: "Neutrality: Shall We Have Revision?"; XCVII (February 1, 1939), 359-362: "The Frontier in American History"; XCIX (June 14, 1939), 148: "America and the Next War" (with others); CI (November 8, 1939), 74-80: "Looking Backward."

New Review, II (June, 1914), 321-324: "The Key to the Mexican Problem."

New York World Telegram, February 25, 1935: "Beard's Criticism of William Randolph Hearst [Speech before the National Education Association Convention, Atlantic City, N. J., February 24, 1935]."

Our World, V (April, 1924), 11-21: "Goto and the Rebuilding of Tokyo."

Outlook, CLII (May 29, 1929), 179: "The President and Congress"; CLIII (September 4, 1929), 17: "Another Job for Mr. Hoover."

Political Quarterly, VIII (October, 1937), 495-506: "The Future of Democracy in the United States."

Political Science Quarterly, XX (June, 1905), 351-384: "Record of Political Events from November 9, 1904, to May 1, 1905" (with Alvin S. Johnson); XX (December, 1905), 740-776: "Record of Political Events from May 1 to November 7, 1905" (with Johnson); XXII (December, 1907), 748-776: "Record of Political Events from May 1 to November 5, 1907" (with Carlton J. H. Hayes); XXIII (June, 1908), 351-384: "Record of Political Events from November 5, 1907, to May 1, 1908" (with Hayes); XXIII (December, 1908), 746-776: "Record of Political Events from May 1 to November 3, 1908" (with Hayes); XXIV (March, 1909), 95-114: "The Constitution of Oklahoma"; XXIV (June, 1909), 343-376: "Record of Political Events from November 3, 1908, to May 1, 1909" (with Hayes); XXIV (December, 1909), 589-614, 730-760: "The Ballot's Burden" and "Record of Political Events from May 1, to November 3, 1909" (with Hayes); XXVI (September, 1911), 381-414: "The Syndication of the Speakership" (with Charles R. Atkinson); XXVII (March, 1912), 1-35: "The Supreme Court—Usurper or Grantee?"

Proceedings of the Association of History Teachers of the Middle States and Maryland, XXII (1924), 46-54: "History and Travel"; XXIX (1931), 12-21: "A Historian's Quest for Light."

Progressive Education, XV (March, 1938), 243: "History as Actuality."

Public Management, XI (July, 1929), 501: "Life Is Not a Table of Logarithms."

Review of Reviews, LXVIII (September, 1923), 296-298: "Japan's Statesman of Research"; LXVIII (October, 1923), 373-382: "Rebuilding in Japan"; LXIX (May, 1924), 523-527: "The Awakening of Japanese Cities"; LXIX (June, 1924), 608-624: "New York: The Metropolis of Today"; LXXI (March, 1925), 268-270: "Reconstruction in Tokyo" (with K. Sawada).

St. Louis Post-Dispatch, Sixtieth Anniversary Section, December 11, 1938: "The Stream of Tendencies in American Government."

Saturday Evening Post, CCXX (October 4, 1947), 172: "Who's to Write the History of the War?"

Saturday Review of Literature, V (October 20, 1928), 272-273: "Culture and Agriculture"; VI (September 7, 1929), 101-102: "History and Culture" (with Mary Beard); VI (April 5, 1930), 894-895: "Toward Civilization"; XI (December 22, 1934), 381-383: "Behind the New Deal."

Scholastic, XXV (November 10, 1934), 12+: "War Springs from Peace."

School and Society, II (December 25, 1915), 904-911: "Methods of Training for Public Service"; VI (October 13, 1917), 446-447: "Letter of Resignation from Columbia University"; XXXV (February 27, 1932), 296-297: "Professional and Patriotic Obligation" (with others); XLIII (February 29, 1936), 278-283: "The Scholar in an Age of Conflicts" (repr. in *National Education Association Department of Superintendence Official Report* [1936], 114-120; *National Education Association Proceedings* [1936], 438-444; *Nation's Schools*, XVII [March, 1936], 21-22; *Bulletin of the American Association of University Professors*, XXII [May, 1936], 324-328; abr. in *National Education Association Journal*, XXV [April, 1936], 105); L (August 19, 1939), 228-235: "Essentials of Democracy" (repr. in Congress on Education for Democracy, *Education for Democracy* [Teachers College, Columbia University, 1939], 29-41; *Vital Speeches*, V [September 15, 1939], 729-732; abr. in *National Education Association Journal*, XXVIII [October, 1939], 195-196).

School Life, XVIII (January, 1933), 86: "List of Books on Economics."

Scribner's Magazine, XC (December, 1931), 571-578: "Rushlights in Darkness"; XCI (January, 1932), 2-7: "Search for the Centre"; XCIII (April, 1933), 209-214: "The Case for Bureaucracy" (with William Beard); XCVII (February, 1935), 65-70: "National Politics and the War."

Social Education, II (September, 1938), 383-385: "A Memorandum from an Old Worker in the Vineyard."

Social Forces, XI (May, 1933), 505-510: "Limitations to the Application of Social Science Implied in Recent Social Trends."

Social Frontier, I (October, 1934), 13-15: "Property and Democracy"; I (March, 1935), 18-20: "Freedom of Teaching" (abr. in *Michigan Education Journal and Moderator Topics*, XII [May, 1935], 419-420; repr. in *Freedom of Speech*, Julia E. Johnson, comp. [Wilson, 1936], 149-152); I (April, 1935), 6, 13-15: "Address at Meeting of Teachers at Atlantic City, February 24, 1935" (excerpts in *New Republic*, LXXXII [March 6, 1935], 86) and "The Educator in the Quest for National Security" (repr. as "The Quest for National Security" in *National Education Association Proceedings* [1935], 510-515; *National Education Association Department of Superintendence Official Report* [1935], 33-38;

Baltimore Bulletin of Education, XIII [March, 1935], 41-53; *American Association of University Women Journal,* XXVIII [April, 1935], 141-144; *School and Society,* XLI [June 1, 1935], 721-725; *National Education Association Journal,* XXV [May, 1936], 139-140; abr. in *Education Digest,* II [September, 1936], 1-4); III (June, 1937), 269-271: "The Court Issue"; IV (October, 1937), 9-10: "A Lesson in Civics"; IV (December, 1937), 75-79: "Emerson as an American Dream-er."

Social Research, IV (May, 1937), 391-398: "Democracy and Education in the United States."

Social Studies, XXV (January, 1934), 5-6: "Announcement of Change in Editorial Management"; XXV (May, 1934), 215-217: "The Task before Us" (with William G. Carr).

Survey, XL (July 13, 1918), 422, 436-437: "John Purroy Mitchel"; LVI (April 15, 1926), 85-87: "Some Regional Realities"; LVI (May 1, 1926), 189: "America and the Far East: The Issues of Pacific Policy" (with Mary Beard); LVIII (April 1, 1927), 5-7, 51-59, 61: "Ten Years Back" (with Mary Beard); LXI (November 15, 1928), 213-215: "The City's Place in Civilization" (repr. in *American City,* XXXIX [November, 1928], 101-103; *National Municipal Review,* XVII [December, 1928], 726-731).

Survey Graphic, XXVI (April, 1937), 201-203: "The Rise of the Democratic Idea in the United States"; XXVI (December, 1937), 679-682: "The Turn of the Century."

Teachers College Record, XVII (May, 1916), 215-226: "Politics and Education."

Today, III (December 22, 1934), 6-7, 24: "Are Third Parties Futile?"; IV (June 29, 1935), 3-4, 23: "Peace Loads the Guns"; IV (September 14, 1935), 3-4, 21: "America Must Stay Big."

Trans-Pacific, VIII (January, 1923), 79-81: "Outlook of City Improvements in Tokyo"; XII (May 2, 1925), 20: "Tokyo Reconstructed" (with K. Sawada).

Virginia Quarterly Review, VII (October, 1931), 500-506: "Captains Uncourageous'"; XV (October, 1939), 500-514: "The Idea of Let Us Alone."

Weekly News Review, XIV (September 9, 1935), 8: "Great Constitutional Issues before the Nation"; XIV (September 16, 1935), 8: "Constitution, as Finally Adopted, Compromise of Opposing Forces" (with Clay Coss); XIV (September 23, 1935), 8: "Flexibility of Constitution Permits Disputes over Its Real Meaning"; XIV (September 30, 1935), 8: "Advocates of Constitutional Change Do Not Aim to Destroy State Powers"; XIV (October 7, 1935), 8: "Commerce Clause of Constitution Is Source of Much Debate and Friction"; XIV (October 14, 1935), 8: "Extent of Congress' Taxing Power May Soon Meet Supreme Court Test"; XIV (October 28, 1935), 8: "Court Issues Arise over Power of Congress to End Holding Companies"; XIV (November 18, 1935), 8: "Modern Industry Raises Issue of Greater Government Regulation"; XIV (December 2, 1935), 8: "Federal Judge Takes Broad View of Commerce Clause in Coal Case"; XIV (December 16, 1935), 8: "Suggestions Made to Curb Power of Supreme Court over Congress"; XV (September 7–October 26, 1936): "As the Parties See It"; XV (November 9–December 14, 1936, January 4–March 8, March 22–April 26, May 10–May 24, 1937): "Personal Sketches of American Presidents"; XVII (September 12–October 10, October 24–October 31, November 14–November 21, 1938): "America—Yesterday and Today" (with Clay Coss); XVII (January 9–May 8, May 22–May 29, 1939): "Makers of America"; XVIII (October 2–October 30, November 13–December 11, 1939, January 8, February 5, February 19, March 4–March 11, April 1–April 15, May 20–May 27, 1940): "America—Yesterday and Today"; XIX (September 9–October 21, 1940, January 13, January 27–February 3, February 17–February 24, 1941): "Backgrounds of Today's Problems."

World Tomorrow, X (November, 1927), 438-442: "Recent Gains in Government."

Yale Review, n.s. XVII (October, 1927), 65-77: "Conflicts in City Planning"; n.s. XVIII (March, 1929), 456-479: "The Political Heritage of the Twentieth Century"; n.s. XXII (September, 1932), 35-51: "Congress under Fire."

Young Oxford, I (October, 1899), 17-18: "Self-Education"; I (December, 1899),
16: "What Is Worth While in Education"; II (November, 1900), 79: "A Trib-
ute to Co-operators"; II (December, 1900), 96-100: "Co-operation and the New
Century"; II (February, 1901), 171-174: "Men Who Have Helped Us: I. Wil-
liam Cobbett, Friend of Man"; II (March, 1901), 206-209: "Men Who Have
Helped Us: II. Robert Owen"; II (March, 1901), 221: "Ruskin Hall and
Temperance Reform"; II (April, 1901), 246-248: "Men Who Have Helped Us:
III. Thomas Carlyle"; II (May, 1901), 290-293: "Men Who Have Helped Us:
IV. William Morris"; II (June, 1901), 338-341: "Lessons from Science"; II
(July, 1901), 358-360: "Men Who Have Helped Us: VI. Mazzini"; II (Septem-
ber, 1901), 439-441: "Men Who Have Helped Us: VII. Charles Darwin"; III
(October, 1901), 24-25: "A Living Empire, I"; III (November, 1901), 39-43:
"A Living Empire, II"; IV (December, 1901), 79-81: "An Ideal Labour Col-
lege."

ESSAYS BY BEARD IN CO-OPERATIVE WORKS:

Adult Education and Democracy (American Association for Adult Education,
1936): "What Is This Democracy?" (excerpts in Federal Council of Churches
of Christ in America Department of Research and Education, *Information
Service,* XV [September 26, 1936], 1-2).
Archibald Henderson, the New Crichton, Samuel S. Hood, ed. (Beechhurst Press,
1949), 71-72, 73-75: "Baconian Scholar" and "Mr. Henderson's North Carolina."
The Constitution Reconsidered, Conyers Read, ed. (Columbia University Press,
1938), 159-166: "Historiography and the Constitution."
Democracy in Reconstruction, Frederick A. Cleveland and Joseph Schafer, eds.
(Boston, Houghton Mifflin, 1919), 486-491: "The Evolution of Democracy: A
Summary."
Encyclopaedia of the Social Sciences, Edwin R. A. Seligman and Alvin Johnson,
eds. (Macmillan, 1930), I, 145-163: "The Development of Social Thought and
Institutions: Individualism and Capitalism."
Essays in Intellectual History Dedicated to James Harvey Robinson (Harper,
1929), 107-124: "The Inside of Germany's War Politics."
Essays on Research in the Social Sciences, sponsored by the Brookings Institution
Committee on Training (Washington, The Brookings Institution, 1931), 51-63:
"Method in the Study of Political Science as an Aspect of Social Science."
The People, Politics, and the Politician, A. N. Christensen and E. M. Kirk-
patrick, eds. (Holt, 1941), 49-54, 338-349: "Adopting the National Constitu-
tion" (with Mary R. Beard) and "Whom Does Congress Represent."
Research in the Social Sciences, Wilson Gee, ed. (Macmillan, 1929), 269-291:
"Political Science."
Report of the Committee on Policy of the American Political Science Association
(George Banta Publishing Co., Menasha, Wis., 1930), 25-32: "Conditions Fav-
orable to Creative Work in Political Science."
*Theory and Practice in Historical Study: A Report of the Committee on His-
toriography,* Merle E. Curti, ed. (*Social Science Research Council Bulletin,* no.
54 [1946]), 1-14, 136-137, 103-108: "Grounds for a Reconsideration of Historiography," "Signed Footnote" (with Alfred Vagts), "Problems of Terminology in Historical Writing: The Need for Greater Precision in the Use of
Historical Terms."
Training for Municipal Service (*Municipal Research,* no. 68 [Bureau of Municipal Research, 1915]), 5-14: "The Problem of Training for the Public Service."
The Work Unit in Federal Administration (*Public Administration Service Publication,* no. 56, Chicago [1937]), 1-3: "The Role of Administration in Government."
Workers' Education: A Symposium, New York? 1919?: "The New School for Social Research."

TESTIMONY BEFORE CONGRESSIONAL COMMITTEES:

"Statement of Dr. Charles A. Beard," March 19, 1935, *To Make Better Provision for the Government of the Military and Naval Forces of the United States by the Suppression of Attempts to Incite the Members Thereof to Disobedience: Hearings before the Committee of Military Affairs and Subcommittee No. 10 House of Representatives on House Resolution 5845*, 74 Cong., 1 Sess., 49-54.

"Statement of Dr. Charles A. Beard, Historian," February 10, 1938, *To Establish the Composition of the United States Navy: Hearings before the Committee on Naval Affairs, House of Representatives on House Resolution 9218 to Establish the Composition of the United States Navy, to Authorize the Construction of Certain Naval Vessels, and for Other Purposes*, 75 Cong., 3 Sess., 2133-2146 (repr. in "Testimony before the House Naval Affairs Committee," *Christian Science Monitor Weekly*, March 9, 1938).

"Statement of Charles A. Beard, New Milford, Conn.," February 4, 1941, *To Promote the Defense of the United States: Hearings before the Committee on Foreign Relations United States Senate on Senate [Bill] 275*, 77 Cong., 1 Sess., 307-313.

"Statement of Dr. Charles A. Beard, April 3, 1948," *Universal Military Training: Hearings before the Committee on Armed Services United States Senate*, 80 Cong., 2 Sess., 1053-1057.

BOOK REVIEWS BY BEARD:

The names of the periodicals in which the reviews appeared are abbreviated: AHR—*American Historical Review;* APSR—*American Political Science Review;* CH—*Current History;* CS—*Common Sense;* N—*Nation;* NMR—*National Municipal Review;* NR—*New Republic;* PSQ—*Political Science Quarterly;* SRL—*Saturday Review of Literature;* VQR—*Virginia Quarterly Review;* and YR—*Yale Review,* new series.

Abbott, Frank F., and Johnson, Allan C., *Municipal Administration in the Roman Empire,* NMR, XVI (September, 1927), 587-588.

Adams, Ephriam D., *Great Britain and the American Civil War,* NR, XLIV (September 30, 1925—Part 2), 5-6.

Adams, George B., *The Political History of England, 1066-1216,* PSQ, XXI (September, 1906), 531-535.

Adams, Henry, *The Degradation of the Democratic Dogma,* NR, XXII (March 31, 1920), 162-163.

Adamson, Robert, *Municipal Year Book of the City of New York (1913),* NMR, III (April, 1914), 428-429.

Alexander, De Alva S., *A Political History of the State of New York,* PSQ, XXII (March, 1907), 141-143.

Angell, Norman, *From Chaos to Control* (Halley Stewart Lectures, 1932), SRL, IX (June 10, 1933), 637-639.

Ballard, Adolphus, *The Domesday Boroughs,* PSQ, XX (March, 1905), 158-159.

Barnes, Harry Elmer, *The Genesis of the World War,* CH, XXIV (July, 1926), 730-735.

Batault, Georges, *La Guerre absolue,* NR, XXVIII (September 21, 1921), 109-110.

Becker, Carl L., *The Heavenly City of the Eighteenth-Century Philosophers,* AHR, XXXVIII (April, 1933), 590-591.

———, *The United States: An Experiment in Democracy,* N, CXI (October 13, 1920), 416-417.

———, Clark, John M., and Dodd, William E., *The Spirit of '76 and Other Essays,* NR, LII (August 24, 1927), 23-24.

Beckerath, Herbert von, *Modern Industrial Organization,* APSR, XXVII (October, 1933), 833-835.

Bennett, Jesse L., *The Essential American Tradition: An Anthology,* NR, XLIII (July 29, 1925), 269-270.

Bentley, Arthur F., *The Process of Government: A Study of Social Pressures*, PSQ, XXIII (December, 1908), 739-741.
Bérard, Victor, *La France et Guillaume II*, AHR, XII (July, 1907), 895-897.
Bingham, Alfred, *Man's Estate*, CS, VII (June, 1939), 24-25.
Bowley, Arthur L., *The Need and Purpose of the Measurement of Social Phenomena*, NMR, V (July, 1916), 518.
Bowman, Isaiah, *The New World*, NR, LVIII (April 17, 1929), 257-258.
Brady, Robert A., *Business as a System of Power*, APSR, XXXVII (April, 1943), 329-330.
Broderick, George C., and Frotheringham, John K., *The Political History of England, 1801-1837*, PSQ, XXII (September, 1907), 522-523.
Bryce, James, *Bryce's American Commonwealth: Fiftieth Anniversary*, Robert C. Brooks, ed., APSR, XXXIV (February, 1940), 131.
California Committee on Efficiency and Economy, *Report to Governor William D. Stephens and His Message to the Legislature in Relation Thereto March 12, 1919*, NMR, VIII (December, 1919), 727-728.
Campbell, Thomas D., *Russia: Market or Menace?* NR, LXX (April 27, 1932), 305-306.
Carr, Albert, *America's Last Chance*, APSR, XXXV (February, 1941), 155-156.
Catlin, George E. G., *The Science and Method of Politics*, APSR, XXI (August, 1927), 652-653.
Chafee, Zechariah, *Freedom of Speech*, NMR, X (April, 1921), 247-248.
Chamberlin, William Henry, *The Russian Revolution*, APSR, XXX (February, 1936), 174-175.
Channing, Edward, *A History of the United States*, vol. IV, NR, XI (July 7, 1917), 282-283; vol. V, NR, XXIX (January 4, 1922), 160-161; vol. VI, NR, XLIV (November 11, 1925), 310-311.
Chase, Stuart, *Men and Machines*, YR, XIX (September, 1929), 159-161.
Chinard, Gilbert, *Thomas Jefferson: The Apostle of Americanism*, N, CXXIX (December 4, 1929), 686.
Chugerman, Samuel, *Lester F. Ward: The American Aristotle*, NR, CI (November 15, 1939), 119.
Churchill, Winston S., *Liberalism and the Social Problem*, PSQ, XXV (September, 1910), 529-531.
Cleveland, Frederick A., and Buck, Arthur E., *The Budget and Responsible Government*, N, CXI (September 4, 1920), 275.
Cole, George D. H., *A Guide through World Chaos*, APSR, XXVII (February, 1933), 118-119.
Collingwood, Robin G., *The Idea of History*, AHR, LII (July, 1947), 704-708.
Commission of Inquiry on Public Service Personnel, *Better Government Personnel*, APSR, XXIX (April, 1935), 296-297.
Commons, John R., *Industrial Government*, N, CXIII (November 9, 1921), 543.
Cooke, Morris L. Llewellyn, *Our Cities Awake: Notes on Municipal Activities and Administration*, NR, XVII (January 25, 1919), 381-383.
Curti, Merle E., *Peace or War: The American Struggle, 1636-1936*, NR, LXXXVI (April 15, 1936), 289.
Davis, George T., *A Navy Second to None*, NR, CII (February 26, 1940), 283-284.
Dennett, Tyler, *Roosevelt and the Russo-Japanese War*, NR, XLIII (June 3, 1925), 52-53.
Deville, Gabriel, *Histoire socialiste: du 9 thermidor au 18 brumaire*, PSQ, XXI (March, 1906), 111-120.
DeWitt, Benjamin P., *The Progressive Movement*, NMR, IV (October, 1915), 682-683.
Dodd, Walter F., *Modern Constitutions*, PSQ, XXIV (September, 1909), 524-525.
Duguit, Léon, *Traité de droit constitutionnel*, PSQ, XXVII (September, 1912), 518-519.
———, *Les Transformations du droit public*, PSQ, XXIX (June, 1914), 340-341.
Earle, Edward Meade, ed., *The Federalist: A Commentary on the Constitution of the United States; Being a Collection of Essays Written in Support of the*

Constitution Agreed upon September 17, 1787, by the Federal Convention, AHR, XLIII (April, 1938), 651-652.

Eckardstein, Baron Hermann von, *Ten Years at the Court of St. James,* NR, XXXII (September 27, 1922), 5.

Ely, Richard T., *Property and Contract in Their Relation to the Distribution of Wealth,* PSQ, XXX (September, 1915), 510-511.

Errera, Paul, *Das Staatsrecht des Königreichs Belgien,* PSQ, XXV (September, 1910), 533-534.

Eyschen, Paul, *Das Staatsrecht des Grossherzogtums Luxemburg,* PSQ, XXV (September, 1910), 533-534.

Farrand, Max, *The Records of the Federal Convention of 1787,* PSQ, XXVI (September, 1911), 551-553.

Fenwick, Charles G., *Political Systems in Transition: War-Time and After,* N, CXII (February 23, 1921), 297-298.

Fischer, Louis, *Oil Imperialism,* NR, XLIX (December 8, 1926), 82-83.

Fisher, Herbert A. L., *The Republican Tradition in Europe,* PSQ, XXVII (September, 1912), 512-513.

Fitzpatrick, John C., ed., *The Diaries of George Washington, 1748-1799,* NR, XLVI (April 21, 1926), 279.

Forbes, Russell, *Governmental Purchasing,* NMR, XVIII (September, 1929), 580.

Fox, Richard M., *The Triumphant Machine,* SRL, V (June 1, 1929), 1071.

Friedrich, Carl Joachim, *Foreign Policy in the Making,* CS, VIII (June, 1939), 25.

French, Allen, *The Day of Concord and Lexington,* NR, XLIII (July 15, 1925), 215-216.

Gabriel, Ralph H., *The Course of American Democratic Thought: An Intellectual History since 1815,* AHR, XLVI (October, 1940), 164-165.

Gaus, John M., *Great Britain: A Study of Civic Loyalty,* APSR, XXIII (November, 1929), 1005-1007.

Glaser, Friedrich, ed., *Wirtschaftspolitische Annalen,* PSQ, XXIV (March, 1909), 165-167.

Grey, Viscount [Edward], *Twenty-five Years, 1892-1916,* NR, XLIV (October 7, 1925), 172-175.

Grumbach, Solomon, *Das annexionistische Deutschland,* NR, XI (July 14, 1917), 309-310.

Guest, L. Haden, *The Struggle for Power in Europe, 1917-21,* NR, XXX (March 29, 1922), 144-145.

Gulick, Luther H., *The Evolution of the Budget in Massachusetts,* N, CXI (September 4, 1920), 275.

Gundolf, Friedrich, *Anfänge deutscher Geschichtsschreibung,* PSQ, LIV (March, 1939), 138.

Hacker, Louis M., and Kendrick, Benjamin B., *The United States since 1865,* NR, LXX (March 30, 1932), 187.

Halle, Ernst von, *Die Weltwirtschaft: Ein Jahr- und Lesebuch,* PSQ, XXIV (March, 1909), 165-167.

Harper, Samuel N., *Civic Training in Soviet Russia,* APSR, XXIII (November, 1929), 1005-1007.

Hatschek, Julius, *Englisches Staatsrecht,* PSQ, XXII (December, 1907), 719-723.

Haworth, Paul L., *The United States in Our Own Times, 1865-1920,* N, CXI (October 13, 1920), 416-417.

Hayes, Carlton J. H., *A Brief History of the Great War,* NR, XXV (December 22, 1920), 114-115.

Haynes, Fred E., *Third Party Movements since the Civil War,* NR, IX (November 18, 1916), 22-24.

Haynes, George H., *The Senate of the United States,* NR, XCVIII (February 8, 1939), 26.

Henderson, Archibald, *North Carolina: The Old North State and the New,* VQR, XVII (Autumn, 1941), 600-603.

Hobson, John A., *The Crisis of Liberalism*, PSQ, XXV (September, 1910), 529-531.
Hobson, Samuel G., *National Guilds and the State*, NR, XXV (December 8, 1920), 50-51.
Hodgkin, Thomas, *The Political History of England to 1066*, PSQ, XXI (December, 1906), 699-702.
Humphreys, John H., *Proportional Representation*, PSQ, XXVII (March, 1912), 137-138.
Hunt, Gaillard, *The Department of State of the United States*, PSQ, XXIX (December, 1914), 710-711.
Hunter, Robert, *Poverty*, PSQ, XX (June, 1905), 341-343.
Huntington-Wilson, Francis M., *Money and the Price Level*, NR, LXXIV (March 15, 1933), 134-135.
Ise, John, *The United States Forest Policy*, N, CXII (February 2, 1921), 187.
Jameson, J. Franklin, *The American Revolution Considered as a Social Movement*, NR, XLVII (August 11, 1926), 344.
Jaurès, Jean, *Histoire socialiste jusqu'au 9 thermidor*, 4 vols., PSQ, XXI (March, 1906), 111-120.
Jellinek, George, Laband, Paul, and Piloty, Robert, eds., *Jahrbuch des öffentlichen Rechts*, PSQ, XXIV (March, 1909), 165-167.
Kerney, James, *The Political Education of Woodrow Wilson*, NR, XLVI (May 12, 1926), 372-373.
Kirkland, Edward C., *A History of American Economic Life*, SRL, IX (August 13, 1932), 42.
Korff, Sergiei A., *Russia's Foreign Relations during the Last Half Century*, NR, XXX (March 29, 1922), 144-145.
Laband, Paul, *Deutsches Reichsstaatsrecht*, PSQ, XXV (September, 1910), 533-534.
Laidler, Harry W., *History of Socialist Thought*, NR, LI (July 13, 1927), 208-209.
Larson, Laurence M., *The King's Household in England before the Norman Conquest*, PSQ, XX (December, 1905), 738-739.
Laski, Harold J., *The Foundations of Sovereignty and Other Essays*, N, CXIII (October 26, 1921), 482-483.
———, *A Grammar of Politics*, NR, XLV (December 9, 1925), 91-92.
———, *Political Thought in England from Locke to Bentham*, NR, XXIV (November 17, 1920), 303-304.
———, *Where Do We Go from Here?* APSR, XXXV (February, 1941), 155-156.
Lebon, André, *Das Verfassungsrecht der französischen Republik*, PSQ, XXV (September, 1910), 533-534.
Lenin, Vladimir Ilich, *The Revolution of 1917* and *Toward the Seizure of Power*, NR, LXXV (May 17, 1933), 22-24.
Lennes, Nels J., *Whither Democracy*, NR, LI (August 10, 1927), 314-315.
Liefmann, Robert, *Cartels, Concerns, and Trusts*, N, CXXXVI (May 31, 1933), 618-619.
Lindeman, Eduard C., *Wealth and Culture*, SRL, XIII (March 14, 1936), 20-21.
Lodge, Henry Cabot, ed., *Selections from the Correspondence of Theodore Roosevelt and Henry Cabot Lodge, 1884-1918*, NR, XLIII (June 17, 1925), 103-104.
Loeb, Harold, and Associates, *The Chart of Plenty*, NR, LXXXII (March 20, 1935), 164.
Lynd, Robert S., *Knowledge for What?* APSR, XXXIII (August, 1939), 711-712.
McCall, Samuel W., *The Life of Thomas Brackett Reed*, PSQ, XXX (September, 1915), 530-531.
MacCunn, John, *The Political Philosophy of Burke*, AHR, XIX (October, 1913), 170-171.
McLaughlin, Andrew C., *A Constitutional History of the United States*, NR, XCII (September 15, 1937), 162-164.
———, *The Courts, the Constitution and Parties: Studies in Constitutional History and Politics*, AHR, XVIII (January, 1913), 378-379.

Macmahon, Arthur, and Millett, John D., *Federal Administrators*, NR, CII (May 20, 1940), 678-679.

McMaster, John B., *A History of the People of the United States during Lincoln's Administration*, NR, LI (June 29, 1927), 156-157.

Mandelbaum, Maurice, *The Problem of Historical Knowledge: An Answer to Relativism*, AHR, XLIV (April, 1939), 571-572.

Marriott, John A. R., *Second Chambers: An Inductive Study in Political Science*, PSQ, XXV (December, 1910), 721-723.

Marsh, Benjamin, *Taxation of Land Values in American Cities*, PSQ, XXVI (December, 1911), 714-715.

Mathews, John Mabry, *The Conduct of American Foreign Relations*, NR, XXX (March 29, 1922), 144-145.

Maurer, James H., *It Can Be Done*, NR, XCVIII (February 22, 1939), 81-82.

May, Thomas Erskine, *The Constitutional History of England since the Accession of George III*, ed. and cont. by Francis Holland, PSQ, XXVII (December, 1912), 701-704, and NR, XVI (October 19, 1918), 350-351.

Megaro, Gaudens, *Mussolini in the Making*, AHR, XLV (January, 1940), 393-394.

Merriam, Charles E., *American Political Ideas, 1865-1917*, NR, XXV (January 19, 1921), 235-236.

————, *The Making of Citizens*, APSR, XXVI (February, 1932), 150-151.

————, *The New Democracy and the New Despotism*, APSR, XXXIII (October, 1939), 884-886.

————, *Primary Elections*, PSQ, XXIV (June, 1909), 316-317.

Michels, Robert, *Political Parties: A Sociological Study of the Oligarchical Tendencies of Modern Democracy*, PSQ, XXXII (March, 1917), 153-155.

Mims, Edwin, *The Advancing South*, NR, XLVII (June 23, 1926), 144-145.

Morgan, George, *James Monroe*, N, CXIV (April 26, 1922), 499-500.

Morison, Samuel Eliot, *The Life and Letters of Harrison Gray Otis*, PSQ, XXIX (December, 1914), 716-718.

————, *The Maritime History of Massachusetts, 1783-1860*, NR, XXIX (January 25, 1922), 253-254.

Muir, Ramsay, *How Britain Is Governed*, NMR, XIX (August, 1930), 550.

Müller-Armack, Alfred von, *Entwicklungsgesetze des Kapitalismus*, N, CXXXVI (March 22, 1933), 323.

Murdock, Harold, *The 19th of April, 1775*, NR, XLIII (July 15, 1925), 215-216.

National Municipal League Committee on Municipal Program, *A Model City Charter and Municipal Home Rule*, APSR, X (August, 1916), 602-605.

Neurath, Otto, *Modern Man in the Making*, SRL, XX (September 30, 1939), 10-11.

Nevins, Allan, ed., *American Press Opinion: Washington to Coolidge*, NR, LVII (February 13, 1929), 254.

————, ed., *The Diary of John Quincy Adams*, NR, LVII (February 13, 1929), 354.

————, *Gateway to History*, N, CXLVII (September 24, 1938), 300-302.

————, *John D. Rockefeller: The Heroic Age of American Enterprise*, APSR, XXXV (October, 1941), 977-980.

New York City Commission on Congestion of Population, *Report*, PSQ, XXVI (December, 1911), 714-715.

Newell, Frederick H., *Water Resources: Present and Future Uses*, N, CXII (February 2, 1921), 187.

O'Brien, George, *An Essay on Medieval Economic Teaching*, N, CXI (October 27, 1920), 480.

Panaretoff, Stephen, *Near Eastern Affairs*, NR, XXX (March 29, 1922), 144-145.

Parrington, Vernon L., *Main Currents in American Thought*, N, CXXIV (May 18, 1927), 560-562.

Pasvolsky, Leo, *Russia in the Far East*, NR, XXX (March 29, 1922), 144-145.

Paul, Eden, and Paul, Cedar, *Creative Revolution: A Study in Communist Ergatocracy*, N, CXII (March 2, 1921), 342.

———, *Prolecult*, N, CXIV (February 15, 1922), 196.
Pease, Edward R., *The Case for Municipal Drink*, PSQ, XIX (December, 1904), 697-699.
Penty, Arthur J., *A Guildsman's Interpretation of History*, N, CXI (December 29, 1920), 783.
Pettus, Daisy C., ed., *The Rosalie Evans Letters from Mexico*, NR, XLVIII (October 13, 1926), 225-226.
Porter, Kirk, *History of Suffrage in the United States*, NMR, VIII (September, 1919), 495.
President's Research Committee on Social Trends, *Recent Social Trends in the United States*, YR, XXII (March, 1933), 595-597.
Puleston, William D., *The Life and Works of Captain Alfred Thayer Mahan*, NR, XCIX (June 28, 1939), 221-225 (with Alfred Vagts).
Rauch, Basil, *The History of the New Deal*, APSR, XXXIX (February, 1945), 196-197.
Rauschenbush, Stephen, *The March of Fascism*, YR, XXIX (September, 1939), 167-169.
Reinsch, Paul S., *An American Diplomat in China*, NR, XXX (March 29, 1922), 144-145.
———, *Secret Diplomacy*, NR, XXX (March 29, 1922), 144-145.
Repington, Charles à Court, *After the War*, NR, XXX (March 29, 1922), 144-145.
Rhodes, James Ford, *History of the United States, 1877-1896*, NR, XXI (December 17, 1919), 82-83.
Rightor, Chester E., *City Manager in Dayton*, NMR, IX (January, 1920), 45-46.
Ripert, Henry, *La Présidence des assemblées politiques*, PSQ, XXVI (March, 1911), 145-146.
Rippy, J. Fred, *The United States and Mexico*, NR, XLVIII (October 13, 1926), 225-226.
Robson, William A., ed., *Public Enterprise*, APSR, XXXI (December, 1937), 1157-1159.
Round, J. Horace, *Peerage and Pedigree*, PSQ, XXV (September, 1910), 527-528.
Ryan, Oswald, *Municipal Freedom*, NMR, IV (October, 1915), 681-682.
Sandburg, Carl, *Abraham Lincoln: The War Years*, VQR, XVI (Winter, 1940), 112-116.
Sanger, Charles P., *The Place of Compensation in Temperance Reform*, PSQ, XIX (December, 1904), 697-699.
Schlesinger, Arthur M., *The Colonial Merchants and the American Revolution, 1763-1776*, NR, XIV (April 6, 1918), 301-302.
———, *The Rise of the City*, AHR, XXXVIII (July, 1933), 779-780.
Schneider, Herbert W., *Making the Fascist State*, NR, LVII (January 23, 1929), 277-278.
———, and Clough, Shepard B., *Making Fascists*, APSR, XXIV (February, 1930), 181-182.
Seymour, Charles, ed., *The Intimate Papers of Colonel House*, vols. I and II, NR, XLVI (March 17, 1926), 109-111; vols. III and IV, APSR, XXIII (February, 1929), 190-191.
Shambaugh, Benjamin F., ed., *Applied History*, PSQ, XXX (March, 1915), 173-174.
Shelton, Douglas, *The Life and Letters of Sir Wilfred Laurier*, NR, XXXI (August 9, 1922), 313.
Siegfried, André, *America Comes of Age*, NR, LI (June 8, 1927), 75-76.
Slemp, C. Bascom, *The Mind of the President*, NR, XLVII (May 26, 1926), 38-39.
Small, Albion W., *Between Eras from Capitalism to Democracy*, NMR, II (October, 1913), 771-772.
Smith, J. Allen, *The Spirit of American Government*, PSQ, XXIII (March, 1908), 136-137.
Sprout, Harold, and Sprout, Margaret, *The Rise of American Naval Power*, NR, XCIX (June 28, 1939), 221-225 (with Alfred Vagts).

Stimson, Frederic J., *The American Constitution*, PSQ, XXIII (June, 1908), 340-343.

Taft, William Howard, *Popular Government*, PSQ, XXXIII (December, 1918), 594-596.

Tout, Thomas F., *The Political History of England, 1216-1377*, PSQ, XXI (December, 1906), 699-702.

Toynbee, Arnold J., *A Study of History*, vols. I-III, AHR, XL (January, 1935), 307-309; vols. IV-VI, AHR, XLV (April, 1940), 593-594.

———, *Survey of International Affairs, 1924*, NR, XLIX (December 8, 1926), 82-83; *1926*, NR, LVIII (April 17, 1929), 257-258.

Tugwell, Rexford G., *Industrial Discipline and the Governmental Arts*, APSR, XXVII (October, 1933), 833-835.

Turner, Frederick J., *The Frontier in American History*, NR, XXV (February 16, 1921), 349-350.

Ulbrich, Josef, *Das österreichische Staatsrecht*, PSQ, XXV (September, 1910), 533-534.

Van Kleeck, Mary, *Miners and Management*, APSR, XXVIII (August, 1934), 699-700.

Van Loon, Hendrik W., *The Story of Mankind*, NR, XXIX (December 21, 1921), 105.

Viallate, Achille, ed., *La Vie politique dans les deux mondes*, PSQ, XXIV (March, 1909), 165-167.

Vinogradoff, Paul, *The Growth of the Manor*, PSQ, XXI (March, 1906), 165-167.

Walling, William E., *Progressivism and After*, NMR, IV (January, 1915), 132-133.

Walsh, Correa M., *The Political Science of John Adams: A Study in the Theory of Mixed Government and the Bicameral System*, PSQ, XXX (September, 1915), 521-522.

Walsh, Edmund A., ed., *The History and Nature of International Relations*, NR, XXX (March 29, 1922), 144-145.

Wandell, Samuel H., and Minnigerode, Meade, *Aaron Burr*, SRL, II (November 28, 1925), 337.

Ward, Harry F., *The New Social Order*, NR, XXIII (July 14, 1920), 208-209.

Ware, Caroline F., ed., *The Cultural Approach to History*, AHR, XLVI (July, 1941), 844-846.

Waterhouse, Paul, and Unwin, Raymond, *Old Towns and New Needs; Also the Town Extension Plan*, NMR, II (July, 1913), 561.

Watson, David K., *The Constitution of the United States*, PSQ, XXVI (September, 1911), 549-551.

Webb, Sidney, and Webb, Beatrice, *A Constitution for the Socialist Commonwealth of Great Britain*, N, CXI (December 8, 1920), 664-666.

———, *English Local Government from the Revolution to the Municipal Corporations Act: The Parish and the County*, PSQ, XXIII (March, 1908), 144-147.

———, *The History of Liquor Licensing in England, Principally from 1700 to 1830*, PSQ, XIX (March, 1904), 152-154.

Weber, Elizabeth Ann, *The Duk-Duks*, APSR, XXIII (November, 1929), 1005-1007.

Wells, Herbert G., *Washington and the Riddle of Peace*, N, CXIV (March 8, 1922), 289-290.

Welschinger, Henri, *L'Alliance franco-russe*, NR, XXIX (February 22, 1922), 375-376.

Weyl, Walter, *The End of the War*, NR, XV (July 6, 1918), 297-299.

White, Leonard D., ed., *Essays in Honor of Charles E. Merriam: The Future of Government in the United States*, APSR, XXXVI (October, 1942), 953-954.

Wilcox, Delos F., *Municipal Franchises*, PSQ, XXVII (December, 1912), 713-715.

Wilson, Woodrow, *The New Freedom: A Call for the Emancipation of the Generous Energies of a People*, PSQ, XXIX (September, 1914), 506-507.

Wingfield-Stratford, Esmé, *The History of British Civilization*, NR, LVII (February 6, 1929), 327-328.

Workers Education Bureau, *Workers' Education in the United States*, NR, XXVIII (November 9, 1921), 327-328.
Works Progress Administration, *Index of Research Projects*, vol. I, NR, XCIX (July 12, 1939), 286-287.
Young, George, *Diplomacy, Old and New*, NR, XXX (March 29, 1922), 144-145.
Zweig, Egon, *Die Lehre vom Pouvoir Constituant: Ein Beitrag zum Staatsrecht der französischen Revolution*, PSQ, XXIV (September, 1909), 522-523.

PREFACES, FOREWORDS, AND INTRODUCTIONS BY BEARD:

Adams, Brooks, *The Law of Civilization and Decay: An Essay on History*. Knopf, 1943.
Breithut, Frederick E., *The Engineer in Public Service*. Bureau of Municipal Research, 1916.
Bureau of Municipal Research, *The Accounting and Reporting Methods of the State of New York*. 1916.
———, *Budget Systems: A Discussion before the New York Constitutional Convention*. 1915.
———, *The History of Appropriations in the Legislative Session of 1916, New York State*. 1916.
———, *Japanese Administration and Finance*. 1917.
———, *The New York City Budget*. 1917.
———, *The New York State Legislative Budget and Financial Measures for 1918*. 1918.
———, *State Administration: Discussions of Proposed Amendments for the Reorganization of the Executive Branch before the New York Constitutional Convention*. 1915.
Bury, John Bagnell, *The Idea of Progress: An Inquiry into Its Origin and Growth*. Macmillan, 1932.
Frank, John P., *Mr. Justice Black: The Man and His Opinions*. Knopf, 1949.
Gilchrist, Huntington, *The Governor's Budget in Maine, 1917*. Bureau of Municipal Research, 1917.
Haines, Charles G., and Dimock, Marshall E., eds., *Essays on the Law and Practice of Governmental Administration: A Volume in Honor of Frank Johnson Goodnow*. Baltimore, Johns Hopkins Press, 1935.
Hibben, Paxton, *The Peerless Leader: William Jennings Bryan*. Farrar and Rinehart, 1929.
Knight, Melvin M., *Morocco as a French Economic Venture: A Study of Open-Door Imperialism*. Appleton-Century, 1937.
Konefsky, Samuel J., *Chief Justice Stone and the Supreme Court*. Macmillan, 1945.
Lief, Alfred, ed., *The Social and Economic Views of Mr. Justice Brandeis*. Vanguard, 1930.
McCaleb, Walter F., *The Aaron Burr Conspiracy*. Wilson-Erickson, 1903.
Maclay, Edgar S., ed., *The Journal of William Maclay, United States Senator from Pennsylvania, 1789-1791*. Albert and Charles Boni, 1927.
Powell, Fred W., *Recent Movement for State and Government Reform, 1911-1917*. Bureau of Municipal Research, 1917.
Stourm, René, *The Budget*. Appleton, 1917.
Tsurumi, Yusuke, *The Mother*. R. D. Henkle, 1932.
Watts, Franklin, ed., *Voices of History: Great Speeches and Papers of the Year 1941*. Franklin Watts, 1942.

LETTERS TO THE EDITOR:

New Republic, I (December 12, 1914), 22-23: "Women Suffrage and Strategy"; I (January 9, 1915), 23: "Section Four and Suffrage"; XI (June 2, 1917), 136-138: "The Perils of Diplomacy"; XIII (December 29, 1917), 249-250: "A Statement [on resignation from Columbia University]"; XVII (January 18, 1919), 343: "The Supreme Issue"; XXVII (August 17, 1921), 328: "Go Easy on the Professors"; XXVIII (November 16, 1921), 349: "The Federal Reserve System and Labor"; XXX (April 12, 1922), 201: [Reply to Paul S. Reinsch on] "Why China Entered the War"; XXXII (September 27, 1922), 128-129: Reply to Lippmann's essay on the *Economic Basis of Politics;* XLVI (April 14, 1926), 226-227: "Woodrow Wilson and Science"; LIV (March 21, 1928), 157: "Mr. Lennes Excepts"; LXIX (November 25, 1931), 47: Reply to Mr. Karl Gerber's "Economic Interpretation of Navies"; LXIX (December 16, 1931), 137: "Who Runs the Japanese Government?"; LXXII (October 19, 1932), 264: "An Amazing Book [*Red Smoke* by Freeman]"; LXXV (June 28, 1933), 183-184: "Letting Down the Bars"; LXXV (August 2, 1933), 318: "Relative Normality [reply to Mr. Robert Rockafellow]"; LXXVII (January 3, 1934), 227: "Invitation to Bronx Cheer [comment on Professor Frederick Schönemann]"; LXXVIII (March 21, 1934), 161: "Freedom to Laugh [reply to Homer G. Richey]"; LXXIX (June 13, 1934), 130: "An Opening for Idiots"; LXXXI (January 30, 1935), 334: "On Liberalism"; LXXXVII (June 17, 1936), 177-178: "New Light on Bryan and War Policies"; LXXXVIII (August 26, 1936), 77: "The Living Constitution [reply to Mr. Witmer]"; LXXXIX (February 3, 1937), 413: "The Case of Glenn Frank"; XCIX (May 17, 1939), 48-49: "Realism on Money"; C (September 6, 1939), 133: "Mr. Bingham's Intent"; CII (September 23, 1940), 411: "How They Are Voting."

New York Times, July 18, 1915, on woman physicians; September 17, 1923, on Japan's problems; March 28, 1936, reply to editorial discussing Beard on Germany in foreign affairs; July 30, 1936, on Nobel peace prize; January 23, 1938, on frontier folk; February 13, 1938, reply to James Truslow Adams's letter; November 15, 1939, reply to letter on Beard's *Giddy Minds and Foreign Quarrels.*

Outlook, CLVI (October 1, 1930), 200: "Killing the Intellect."

Saturday Review of Literature, XII (August 17, 1935), 9, 22-23: "History and Social Science."

Survey Graphic, XXII (May, 1933), 269: "The Fels Plan for a Federal Trade System."

MAJOR ARTICLES AND REFERENCES ABOUT BEARD:

Blinkoff, Maurice, *The Influence of Charles A. Beard upon American Historiography* (Buffalo, University of Buffalo, 1936).

Borning, Bernard C., "The Political Philosophy of Young Charles A. Beard," *American Political Science Review,* XLIII (December, 1949), 1165-1178.

——, "Political Ideas of Charles A. Beard" (Ph.D. dissertation, University of Minnesota, 1932).

Boudin, Louis, *Government by Judiciary* (William Godwin, 1932), I, 90-91, 104-109, 568-583, and *passim.*

Commager, Henry S., *The American Mind: An Interpretation of American Thought and Character since the 1880's* (New Haven, Yale University Press, 1950), 303-309, 328-331, and *passim.*

Curti, Merle, "Charles Austin Beard," *Year Book of the American Philosophical Society, 1948,* 242-244.

——, "A Great Teacher's Teacher," *Social Education,* XIII (October, 1949), 263-267.

Edman, Irwin, *Philosopher's Holiday* (Viking, 1938), 129-133.

Giddens, Paul H., "Views of George Bancroft and Charles A. Beard on the Making of the Constitution," *Journal of American History,* XXVII (3d qtr., 1933), 129-141.

Gideonse, Harry D., "National Collectivism and Charles A. Beard," *Journal of Political Economy,* XLIII (December, 1935), 778-799.

Glaser, William A., "Critique of Two Economic Interpretations of Politics: Charles A. Beard and A. M. Simons" (Ph.D. dissertation, Harvard University, 1952).

Goldman, Eric F., "A Historian at Seventy," New Republic, CXI (November 27, 1944), 696-697.

———, "Origins of Beard's Economic Interpretation of the Constitution," Journal of the History of Ideas, XIII (April, 1952), 234-249.

———, Rendezvous with Destiny (Knopf, 1952), passim.

Herring, Hubert, "Charles A. Beard: Free Lance among the Historians," Harper's Magazine, CLXXVIII (May, 1939), 641-652.

Hofstadter, Richard, "Beard and the Constitution: The History of an Idea," American Quarterly, II (Fall, 1950), 195-213.

Hook, Sidney, "Charles Beard's Political Testament," Nation, CLVII (October 23, 1943), 474-476.

Josephson, Matthew, "Charles A. Beard: A Memoir," Virginia Quarterly Review, XXV (October, 1949), 585-602.

———, "The Hat on the Roll-Top Desk," New Yorker, XVII (February 14, 1942), 24-28; XVIII (February 21, 1942), 21-28.

Kallen, Horace M., "In Remembrance of Charles Beard, Philosopher-Historian," Social Research, XVIII (June, 1951), 243-249.

Kraus, Michael, A History of American History (Farrar and Rinehart, 1937), 461-466.

———, The Writing of American History (Norman, University of Oklahoma Press, 1953), 173-174, 366, 367-373, and passim.

Lamm, Lucian, and Feins, Daniel M., "Charles A. Beard," Social Education, V (April, 1941), 263-268.

Lerner, Max, "Beard's 'Economic Interpretation,'" New Republic, XCIX (May 10, 1939), 7-11.

———, "Charles Beard: Civilization and the Devils," New Republic, CXIX (November 1, 1948), 21-24.

———, "Charles Beard Confronts Himself," Nation, CXLII (April 8, 1936), 452-454.

———, "Charles Beard's Stormy Voyage," New Republic, CXIX (October 25, 1948), 20-23.

———, Ideas Are Weapons: The History and Uses of Ideas (Viking, 1940), 152-173, 432-435, and passim.

———, "The Political Theory of Charles A. Beard," American Quarterly, II (Winter, 1950), 303-321.

Levin, Peter R., "Charles A. Beard: Wayward Liberal," Tomorrow, VIII (March, 1949), 36-40.

Macmahon, Arthur W., "Charles Austin Beard as a Teacher," Political Science Quarterly, LXV (March, 1950), 1-19.

Miller, Perry, "Charles A. Beard," Nation, CLXVII (September 25, 1948), 344-346.

Morison, Samuel Eliot, "Did Roosevelt Start the War? History through a Beard," Atlantic Monthly, CLXXXII (August, 1948), 91-97.

Phillips, Harlan B., "Charles Beard: The English Lectures, 1899-1901," Journal of the History of Ideas, XIV (June, 1953), 451-456.

———, "Charles Beard, Walter Vrooman, and the Founding of Ruskin Hall," South Atlantic Quarterly, L (April, 1951), 186-191.

Pixton, John E., Jr., "The Ghost of Charles Beard," Christian Century, LXIX (October 1, 1952), 1120-1122.

Reed, John J., "Economic Interpretation of the Constitution," Social Studies, XXXIV (January, 1943), 23-28.

Smith, Theodore C., "The Writing of American History in America, from 1884 to 1934," American Historical Review, XL (April, 1935), 439-449.

Thomas, Robert E., "A Reappraisal of Charles A. Beard's Economic Interpretation of the Constitution of the United States," American Historical Review, LVII (January, 1952), 370-375.

———, "The Virginia Convention of 1788: A Criticism of Beard's *An Economic Interpretation of the Constitution*," *Journal of Southern History*, XIX (February, 1953), 63-72.

Villard, Oswald G., "Charles A. Beard, Patriot," *Progressive*, XII (October, 1948), 21-22.

Ware, Alexander, "The Beards, Chroniclers of Time," *Christian Science Monitor Magazine*, July 22, 1939.

Whitaker, Arthur Preston, "Charles Austin Beard," *Revista de historia America*, no. 26 (December, 1948), 419-423.

White, Morton G., *Social Thought in America: The Revolt against Formalism* (Viking, 1949), 32-46, 107-127, 220-235, and *passim*.

Who's Who in This Volume

HOWARD K. BEALE, Ph.B. in 1921 at the University of Chicago and A.M. in 1922 and Ph.D. in 1927 at Harvard University, is professor of history at the University of Wisconsin. He is author of *The Critical Year—A Study of Andrew Johnson and Reconstruction*, 1930; *Are American Teachers Free? An Analysis of Restraints upon the Freedom of Teaching in American Schools*, 1936; *Educational Freedom and Democracy* (with H. B. Alberty and B. H. Bode), 1938; *A History of Freedom of Teaching in American Schools*, 1941. He edited *The Diary of Edward Bates*, 1933. While he was writing two books for the Commission on Social Studies in the Schools he had frequent contacts with Beard at the meetings of that Commission, of which Beard was a leading member. Beard read and criticized the two manuscripts prepared for the Commission and a third one prepared for the Committee on Historiography of the Social Science Research Council, of which Beard was a member.

GEORGE S. COUNTS, A.B. at Baker University in 1911, Ph.D. at the University of Chicago in 1916, and honorary LL.D. at Baker University in 1935, is professor of education at Teachers College of Columbia University, where he has taught since 1927. He is author of *Arithmetic Tests and Studies in the Psychology of Arithmetic*, 1917; *The Selective Character of American Secondary Education*, 1922; *Principles of Education* (with J. C. Chapman), 1924; *The Senior High School Curriculum*, 1926; *The Social Composition of Boards of Education*, 1927; *School and Society in Chicago*, 1928; *Secondary Education and Industrialism*, 1929; *The American Road to Culture*, 1930; *A Ford Crosses Soviet Russia*, 1930; *The Soviet Challenge to America*, 1931; *Dare the School Build a New Social Order?* 1932; *The Social Foundations of Education*, 1934; *The Prospects of American Democracy*, 1938; *The Schools Can Teach Democracy*, 1939; *The Education of Free Men* (for the Educational Policies Commission), 1941; *America, Russia, and the Communist Party* (with John L. Childs), 1942; *Education and the Promise of America* (Kappa Delta Pi lecture), 1945; *The Country of the Blind—The Soviet System of Mind Control* (with Nuncia Lodge), 1949; *American Education through the Soviet Looking Glass*, 1951; *Education and American Civilization*, 1952. In 1947 he translated *New Russia's Primer* by M. Ilin under the title *I Want to Be like Stalin*. He was editor of the *Social Frontier*, 1934-1937, a member of the Educational Policies Commission of the National Education Association, 1936-1942, and president of the American Federation of Teachers, 1939-1942. He has worked with Beard in various committees on educational policies and the problem of civil liberties. From 1929 to 1934 he served with Beard on the Commission on Social Studies in the Schools of the American Historical Association, and he and Beard were members of the small committee that drafted the *Conclusions and Recommendations* of that Commission. Long a close personal friend, he visited frequently in the Beard home.

EDMUND DAVID CRONON, A.B. at Oberlin College in 1948 and A.M. in 1949 and Ph.D. at the University of Wisconsin in 1953, Fulbright fellow at the University of Manchester, 1950-1951, University fellow at the University of Wisconsin, 1952-1953, and instructor in history at Yale University since 1953, is the author of *Marcus Garvey and the Universal Negro Improvement Association* (in press) and a Ph.D. dissertation, "Good Neighbor Ambassador: Josephus Daniels in Mexico."

MERLE CURTI, A.B. *summa cum laude* in 1920, A.M. in 1921, and Ph.D. in 1927, all at Harvard University, is Frederick Jackson Turner professor of history at the University of Wisconsin, where he has taught since 1942. He is author of *Austria and the United States, 1848-1852*, 1926; *The American Peace Crusade*, 1929; *Bryan and World Peace*, 1931; *Social Ideas of American Educators*, 1934; *Peace or War—The American Struggle, 1636-1936*, 1936; *The Learned Blacksmith: The Letters and Journals of Elihu Burritt*, 1937; *American Issues* (with Willard Thorp and Carlos Baker), 1941; *The Growth of American Thought* (Pulitzer Award), 1943; *Roots of American Loyalty*, 1946; and *A History of the University of Wisconsin* (with Vernon Carstensen), 1949. He edited *Theory and Practice in Historical Method*, the report of the Committee on Historiography that appeared as Bulletin 54 of the Social Science Research Council. He was visiting professor to Indian universities on the Watumull Foundation in 1946-1947. He has served on the council of the American Historical Association, 1937-1942, and as vice-president, 1952-1953. In the Mississippi Valley Historical Association he has served on the board of editors, 1938-1941, as vice-president, 1950-1951, and as president, 1951-1952. He has also been on the board of advisers of the American Council of Learned Societies, a member of the Social Science Research Council, vice-president of the American Studies Association, 1951-1952, and a senator of Phi Beta Kappa. While he was writing one of the volumes for the Commission on Social Studies he attended its meetings and saw much of Beard. Later Curti was chairman of the Committee on Historiography of the Social Science Research Council, of which Beard was an actively participating member. For two decades a personal friend of Beard, Curti has been an occasional guest at New Milford.

JACK FROOMAN, S.B. at the University of Illinois in 1948 and S.M. in 1949 and M.S.L.S. in 1952, both at the University of Wisconsin, is reference librarian in the John McIntire Public Library, Zanesville, Ohio. He is a former teacher in the Chicago public schools and is the author of an unpublished thesis, "The Wisconsin Peace Movement, 1915-1919."

ERIC F. GOLDMAN, A.B. in 1934, A.M. in 1935, Ph.D. in 1938 at the Johns Hopkins University, sometime contributing editor of *Time Magazine*, is associate professor of history at Princeton University where he has taught since 1943. He is author of *John Bach McMaster*, 1943; *Charles J. Bonaparte*, 1943; *Two Way Street: The Emergence of the Public Relations Counsel*, 1948; and *Rendezvous with Destiny: A History of Modern American Reform,* 1952. In 1941 he edited *Historiography and Urbanization: Essays in American History in Honor of W. Stull Holt,* and since 1948 has been social science book editor of the *Key Reporter.* In 1953 he was awarded the Frederick Bancroft Prize in American history. Goldman was an intimate friend of Beard from 1940 until Beard's death. For 1953-1954 he is visiting professor at the University of Vienna.

LUTHER H. GULICK, A.B. in 1914, A.M. in 1915, and Litt.D. in 1939, all at Oberlin College, Ph.D. in 1920 at Columbia University, and LL.D. at Whitman College in 1952, is president of the Institute of Public Administration in New York City. He is author of *Evolution of the Budget in Massachusetts,* 1920; *Modern Government in a Colonial City,* 1922; *The National Institute of Public Administration: a Progressive Report,* 1928; *An Adventure in Democracy,* 1928; *Notes on the Theory of Organization,* 1937; *Science, Values, and Public Administration,* 1937; *Administrative Reflections from World War II,* 1948; *American Forest Policy,* 1952. He is coauthor of *Municipal Finance,* 1926; *Better Government Personnel,* 1935; *Report of the President's Committee on Administrative Management,* 1937; *The New York Primer,* 1939; *Federal-State-Local Government Fiscal Relations,* 1943; and *After Defense, What?* 1941. He has edited *Papers on the Science of Administration,* 1937, and *Improved Personnel in Government Service,* 1937. He has served as president of the American Political Science Association, on the Council of the American Society for Public Administration, on the board of trustees of the National Planning Association, as chairman of the Public Affairs Committee, as a member of the National Management Council, as executive director of the Mayor's Committee on Management Survey of the City of New York, and on numerous international, federal, state, and local committees dealing with problems of public administration. He was a friend of Beard for thirty-five years. From 1915 to 1917 he was a student of Beard's at Columbia University. Then he was a member of Beard's staff at the New York Bureau of Municipal Research and at the Training School for Public Service. Ultimately he succeeded Beard as director of both institutions.

WALTON H. HAMILTON, A.B. at the University of Texas in 1907, Ph.D. at the University of Michigan in 1913, and honorary A.M. at Yale University in 1928, professor emeritus of the Yale University Law School, where he taught from 1928 to 1948, is now practicing law in Washington, D. C. He is author of *Current Economic Problems,* 1915; *The Control of Wages* (with Stacy May), 1923; *The Case of Bituminous Coal* (with Helen R. Wright), 1925; *A Way of Order for Bituminous Coal* (with Helen R. Wright), 1928; *The Power to Govern: The Constitution Then and Now* (with Douglass Adair), 1937; *Price and Price Policies,* 1938; *The Pattern of Competition,* 1940; *Anti-Trust, in Action* (with Irene Till) (United States Temporary National Economic Committee, *Monograph,* no. 16), 1940; *Patents and Free Enterprise,* 1941. He has served as a member of the National Recovery Administration Board, 1934-1935, as delegate to the International Labor Office Conference in Geneva, 1935, and as special assistant to the attorney general, 1938-1945.

RICHARD HOFSTADTER, A.B. at the University of Buffalo in 1937 and A.M. in 1938 and Ph.D. in 1942, both at Columbia University, is professor of history at Columbia University, where he has taught since 1946. He is author of *Social Darwinism in American Thought, 1860-1915,* 1945, and *The American Political Tradition,* 1948.

HAROLD J. LASKI, a graduate of Oxford University in 1914 and lecturer at Harvard University, 1916-1920, was professor of political science at the London School of Economics from 1920 until his death in March, 1950. He is author of *Authority in the Modern State*, 1919; *Political Thought in England from Locke to Bentham*, 1920; *The Foundations of Sovereignty and Other Essays*, 1921; *Karl Marx*, 1922; *A Grammar of Politics*, 1925; *Communism*, 1927; *The Dangers of Obedience and Other Essays*, 1930; *Liberty in the Modern State*, 1930; *The Socialist Tradition in the French Revolution*, 1930; *An Introduction to Politics*, 1931; *Studies in Law and Politics*, 1932; *Democracy in Crisis*, 1933; *The State in Theory and Practice*, 1935; *The Rise of European Liberalism*, 1936; *Parliamentary Government in England*, 1938; *The Danger of Being a Gentleman and Other Essays*, 1939; *The American Presidency*, 1940; *Where Do We Go from Here?* 1940; *Reflections on the Revolution of Our Time*, 1943; *Faith, Reason, and Civilization*, 1944; and *The American Democracy*, 1948. He has played an active role in the British Labour Party and has frequently made lecture tours to America. He first became acquainted with Beard thirty-five years ago and from 1919 to 1920 he was a colleague of Beard's at the New School for Social Research.

GEORGE R. LEIGHTON, who attended Phillips Exeter Academy, 1919-1921, and Harvard University, 1922-1926, is a member of the staff of the Republican Policy Committee of the United States Senate. From 1932 to 1944 he was one of the editors of *Harper's Magazine*. He is the author of *Five Cities*, 1939, and *The Wind That Swept Mexico* (with Anita Brenner), 1943. He has written extensively for periodicals. Leighton and Beard became friends when Leighton persuaded Beard to do an article for *Harper's* in 1932. Thereafter they had frequent contacts, especially while Beard was working on "Giddy Minds and Foreign Quarrels" for *Harper's* in 1939.

MAX LERNER, A.B. at Yale in 1923, A.M. at Washington University of St. Louis in 1925, Ph.D. at Robert Brookings Graduate School of Economics and Government in 1927, has been professor of American civilization at Brandeis University since 1949. He has taught at Sarah Lawrence College, 1932-1935, Harvard University, 1935-1936, and Williams College, 1938-1943. He has been editor of the *Encyclopaedia of the Social Sciences*, of the *Nation*, 1936-1938, and of *P.M.*, 1943-1948, and is now a columnist on the *New York Post*. He is author of *It Is Later Than You Think*, 1938; *Ideas Are Weapons*, 1939; *Ideas for the Ice Age*, 1941; *The Mind and Faith of Justice Holmes*, 1943; *Public Journal*, 1945; and *Actions and Passions: Notes on the Multiple Revolution of Our Time*, 1949.

ARTHUR W. MACMAHON, A.B. in 1912, A.M. in 1913, and Ph.D. in 1923, all at Columbia University, is Eaton professor of public administration at Columbia University, where he has taught since 1913. He is author of *Statutory Sources of New York City Government*, 1923; *Department Management*, 1937; *The Postwar International Information Program of the United States*, 1945; and coauthor of *Federal Administrators*, 1939, and *Administration of Federal Work Relief*, 1941. He was editor of the New York Charter Revision Commission, 1921-1923, counselor in the United States Department of State, 1943-1945, a member of the President's Loyalty Review Board, 1947-1950, and president of the American Political Science Association, 1947. He first knew Beard as volunteer coach of the Columbia debating team, when he was an undergraduate on the squad, 1908-1912. Then Macmahon as a young instructor worked with Beard daily as his assistant from 1913 to 1917. In 1916-1917 he worked on several projects under Beard's direction at the New York Bureau of Municipal Research. In the 1920's he helped Beard revise his general text in American government and in 1947 as president of that Association arranged Beard's final appearance before the American Political Science Association. Macmahon knew Beard therefore for forty-one years and was his close friend for thirty-six.

GEORGE SOULE, A.B. at Yale University in 1908, is professor of economics at Bennington College and has been professor of economics at Columbia University summer session, 1949-1952. From 1924 to 1947 he was an editor of the *New Republic*, to which Beard was a frequent contributor. Since 1922 he has been a director at large of the National Bureau of Economic Research. Soule is author of *A Planned Society*, 1934; *The Coming American Revolution*, 1935; *The Strength of Nations*, 1942; *Prosperity Decade*, 1947; *Introduction to Economic Science*, 1948; *Economic Forces in American History*, 1952; and *Ideas of the Great Historians*, 1952. Soule knew Beard from the time of World War I, lived near him in Connecticut, and frequently discussed public opinion questions with him.

Notes

REFERENCES to works by Charles A. Beard are given in greatly shortened form. Full listings may be found in the bibliography.

CHARLES BEARD: AN ENGLISH VIEW

1 *The Office of Justice of the Peace in England, in Its Origin and Development.*

2 J. Franklin Jameson, *The American Revolution Considered as a Social Movement* (Princeton, Princeton U. Press, 1926).

3 Vernon L. Parrington, *Main Currents in American Thought: An Interpretation of American Literature from the Beginnings to 1920*, 3 vols. (New York, Harcourt, Brace, 1927-1930).

4 Arthur M. Schlesinger, *The Colonial Merchants and the American Revolution, 1763-1776* (New York, Columbia U. Press, 1918).

5 Clarence W. Alvord, *The Mississippi Valley in British Politics*, 2 vols. (Cleveland, Arthur H. Clark, 1917).

6 James Ford Rhodes, *History of the United States from the Compromise of 1850 to the Final Restoration of Home Rule at the South in 1877*, 7 vols. (New York, Macmillan, 1892-1906).

7 *An Economic Interpretation of the Constitution of the United States*, 13.

8 *Ibid.*, 324.

9 *Economic Origins of Jeffersonian Democracy*, 3-4, 467.

10 I may, perhaps, venture to say that the two later volumes in the series, *America in Midpassage* (1939) and *The American Spirit* (1942), seem to me of far less value than their predecessors. The Beards' view of the Civil War is criticised with great learning, though not, I think, with success, by Professor Allan Nevins in his illuminating *Ordeal of the Union*, 2 vols. (New York, Scribners, 1947).

11 *The Republic*, 115.

12 *Ibid.*, 246, 252, 260.

13 *Ibid.*, 239.

14 *The Open Door at Home*, 15.

15 *The Republic*, 340.

16 *Ibid.*, 341.

17 *Loc. cit.*

18 *Ibid.*, 342.
19 *Ibid.*, 343.

CHARLES BEARD'S POLITICAL THEORY

1 The essay written originally for this volume has been published in the *American Quarterly*, II (Winter, 1950), 303-321. The editor is greatly indebted to the *American Quarterly* and the University of Pennsylvania for permission to republish.

2 *An Economic Interpretation of the Constitution of the United States*, 3.

3 *The American Spirit*, 347-354.

4 Introduction to John P. Frank, *Mr. Justice Black*, vii-ix.

5 *American Political Science Review*, XXVI (February, 1932), 28-44.

6 John W. Burgess, *Political Science and Comparative Constitutional Law* (Boston, Ginn, 1890), I, 46.

7 *Politics*, 6.

8 *Ibid.*, 11.

9 *Ibid.*, 24.

10 *An Economic Interpretation of the Constitution*, 7.

11 *The American Spirit*, 360-364.

12 *An Economic Interpretation of the Constitution*, 15-16.

13 *Politics*, 24.

14 *Untimely Papers* (New York, B. W. Huebsch, 1919), 140-230.

15 *The Economic Basis of Politics* (1945 ed.), 28.

16 *Ibid.*, 46-49.

17 *Ibid.*, 49-54.

18 *Ibid.*, 56-57.

19 *Ibid.*, 44-47.

20 *An Economic Interpretation of the Constitution*, 8, n. 1.

21 *Loc. cit.*

22 *The Economic Basis of Politics* (1945 ed.), 60.

23 *Whither Mankind*, 1-24.

24 *Toward Civilization*, 297-307.

25 *The Rise of American Civilization*, II, 800.

BEARD AND MUNICIPAL REFORM

1 *The Traction Crisis in New York*, 27.

2 Including Arthur E. Buck, George Carrington, John M. Gaus, John H. Johnson, Morris B. Lambie, Richard MacKenzie, Anne Page, Sedley H. Phinney, Renée Seligman, Paul Studensky, and Channing E. Sweitzer.

3 See *Report of Reconstruction Commission to Governor Alfred E. Smith on Retrenchment and Reorganization in the State Government, October 10, 1919*, 4-5.

4 *Ibid.*, 12.

5 *The Administration and Politics of Tokyo*, 19.

6 *Ibid.*, 23-25.

7 "The Role of Administration in Government," *The Work Unit in Federal Administration*, 3.

8 "It Is Not True," *In Review*, 3-4.

BEARD AND THE CONCEPT OF PLANNING

1 *Harper's Magazine*, CLXIV (December, 1931), 22.

2 *America Faces the Future*, 403.

CHARLES BEARD AND THE CONSTITUTION

1 The essay written originally for this volume has been published in the *American Quarterly*, II (Fall, 1950), 195-213. The editor is greatly indebted to the *American Quarterly* and the University of Pennsylvania for permission to republish.

2 On this see Maurice Blinkoff, *The Influence of Charles A. Beard upon American Historiography* (*University of Buffalo Studies*, XII [May, 1936]), 16ff; Max Lerner, *Ideas Are Weapons* (New York, Viking Press, 1939), 152-169.

3 In the ablest of the critical reviews written at the time of publication, for example, Professor Edward S. Corwin accused Beard of being "bent on demonstrating the truth of socialistic theory of economic determinism and class struggle." *History Teacher's Magazine*, V (February, 1914), 65-66. Twenty years later Professor Corwin was writing that the Constitutional Convention "never for a moment relinquished the intention which it cherished from the outset of utilizing the new system for the purpose of throwing special safeguards about proprietarian interests." *The Twilight of the Supreme Court* (New Haven, Yale U. Press, 1934), 53. See also Corwin's brilliant article, "The Constitution as Instrument and as Symbol," *American Political Science Review*, XXX (December, 1936), 1071-1085, but especially 1072.

4 See John Fiske in *The Critical Period of American History* (Boston, Houghton Mifflin, 1897), 243; Alexander Johnston in his article on the Convention of 1787 in *Lalor's Cyclopedia of Political Science* (New York, Rand, McNally, 1882), I, 638. Woodrow Wilson had pointed out that the Constitution's "plan and structure . . . had been meant to check the sweep and power of popular majorities. . . . The government had, in fact, been originated and organized upon the initiative and primarily in the interest of the mercantile and wealthy classes . . . it had been urged to adoption by a minority under the concerted and aggressive leadership of able men representing a ruling class . . . the pressure of a strong and intelligent class, possessed of unity and informed by a conscious solidarity of material interests." *Division and Reunion* (New York, Longmans, 1893), 12-13. Henry Jones Ford's *The Rise and Growth of American Politics* (New York, Macmillan, 1898), 59, opened its chapter on the Constitution with these words: "The constitutional history of the United States begins with the establishment of the government of the masses by the classes." William Graham Sumner took a similar view in an essay written in 1896 or 1897. See *Essays* (New Haven, Yale U. Press, 1934), II, 340ff, especially 349-350.

5 In the *Annual Report of the American Historical Association for the Year 1900* (Washington, Government Printing Office, 1901), I, 237-463.

6 Chicago, U. of Chicago Press, 1910.

7 Frederick J. Turner in Orin G. Libby, *Geographical Distribution of the Vote* (Madison, U. of Wisconsin Press, 1894), iii, vii.

8 *Ibid.*, 2, 49, 50, 69; see also *ibid.*, 51-52.

9 Introduction to J. Allen Smith, *Growth and Decadence of Constitutional Government* (New York, Holt, 1930), xi.

10 J. A. Smith, *The Spirit of American Government* (New York, Macmillan, 1907), chap. III, especially pp. 29-32.

11 On this movement see Morton G. White, *American Social Thought* (New York, Viking Press, 1949), especially chap. II.

12 This is not a comprehensive inquiry into the sources of Beard's thought; any such undertaking would also note in this connection the influence of such foreign scholars as Frederick W. Maitland, Rudolf von Jhering, Anton Menger, and Rudolf Stammler. See *An Economic Interpretation of the Constitution*, 8-9.

13 *Politics*, 6.

14 Roscoe Pound, "Law in Books and Law in Action," *American Law Review*, XLIV (January, 1910), 21, 34.

15 R. Pound, "Mechanical Jurisprudence," *Columbia Law Review*, VIII (December, 1908), 609-610. See also Pound, "The Need of a Sociological Jurisprudence," *Green Bag*, XIX (October, 1907), 607-615.

16 Frank J. Goodnow, *Social Reform and the Constitution* (New York, Macmillan, 1911), 3.

17 Arthur F. Bentley, *The Process of Government* (Chicago, U. of Chicago Press, 1908), 152, 244, 272, 295.

18 *Ibid.*, 135.

19 *Politics*, 12, 20.

20 See, for example, Theodore C. Smith, "The Writing of American History in America, from 1884 to 1934," *American Historical Review*, XL (April, 1935), 447-449, and Beard's answer, *ibid.*, XLI (October, 1935), 74-87.

21 Edwin R. A. Seligman, *The Economic Interpretation of History* (New York, Columbia U. Press, 1902), 86.

22 *An Economic Interpretation of the Constitution*, 15n.

23 E. R. A. Seligman, *The Economic Interpretation of History*, 166.

24 *An Economic Interpretation of the Constitution*, 6n.

25 Algie M. Simons, *Social Forces in American History* (New York, Macmillan, 1911), 92-96, especially 95-96. Gustavus Myers, *History of the Supreme Court of the United States* (Chicago, Charles H. Kerr, 1912), is somewhat more shrill. See chap. III, especially pp. 129-134.

26 In reconstructing the intellectual atmosphere in which Beard worked, I have drawn primarily on materials cited in *An Economic Interpretation of the Constitution*. The items cited here by Pound, Goodnow, Bentley, J. Allen Smith, Seligman, Simons, Myers, Schaper, Ambler, and Libby were all referred to in that work.

27 In a certain sense, this sort of systematic study, applied to an intellectual and literary elite rather than political leaders, can be traced at least as far back as Alphonse de Condolle, *Histoire des sciences et des savants depuis deux siècles* (Geneva, H. Georg, 1885), and Alfred Odin, *Genèse des grands hommes* (Paris, H. Wetter, 1895). These works were brought to the attention of Americans by Lester Ward in his *Applied Sociology* (Boston, Ginn, 1906). J. McKeen Cattell, who was at Columbia with Beard, applied a similar method in some early studies in *Science*, n.s. XXIV (December 7, 1906), 732-742, and XXXII (November 4, 1910), 633-648. Systematic studies have been made of professionals and intellectuals, educators and school boards, labor leaders and businessmen, as well as politicians and bureaucrats. I have not found a study of any body of *political* personnel that predates Beard's. Among early studies in this field the following are notable: Robert T. Nightingale, "The Personnel of the British Foreign Office and Diplomatic Service," *American Political Science Review*, XXIV (May, 1930), 310-331; Dale A. Hartman, "British and American Ambassadors: 1893-1930," *Economica*, XI (August, 1931), 328-341; and Harold J. Laski, "The Personnel of the British Cabinet, 1801-1924," *Studies in Law and Politics* (New Haven, Yale U. Press, 1932), chap. VIII. Among the best of the more recent applications of the technique to political personnel have been H. Dewey Anderson, "The Educational and Occupational Attainments of Our National Rulers," *Scientific Monthly*, XL (June, 1935), 511-518; Simon Haxey (pseud.), *England's Money Lords: Tory M.P.* (New York, Harrison, Hilton, 1939); Hans Gerth, "The Nazi Party: Its Leadership and Composition," *American Journal of Sociology*, XLV (January, 1940), 517-541; and Franz Neumann, *Behemoth* (New York,

Oxford U. Press., 1942), 365ff. Two challenging recent treatments of the American businessman that suggest similar possibilities for the politician are C. Wright Mills, "The American Business Elite: A Collective Portrait," *Journal of Economic History* (December, 1945), supplement V, 20-44, and William Miller, "American Historians and the Business Elite," *ibid.*, IX (November, 1949), 184-208. For an informal treatment of a political group, see George E. Mowry, "The California Progressive and His Rationale: A Study in Middle Class Politics," *Mississippi Valley Historical Review*, XXXVI (September, 1949), 239-250.

28 Lerner, *Ideas Are Weapons*, 161.

29 *An Economic Interpretation of the Constitution of the United States*, 149. See also *ibid.*, 188, where he describes the Constitution as "an economic document drawn with superb skill by men whose property interests were immediately at stake . . . [which] appealed directly and unerringly to identical interests in the country at large."

30 *Ibid.*, 24.

31 *Ibid.*, 73.

32 *Ibid.*, 151.

33 For Beard's experiences and ideas before 1913, see Bernard C. Borning, "The Political Philosophy of Young Charles A. Beard," *American Political Science Review*, XLIII (December, 1949), 1165-1178.

34 On this see Walter Lippmann, *Drift and Mastery* (New York, Mitchell Kennerley, 1914), especially chap. VIII.

35 "In the American metaphysic," Lionel Trilling observes, "reality is always material reality, hard, resistant, unformed, impenetrable, and unpleasant. And that mind alone felt to be trustworthy which most resembles this reality by most nearly reproducing the sensations it affords." *The Liberal Imagination* (New York, Viking Press, 1950), 13; cf. 4-5.

36 Counting authors rather than titles, Veblen, mentioned 16 times, came first, and Beard, mentioned 11 times, came second; they were followed by Dewey (10), Freud (9), Spengler and Whitehead (7 each), Lenin (6), I. A. Richards (6), and a scattering for others. Beard himself proposed the writings of Brooks Adams, Karl Mannheim's *Ideology and Utopia* (New York, Harcourt, Brace, 1936), and Benedetto Croce's *History: Its Theory and Practice* (New York, Harcourt, Brace, 1921). See Malcolm Cowley and Bernard Smith, eds., *Books That Changed Our Minds* (New York, Doubleday, 1940), 12, 19-20. When titles were counted, Parrington was referred to 5 times. There had been a similar triumph for Beard's thesis in the realm of college teaching. Of 42 college texts examined in 1936, 37 had substantially adopted Beard's position on the Constitution. See M. Blinkoff, *Influence of Charles A. Beard*, 21-36.

37 "Historiography and the Constitution," *The Constitution Reconsidered*, 159-166.

38 On the note of nationalism in the thirties, see Alfred Kazin, *On Native Grounds* (New York, Reynal, 1942), chap. XVI.

39 That Beard was acutely conscious of the historical context of his later thinking on the subject became clear in the chapter he added to his *The Economic Basis of Politics* (1922) on the occasion of its republication in 1945. There he indicated that the economic interpretation of politics, while representing an important note of realism in any social analysis, was far less adequate to the understanding of twentieth century conditions than it had been to nineteenth century industrialism, parliamentary democracy, the *pax Britannica*, and the relatively free market economy. Analyzing the implications of the New Deal at home and fascism and militarism abroad, Beard concluded that the growth

of state intervention in the modern economy had reached a point at which the "political man" is often in a position to give orders to the "economic man" rather than to take them from him. In the United States, for example, the New Deal had made basic economic interests dependent upon the political process to a degree that was significantly different from the conditions of the past. As a result of the rise of fascism and militarism, the "military man" had also entered into full competition with the "economic man" and the "political man" for power over the state. See *The Economic Basis of Politics* (1945 ed.), 71-114.

40 *The Republic*, 21.

41 *Ibid.*, 22-26.

42 Cf. *A Basic History of the United States*, 120, 126-127, 131-132, 136-137, and *The Rise of American Civilization* (1933 ed.), I, 310-311, 315-316, 332-333, 334-335.

CHARLES BEARD: HISTORIAN

1 "Almost the only work in economic interpretation," said Beard in 1913, "which has been done in the United States seems to have been inspired at the University of Wisconsin by Professor Turner, now of Harvard. Under the direction of this original scholar and thinker, the influence of the material circumstances of the frontier on American politics was first clearly pointed out. Under his direction also the most important single contribution to the interpretation of the movement for the federal Constitution was made." *An Economic Interpretation of the Constitution of the United States*, 5. In his classes Beard always emphasized Hildreth as an economic historian in whose footsteps he was following. William T. Hutchinson to H. K. B., March 12, 1949. To Professor Seligman, too, Beard acknowledged great indebtedness; in 1913 he quoted approvingly Seligman's statement: "To economic causes must be traced in the last instance those transformations in the structure of society which themselves condition the relations of social classes and the various manifestations of social life." *An Economic Interpretation*, 15.

2 *An Introduction to the English Historians*, 608.

3 *An Economic Interpretation of the Constitution*, 6, 17, 19. He insisted that in the framing of the Constitution as in the Norman conquest whatever benefits to society or other groups may have resulted, "the direct, impelling motive . . . was the economic advantages which the beneficiaries expected would accrue to themselves first, from their action." *Ibid.*, 17-18.

4 *The Economic Basis of Politics*, 62, 70.

5 *Ibid.*, 29-45.

6 *The Rise of American Civilization*, I, 122-188.

7 *Ibid.*, 201. See also *ibid.*, 202-203, 294, 296.

8 *Ibid.*, 306; *An Economic Interpretation of the Constitution*, 30-32, 40-41, 49-50.

9 *The Rise of American Civilization*, I, 325; *Economic Origins of Jeffersonian Democracy*, 464-465. See also *The Rise of American Civilization*, I, 309-314, 332-333.

10 *Economic Origins of Jeffersonian Democracy*, 466-467. See also *ibid.*, 131-149, 164-166; *The Rise of American Civilization*, I, 336-338, 349-350, 353-354, 378, 392-393.

11 *Economic Origins of Jeffersonian Democracy*, 432; *The Rise of American Civilization*, I, 420.

12 *The Rise of American Civilization*, I, 581-582.

13 *Ibid.*, I, 663-664, 668-669, 671.

14 *Ibid.*, II, 37-38; I, 710; II, 51.   See also *ibid.*, II, 4-6.

15 *Ibid.*, II, 53-54, 105-106.

16 *The American Party Battle.*

17 Richard Enmale, Editor's foreword in James S. Allen, *Reconstruction, The Battle for Democracy (1865-1876)* (New York, International Publishers, 1937), 10. Theodore Smith, on the other hand, charged Beard with undermining sound history with concepts that did originate with Marx.   Theodore C. Smith, "The Writing of American History in America, from 1884 to 1934," *American Historical Review*, XL (April, 1935), 447-449.

18 "That Noble Dream," *American Historical Review*, XLI (October, 1935), 85.

19 *An Economic Interpretation of the Constitution* (1935 ed.), xi.

20 *The American Spirit*, 532-533.

21 *An Introduction to the English Historians*, 623.

22 *The Rise of American Civilization*, I, 4-10, 581-582, 699.   See also *ibid.*, I, 695-703.

23 *An Economic Interpretation of the Constitution*, v, 73, 189.

24 William T. Hutchinson to Merle E. Curti, 1948.   On consulting his lecture notes of 1916 Hutchinson found he had paraphrased Beard as follows: "One effective propaganda method is the method of emphasis and exaggeration.   When I wrote my Economic Interpretation of the Constitution I gave exclusive emphasis to that approach, not because I believed that it was the only correct one, but because it was an important (perhaps the most important) and a neglected one.   But of course the fundamental method with life is that it seems impossible to have anything without having too much or too little of it."

25 *An Economic Interpretation of the Constitution* (1935 ed.), xvi.

26 "Historiography and the Constitution," *The Constitution Reconsidered*, 164.

27 *The Economic Basis of Politics* (1945 ed.), 75, 90-91.

28 *Ibid.*, 71-72, 103-114.

29 "Historiography and the Constitution," 163-164.

30 *Loc. cit.*

31 John Hay, MS. Diary, April 3, 1905.

32 For example, *An Economic Interpretation of the Constitution*, 13-16, 153-154.

33 "They did not assume," he pointed out, "that property . . . [has] no relation to the forms and functions of government or to the structure and operations of political parties.   Nor . . . that government is a mere matter of popular will. . . . On the contrary they recognized that the form of every government . . . is closely connected with the forms and distribution of wealth . . . that all fundamental actions of governments reflect and affect diverse interests in society and that such interests appear inexorably in every complex and civilized society." *America in Midpassage*, 926.

34 *An Economic Interpretation of the Constitution*, 153-154.

35 *The Rise of American Civilization*, I, 310.

36 *An Economic Interpretation of the Constitution* (1935 ed.), xvii.   See also *The Republic* and "What about the Constitution?" *Nation*, CXLII (April 1, 1936), 405-406.

37 Professor James R. Weaver at DePauw University.   See Merle E. Curti, "A Great Teacher's Teacher," *Social Education*, XIII (October, 1949), 266.

38 Beard to Frederick J. Turner, April 24, 1903, Department of History Archives, University of Wisconsin.

39 *An Introduction to the English Historians*, 185.

40 *The Development of Modern Europe*, I, 167; II, 30. See also *ibid.*, I, 157-183.

41 *The Rise of American Civilization*, I, 294; II, 258, 589; *America in Mid-*

passage, 507-508.   See also *The Rise of American Civilization,* I, 294-296, 306, 542; II, 258-259, 588-589.

42 Luther V. Hendricks, *James Harvey Robinson* (New York, King's Crown Press, 1946), 79-80.

43 James H. Robinson, "The Newer Ways of Historians," *American Historical Review,* XXXV (January, 1930), 250.

44 I have not tried to distinguish the contributions of Charles and of Mary Beard to their joint works, because no one knows the nature of their collaboration. Both Merle Curti and I have tried to persuade Mary Beard to enlighten us for the purposes of this volume, but she prefers not to discuss it. Hence, I have always spoken of the joint works as Charles Beard's, since he did accept even the parts he may not have initiated.

45 *The Rise of American Civilization,* I, 725-726.

46 "Historiography and the Constitution," 165.

47 *America in Midpassage,* 926.

48 *The Rise of American Civilization,* II, 254.

49 *America in Midpassage,* 250.

50 Introduction to John B. Bury, *The Idea of Progress* (1932 ed.), ix, xxxi-xxxvi.   For other examples see *The Rise of American Civilization,* I, 443-445, 748-752; II, 530-532.

51 *The Open Door at Home,* 19, 29-32.

52 *America in Midpassage,* 866; *The Nature of the Social Sciences,* 59-60; *The Open Door at Home,* 21-23.

53 *The American Party Battle,* 144; *The Rise of American Civilization,* II, 589.

54 For example, *The Devil Theory of War,* 16, 19-23, 29.

55 At the end of his life Beard wrote: "It is needless to point out to anyone given to precision in the use of language how elusive are such phrases as 'war was inevitable,' 'drawn into war,' 'compelled to take up arms,' 'forced into war,' and 'America has been wantonly attacked.' They connote a determinism of events for the United States, as if President Roosevelt was a mere agent of 'forces' beyond his initiation or control, not an active agent in a conjuncture of circumstances which he had helped to create by deliberate actions on his own part. Of course, it may be assumed that the whole world drama has been determined from the beginning of human time and that all men and women who have taken part in it have been mere actors, mere puppets speaking lines and acting roles assigned to them by fate or 'the nature of things.' If so, so-called human virtues of courage, prescience, wisdom, and moral resolve are to be reckoned as phantoms." *President Roosevelt and the Coming of the War, 1941,* 407, 575, 580-581, 598.

56 *Ibid.,* 575, 580-581, 598.

57 *The Idea of National Interest,* 311; *A Foreign Policy for America,* 9. See also *ibid.,* 11.

58 *America in Midpassage,* 453.   For other examples see *Economic Origins of Jeffersonian Democracy,* 432; *The Rise of American Civilization,* I, 392-393, 420; II, 709-710; *The Open Door at Home,* 112, 130; *America in Midpassage,* 381-383, 388-389, 393-399, 400, 420-422, 424, 453-455, 481-482; *The Idea of National Interest,* 28-29, 116-119, 124-126, 193-194, 330-331.

59 Indeed Beard believed that "few important aspects of domestic development fail to have some bearing upon foreign relations." Geographic conditions, "the store and use of natural resources," and even the manner of enacting and executing domestic legislation affect a nation's relationships abroad. *The Idea of National Interest,* 312, 357.

60 *An Introduction to the English Historians*, 623.
• 61 See, for example, *The Rise of American Civilization*, I, 391; II, 536-537, 709; *America in Midpassage*, 98, 382.

62 *A Foreign Policy for America*, 3.

63 *The Rise of American Civilization*, I, 402, 407.

64 "Written History as an Act of Faith," *American Historical Review*, XXXIX (January, 1934), 219.

65 Max Lerner, *Ideas Are Weapons* (New York, Viking Press, 1939), 170.

66 *The American Spirit*, 543-546.

67 On the other hand he conceded that "dependence on generalities, without reference to particulars, leads to idle speculation." In specializing, however, we must, he insisted, "keep constantly referring to the relations between the narrow field we lay out and the wider field of which it is in truth an inseparable part. . . . Both operations must be kept in mind." *The Nature of the Social Sciences*, 9.

68 Beard's final appeal was that political science be made "three-dimensional instead of superficial and abstract, by anchoring it and every part of it in the substance, concreteness, sweep, and thought of great history—a powerful corrective for the despotism of sentimental abstractions." "Neglected Aspects of Political Science," *American Political Science Review*, XLII (April, 1948), 221-222.

69 Introduction to Bury, *The Idea of Progress*, xi.

70 *The Nature of the Social Sciences*, 72.

71 Review of Maurice Mandelbaum, *The Problem of Historical Knowledge; The Open Door at Home*, 13; "Written History as an Act of Faith," 225.

72 "That Noble Dream," 87.

73 *Politics*, 14-15.

74 *Ibid.*, 30-32.

75 "Written History as an Act of Faith," 221, 225-227; *The Discussion of Human Affairs*, 85-87; *The Nature of the Social Sciences*, 5-7. See also *ibid.*, 37, 41, 47, 58-60; *The Open Door at Home*, 16-18, 24-26; *The American Spirit*, 336-338; *America in Midpassage*, 822-823, 832-834, 859; and *The Discussion of Human Affairs*, 46, 114-117.

76 "Written History as an Act of Faith," 226-227; *The Nature of the Social Sciences*, 59.

77 *The Discussion of Human Affairs*, 88; "Written History as an Act of Faith," 223. See also *ibid.*, 222-224; *The Nature of the Social Sciences*, 56-57.

78 At the end of his life Beard had arrived at an "operating theory" of history that was "ancient and simple." He saw in political affairs three probabilities: (1) "necessity or determinism," (2) "fortune, chance, contingency, conjuncture," and (3) "the living force of the human being" working "within the limits of necessity, struggling for some kind of self-expression." "Neglected Aspects of Political Science," 213-214. See also *The Discussion of Human Affairs*, 111-114.

79 *Politics*, 32; *The Discussion of Human Affairs*, 79; "Signed Footnote," *Theory and Practice in Historical Method*, 137.

80 *The Nature of the Social Sciences*, 5, 38-41, 50-52, 55-56, 58, 71-72; *The Discussion of Human Affairs*, 84-85, 101-103, 111-114, 123-124; *The Rise of American Civilization*, I, 191; "Written History as an Act of Faith," 220, 227; "That Noble Dream," 74-87; *An Economic Interpretation of the Constitution*, 2-4; *ibid.* (1935 ed.), xi-xii.

81 J. Montgomery Gambrill to Merle E. Curti, July 20, 1948.

82 *The Nature of the Social Sciences*, 16-17; "Written History as an Act of Faith," 227-228. See also "That Noble Dream," 74-87.

83 "Written History as an Act of Faith," 222.

84 *An Economic Interpretation of the Constitution,* 3.

85 "That Noble Dream," 74-87; *The Discussion of Human Affairs,* 33, 38, 40-41, 47-48, 53, 119-124; *The Nature of the Social Sciences,* 47, 50-52, 55-58, 62; "Historiography and the Constitution," 165-166; *America in Midpassage,* 913-914.

86 "Written History as an Act of Faith," 228.

87 *An Economic Interpretation of the Constitution* (1935 ed.), ix-xi; "That Noble Dream," 85-86.

88 *The Development of Modern Europe,* I, iv.

89 *Ibid.,* 1-2. See also *Politics,* 34-35; *America in Midpassage,* 914.

90 Sidney B. Fay, Review in the *American Historical Review,* XIV (October, 1908), 190.

91 *Politics,* 14-15. See also *ibid.,* 11-12.

92 *The Nature of the Social Sciences,* 42. See also *ibid.,* 61.

93 Max Lerner, *Ideas Are Weapons,* 163, 170.

94 *Ibid.,* 170.

95 M. E. Curti, "A Great Teacher's Teacher," *loc. cit.,* 263-266, 274.

96 Undated letters from Andrew Stephenson, professor of history, and James R. Weaver, professor of political science, DePauw University; letters of Frederick York Powell, Regius professor of history, Oriel College, Oxford, June 12, 1899, and Moses Coit Tylor, professor of history and political science, Cornell University, January 29, 1900, Department of History Archives, University of Wisconsin.

97 Beard somewhat modified the emphasis of his own earlier conception and might, of course, have changed the emphasis of his view concerning World War II. Furthermore, there have been those, a few of them prominent, who have never accepted the Beardian view. See, for example, Edward S. Corwin's review of *An Economic Interpretation* in *History Teacher's Magazine,* V (February, 1914), 65-66. Corwin presumably has not been converted to Beard's view here criticized, though he later praised *The Republic.* Fred Rodell of the Yale Law School in a review of the 1935 edition (*Yale Law Journal,* XLV [May, 1936], 1327) recognized this remnant of unconvinced opposition when he wrote, "That Charles Beard, reissuing after twenty-two years 'An Economic Interpretation of the Constitution . . .' should find it necessary to introduce the new volume with a patient defense of his work and his motives is a sorry comment on the tenor of American thinking about American history." Still, it remains true that Beard's view of 1913 has remained essentially unchanged, that he was bitterly and widely denounced when he based a book on it in 1913, and that the view then denounced has gained wide and reputable acceptance with the passage of years. Indeed, Professor Rodell said in 1936, "it is both ridiculous and tragic that Dr. Beard's penetrating analysis of the economic motives behind the Constitution is not required reading for every course in American history and every course in American constitutional law." *Loc. cit.*

98 For examples see *The Rise of American Civilization,* I, 391, 394, 420, 431-432; II, 536-537, 709-710; *America in Midpassage,* 98, 382; *Economic Origins of Jeffersonian Democracy,* 432; *The Idea of National Interest,* 311; *A Foreign Policy for America,* 9-11.

99 *The Rise of American Civilization,* II, 671.

100 Introduction to J. P. Frank, *Mr. Justice Black,* v-vi. Cf. this phrasing of the problem by Beard with Lincoln's statement of the same problem in his message to Congress in special session, July 4, 1861.

101 *America in Midpassage,* 948-949.

102 "Such doctrine as Beard's economic interpretation," Lerner declared, "quite apart from the initial shock it gave in 1913, could not help leaving a more con-

tinuing mark on American thought. Beard's book on the Constitution is one of those books that become a legend—which are more discussed than read and which are known more for their title than their analysis. But in a quarter-century its thesis has increasingly seeped into history writing." M. Lerner, *Ideas Are Weapons*, 157-163.

BEARD AND FOREIGN POLICY

1 *Universal Military Training: Hearings before the Committee on Armed Services United States Senate*, 80 Cong., 2 Sess., 1053.

2 Joseph Dorfman, *Thorstein Veblen and His America* (New York, Viking Press, 1934), 500.

3 *The Open Door at Home*, 197, 208.

4 "Giddy Minds and Foreign Quarrels," *Harper's Magazine*, CLXXIX (September, 1939), 338-339.

5 *Ibid.*, 340.

6 Hubert Herring, "Charles A. Beard, Free Lance among the Historians," *Harper's Magazine*, CLXXVIII (May, 1939), 652.

7 *America in Midpassage*, II, 936-938.

8 *The Idea of National Interest*, v-vii.

9 *The Open Door at Home*, 17.

10 *Ibid.*, 139.

11 *Ibid.*, 210, 212-213.

12 *Ibid.*, 223, 224.

13 *Ibid.*, 225, 226.

14 *Ibid.*, 273-274 (The italics are mine).

15 *Ibid.*, 318.

16 *Ibid.*, 317.

17 "National Politics and War," 70.

18 Cordell Hull, *Memoirs* (New York, Macmillan, 1948), I, 544-545.

19 *Ibid.*, 545.

20 Joseph Alsop and Robert Kintner, *Men around the President* (New York, Doubleday, Doran, 1939), 127.

21 *The Old Deal and the New*, 147.

22 *Ibid.*, 148-150.

23 "War—If, How and When?"

24 *American Foreign Policy in the Making, 1932-1940*, 182-183.

25 *Ibid.*, 183, 166, 175.

26 *A Charter for the Social Sciences*, 79-81.

27 *The Old Deal and the New*, 96-97.

28 *Congressional Record*, 76 Cong., 3 Sess., 12114, 12120.

29 *To Promote the Defense of the United States: Hearings before the Committee on Foreign Relations United States Senate, on Senate [Bill] 275*, 77 Cong., 1 Sess., 312.

30 Robert E. Sherwood, *Roosevelt and Hopkins: An Intimate History* (New York, Harper, 1948), 191, 201.

BEARD AS HISTORICAL CRITIC

1 Review of Andrew C. McLaughlin, *A Constitutional History of the United States*.

2 Review of Samuel Chugerman, *Lester F. Ward: The American Aristotle*. In another review Beard tells of his friendship with Mr. Justice Holmes. Review of Alfred Bingham, *Man's Estate*.

3 See also review of Carlton J. H. Hayes, *A Brief History of the Great War.* Beard commented satirically on Hayes' assertion that one of the results of the First World War was the waning of "materialism . . . while 'spiritualism' came to the fore." "The present reviewer," wrote Beard, "not being versed in theology, feels unable to enter into this domain, but he was not aware that the Ouija board had made any serious inroads upon excess profits since the war broke out."

4 Review of Arnold J. Toynbee, *A Study of History,* vols. IV-VI.

5 Most of Beard's early scholarly reviews were published in the *Political Science Quarterly.* Some, however, appeared in the *American Historical Review.*

6 See, for example, reviews of Julius Hatschek, *Englisches Staatsrecht;* Egon Zweig, *Die Lehre vom Pouvoir constituant;* and Léon Duguit, *Traité de droit constitutionnel.* Beard continued to review non-English books after the First World War. See, for example, reviews of Georges Batault, *La Guerre absolue;* Henri Welschinger, *L'Alliance franco-russe;* Friedrich Gundolf, *Anfänge deutscher Geschichtsschreibung;* and Alfred von Müller-Armack, *Entwicklungsgesetze des Kapitalismus.*

7 Beard reviewed many books on municipal affairs and the problems of local self-government for the *National Municipal Review.* See, for example, reviews of Oswald Ryan, *Municipal Freedom;* Raymond Unwin and Paul Waterhouse, *Old Towns and New Needs;* and Chester E. Rightor, *City Manager in Dayton.* For similar reviews in other journals, see, for example, reviews of Morris Llewellyn Cooke, *Our Cities Awake;* Luther H. Gulick, *The Evolution of the Budget in Massachusetts;* and Arthur Macmahon and John D. Millett, *Federal Administrators.* Examples of Beard's reviews of books on the problems of economic planning may be found in reviews of Harry F. Ward, *The New Social Order;* Stuart Chase, *Men and Machines;* Norman Angell, *From Chaos to Control;* and Rexford G. Tugwell, *Industrial Discipline and the Governmental Arts.*

8 See, for example, reviews of Sidney and Beatrice Webb, *The History of Liquor Licensing in England,* and Thomas Erskine May, *Constitutional History of England* in the *New Republic.*

9 In 1907, Beard criticized De Alva S. Alexander because he accepted "too implicitly Henry Adams' sweeping criticism of Clinton's civil service policy." Review of De Alva S. Alexander, *A Political History of the State of New York.*

10 "To tell again what an ordinary student of English history ought to know is certainly a work of supererogation even if it does meet some requirements of the doctoral dissertation," Beard wrote of the early chapters of Laurence Larson's *The King's Household in England before the Norman Conquest.* At the same time, he commented favorably on the latter chapters of the book because they rested on a study of rare manuscripts.

11 Commenting upon David K. Watson's *The Constitution of the United States,* Beard suggested that it "might have been of advantage . . . if Dr. Watson had given more time to analysis and critical comparison of the cases." See also review of John A. R. Marriott, *Second Chambers.*

12 In the period before 1910, for example, Beard was constantly pointing up the relationship of "pure" constitutional history to the broader implications of social and economic history. See, among others, review of Walter F. Dodd, *Modern Constitutions.*

13 Review of George B. Adams, *The Political History of England, 1066-1216.* Later that year, Beard criticized the limitations of narrow political history. "The legislation of the English Justinian [Edward I] is disposed of in some ten pages; the coming of the friars, the rise of the universities and the studies of Bacon

in thirteen pages. . . . It is fair to say, however, that the author is not responsible for this historical perspective but is executing the design of the editors." Review of Thomas F. Tout, *The Political History of England, 1216-1377.*

14 Review of Kirk Porter, *History of Suffrage in the United States.* Many years earlier Beard had written in a similar vein. Adolphus Ballard's *The Domesday Boroughs,* Beard wrote, is "a warning to hasty generalizers. It destroys some time-worn theories that have got as far afield as Fiske's *Civil Government."*

15 Review of A. C. McLaughlin, *The Courts, the Constitution and Parties.*

16 "It is now time," Beard wrote in 1906, "that scholars should be more precise in their terminology." Review of Thomas Hodgkin, *The Political History of England to 1066.*

17 "The philosophic calm of the authors who write fairly and wisely about Napoleon," Beard complained, "is apparently disturbed beyond measure by democratic agitation, Irish demands, and labor movements. Surely, it is not bigotry in a reader to hope that the time was past for writing about 'the bloodthirsty orgies of the French Revolution ushered in by quixotic visions of liberty, equality, and fraternity.' " Review of George Broderick and John K. Frotheringham, *The Political History of England, 1801-1837.*

18 Review of A. J. Toynbee, *A Study of History,* vols. IV-VI.

19 Beard's distaste for academic "dullness" was also reflected in outspoken criticism of textbooks. "The textbook evil," he wrote in 1927, "is the great American academic disease. . . . We insist on giving our students black-letter aids for imbeciles until they reach the age of 30 and receive their doctorates. It is worse than a disease; it is a crime, an offense against style, intelligence, spiritual vigor. As a result, we turn out a great army of 'educated' persons who have never read a book, have merely tried to chew dessicated hay packed between sign-posts. . . . This is no criticism of Mr. [Harry] Laidler. It is a round, general damnation of pedants, among whom the present reviewer must be reckoned as one." Review of Harry W. Laidler, *History of Socialist Thought.*

20 Review of Edward Channing, *A History of the United States,* vol. VI.

21 Review of Leonard D. White, ed., *Essays in Honor of Charles E. Merriam.*

22 See, for example, reviews of G. B. Adams, *The Political History of England, 1066-1216;* J. Hatschek, *Englisches Staatsrecht;* and Arthur F. Bentley, *The Process of Government.*

23 "Many scholars," Beard wrote, "hold with the late Professor York Powell that the formation and expression of ethical judgments do not fall within the historian's province. Historians will differ, according to their class or personal prejudices, in their distribution of praise or blame." Review of Jean Jaurès, *Histoire socialiste jusqu'au 9 thermidor,* and Gabriel Deville, *Histoire socialiste du 9 thermidor au 18 brumaire.*

24 Review of Robert Michels, *Political Parties.* "This is no place to argue with Dr. Michels," Beard wrote. "Moreover pessimism is a matter of temperament, not of philosophy."

25 The report, Beard insisted, reflected "the coming crisis in the empirical method to which American social science has long been in bondage." Concluding his discussion, Beard remarked: "If the Committee had limited its inquiry to social trends which can be treated as genuinely deterministic sequences, and its conclusions to matters of 'strict scientific determination,' the report could probably have been put into the President's vest pocket." Review of the President's Research Committee on Social Trends, *Recent Social Trends in the United States.*

26 Thus, *as early as 1906,* Beard was criticizing prevailing schools of constitutional history and offering an alternative approach. Commenting on a point made by George B. Adams, Beard noted: "This is unhistorical because it ignores the actual course in the development of the law, and, after all, the law is in final analysis the embodiment of concrete interests. . . . Concrete interests arise with the changing forms of economic and social life however they may be in the garb of 'precedent' or 'constitutional' or 'natural law.' . . . The 'right' of the English people to coerce their sovereigns is in reality nothing more than the 'right' which all people have to assert and realize their interest—that is the 'right' of desire, determination, and might. This, however, is theory." Review of G. B. Adams, *The Political History of England, 1066-1216.*

27 Hatschek, Beard complained, was in error when he suggested that the English regarded politics "as a sport—engaged in for the joy of doing rather than the attainment of a goal." "This comparison may be justified in recent times," he wrote, "but it is not true historically." Review of J. Hatschek, *Englisches Staatsrecht.*

28 Review of Paul Vinogradoff, *The Growth of the Manor.*

29 Reviews of Paul Eyschen, *Das Staatsrecht des Grossherzogtums Luxemburg;* Paul Laband, *Deutsches Reichsstaatsrecht;* André Lebon, *Das Verfassungrsrecht der französischen Republik;* and Josef Ulbrich, *Das österreichische Staatsrecht.*

30 Because of Stimson's acceptance of "anarchical jurisprudence," Beard indicated, "we find the sugar trust and Magna Carta on the same page, and Rooseveltian centralization in close juxtaposition with the shire-moot." Beard's review of Stimson was devastating. His comments were replete with such phrases as "It is an error"; "There is no reason for believing"; "It is fantastic"; "It will be astounding to anyone"; etc.

31 Of Bentley, Beard wrote: "In every instance he has made effective use of the idea of 'group interests,' as distinguished from class interests in the Marxian sense. . . . He has undoubtedly written a thought-provoking book that will help to put politics on a basis of realism, where it belongs." See also Beard's noncritical review of J. Allen Smith, *The Spirit of American Government.*

32 "I should be interested to know how it happened," Beard wrote in October, 1920, "that men living in the ideal state portrayed by Mr. O'Brien ever came to choose Protestantism, the French Revolution, and our 'admitted diseased society.' After laborious days among manorial records, capitularies, charters, deeds, statutes, and court rolls, I am of the opinion that religion controlled economic life in the Middle Ages about as much as it did slavery in America, capitalism in France, communalism in old Russia, and syndicalism in Spain. . . . The treasurer of St. Mary's-in-the-Woods may cut the coupons from steel fives with the same sweet insouciance that gave seraphic rest to the bailiff of St. Thomas's-in-the-Fields as he collected beer and barley from the villeins." Review of George O'Brien, *An Essay on Medieval Economic Teaching.* Two months later, Beard wrote: "The idea of an ever-changing world, good and evil, war and peace, love and bitterness, all evolving together is painful to contemplate." Review of Arthur J. Penty, *A Guildsman's Interpretation of History.*

33 See, for example, review of S. and B. Webb, *A Constitution for the Socialist Commonwealth of Great Britain.* "The state," Beard warned the Webbs, "is not and never has been purely 'political'—whatever that may mean." That same week he asked in another review: "Are there not in Russia officers, armies, gaols, gallows, authorities, courts, and the power to compel obedience?" Review of Samuel G. Hobson, *National Guilds and the State.*

[34] Discussing Laski's "fatal" neglect of the relationship of economics to political philosophy, Beard whiplashed Laski's speculations: "Was not eighteenth century political philosophy intimately related with the interests and conduct of the Whigs and Tories? Were not the philosophers, so-called, spokesmen and defenders of the one or the other party? . . . Is this not well established? Will anyone conversant with English history deny it? If it is true then what has ethics, metaphysics, Freud, the psychology old or new, or any other emotional or intellectual coloration to offer that compares with it as a hypothesis of illumination? . . . Like most English liberals his genial narrative savors of the aroma of tea-cups rather than of the rough stuff of reality. Such things partly account for the magnificent impotence of historic liberalism. . . . Mr. Laski has written a conventional story, bolstered up English political mythology, and left the great muddle of so-called 'political thought' just about where he found it. This is to be regretted, for Mr. Laski is not a member of the grand union of annalists, compilers, and chroniclers." Review of Harold Laski, *Political Thought from Locke to Bentham*. See also the review of H. Laski, *The Foundations of Sovereignty and Other Essays*.

[35] See, for example, reviews of George E. G. Catlin, *The Science and Method of Politics;* Ramsay Muir, *How Britain Is Governed;* and Robert Brady, *Business as a System of Power*.

[36] Introduction to Brooks Adams, *The Law of Civilization and Decay* (1943 ed.).

[37] See, for example, review of Welschinger, *L'Alliance franco-russe*.

[38] "Slowly," Beard commented in 1922, "the official myth about the war and its origins is being dissolved by sunlight. . . . Every movement shakes the solid structure of the official thesis." *Ibid*. See also review of Harry Elmer Barnes, *The Genesis of the World War*.

[39] Beard discussed the effects of Wilson's wartime powers as early as 1921. "What becomes of democracy?" he asked. "It requires no very vivid imagination to discover where a series of wars and internal disturbances would lead us." Review of Charles G. Fenwick, *Political Systems in Transition*.

[40] Review of Carl L. Becker, *The United States*.

[41] Review of Frederick Jackson Turner, *The Frontier in American History;* "Culture and Agriculture," *Saturday Review of Literature*, V (October 20, 1928), 272-273; "The Frontier in American History," *New Republic*, XCIX (February 1, 1939), 359-362.

[42] Review of Arthur F. Bentley, *The Process of Government*. "Mr. Bentley's attempt to get below formalism into the governing process as a manifestation of social pressures," Beard wrote at this time, "deserves serious consideration."

[43] Review of F. J. Turner, *The Frontier in American History*.

[44] *Ibid.;* "Culture and Agriculture."

[45] "The Frontier in American History."

[46] Reviews of George Morgan, *James Monroe*, and J. Fred Rippy, *The United States and Mexico*.

[47] See also review of Shepard B. Clough and Herbert W. Schneider, *Making Fascists*.

[48] See also review of Stephen Rauschenbush, *The March of Fascism*.

[49] Review of Alfred von Müller-Armack, *Entwicklungsgesetze des Kapitalismus*.

[50] Review of Allan Nevins, *John D. Rockefeller*.

[51] Beard, however, qualified his enthusiasm over Morison's biography. "Otis," he wryly commented, "was destined to a well-earned oblivion until rescued by the laudable interest of a descendant. There could be no objection at all to

this rescue, if any new material of real importance were yielded on such matters as the Federalist negotiations over the election of Jefferson in 1801, or the true purpose and spirit of the Hartford Convention; but in these and other particulars, the student of history will be disappointed."

52 The relationship between the two men is illustrated in a letter of Beard to Beveridge on August 25 [1925] when Beard started a letter to his friend with, "Why the devil do you call me 'Hon.' I am no Hon. and you are no Japanese. Stop it."

53 Beard to Beveridge, August 25 [1925] and November 29, 1919, Albert J. Beveridge Papers, Library of Congress. All of the letters to Beveridge are in these Beveridge Papers. Beard discussed two of Beveridge's works with him: *The Life of John Marshall*, 4 vols. (New York, Houghton Mifflin, 1917), and *Abraham Lincoln, 1809-1855*, 2 vols. (New York, Houghton Mifflin, 1928).

54 Beard, New Milford, to Beveridge, September 17 [1924].

55 Beard, New York, to Beveridge, April 23 [1925].

56 Beard, New Milford, to Beveridge, December 25 [1925].

57 Beard, New Milford, to Beveridge, September 17 [1924].

58 Beard, New Milford, to Beveridge, August 25 [1925].

59 Beard, New Milford, to Beveridge, September 12, 1925.

60 *Loc. cit.*

61 Beard, New Milford, to Beveridge, August 25 [1925].

62 Beard, New Milford, to Beveridge, August 19 [1925].

63 Beard to Beveridge, October 3, 1925.

64 Beard, New York, to Beveridge, September 29, 1925.

65 Beard, New Milford, to Beveridge, March 13 [1926].

66 Beard, New Milford, to Beveridge, March 22, 1926.

67 Beard, New Milford, to Beveridge, April 3, 19 [1927].

68 Beard, New Milford, to Beveridge, August 14, 1926, and Beard, New York, to Beveridge, April 3 [1927]. See also Beard, New York, to Beveridge, March 13 [1926].

69 Beveridge to Beard, August 18, 1926.

70 *America in Midpassage*, 919.

71 *The Economic Basis of Politics* (1945 ed.), 3.

CHARLES BEARD, THE TEACHER

1 The essay written originally for this volume has been published in the *Political Science Quarterly*, LXV (March, 1950), 1-19. The editor is greatly indebted to the *Political Science Quarterly* for permission to republish.

2 At Amherst College in 1916, published as *The Economic Basis of Politics;* at Dartmouth College in 1922, published as *Cross Currents in Europe To-day*.

3 Preface.

4 George H. Palmer, *The Ideal Teacher* (Boston, Houghton Mifflin, 1910), 8, 25-26.

5 Charles Warren, "A Plea for Personality in Professors," *Harvard Graduates Magazine*, XXI (September, 1912), 53.

6 "Address on the Commemoration of the Fiftieth Anniversary of the Arrival of Louis Agassiz in the United States," quoted in *Great Teachers*, Houston Peterson, ed. (New Brunswick, Rutgers U. Press, 1946), 204.

7 Henry Adams, *The Education of Henry Adams* (Boston, Houghton Mifflin, 1918), 60.

8 *American Political Science Review*, XXI (February, 1927), 4.

[9] "Political Science," *Research in the Social Sciences*, 287.

[10] *Politics*, 9-10.

[11] "The Study and Teaching of Politics," *Columbia University Quarterly*, XII (June, 1910), 269.

[12] Alfred N. Whitehead, *The Aims of Education and Other Essays* (New York, Macmillan, 1929), 23.

[13] Oliver Elton, *Frederick York Powell: A Life and a Selection from His Letters and Occasional Writings* (Oxford, Clarendon Press, 1906), I, 314.

[14] *The Industrial Revolution*, 81.

[15] *Politics*, 10.

[16] Ernest Barker, *The Study of Political Science and Its Relation to Cognate Studies* (Cambridge [Eng.], University Press, 1928), 33.

[17] Roland H. Bainton, " 'Poppy' Burr," in *Great Teachers*, Houston Peterson, ed., 177.

[18] Irwin Edman, *Philosopher's Holiday* (New York, Viking Press, 1938), 130-131.

[19] "The Ideal Teacher," in *Unseen Harvests: A Treasury of Teaching*, Claude M. Fuess and Emory S. Basford, eds. (New York, Macmillan, 1947), 342.

[20] Sidney Hook, *Education for Modern Man* (New York, Dial Press, 1946), 192.

[21] "Political Science," 289-290.

[22] *Proceedings of the American Political Science Association*, X (1914), 258.

[23] "The Study and Teaching of Politics," 269.

[24] "United States," *Encyclopaedia of the Social Sciences* (New York, Macmillan, 1930), I, 330.

[25] Henry S. Canby, *Alma Mater: The Gothic Age of the American College* (New York, Farrar & Rinehart, 1936), 67.

[26] *Politics*, 24.

[27] Introduction to Charles G. Haines and Marshall E. Dimock, eds., *Essays on the Law and Practice of Governmental Administration*, vi.

[28] Dwight Waldo, *The Administrative State: A Study of the Political Theory of American Public Administration* (New York, Ronald Press, 1948), 37.

[29] *Philosophy, Science and Art of Public Administration*, 5.

[30] "Political Science," 291.

[31] Henry Adams, *The Education of Henry Adams*, 300.

CHARLES BEARD, THE PUBLIC MAN

[1] *President Roosevelt and the Coming of the War, 1941*, 577.

[2] *New York Herald Tribune*, April 30, 1935.

[3] Letter on resignation from Columbia University, *New Republic*, XIII (December 29, 1917), 249-250.

[4] *Ibid.*, 250. See also Matthew Josephson, "The Hat on the Roll-top Desk," *New Yorker*, XVII (February 14, 1942), 24-28; XVIII (February 21, 1942), 21-28.

[5] Beard to Nicholas Murray Butler, October 8, 1917, *New York American*, October 9, 1917, and *School and Society*, VI (October 13, 1917), 446-447.

[6] *Social Frontier*, I, no. 7 (April, 1935), 6. See also *ibid.*, 13-14.

[7] *Life*, XVI (March 20, 1944), 64.

BEARD'S HISTORICAL WRITINGS

[1] P. Unwin of George Allen and Unwin Ltd., London, to Howard K. Beale, April 8, 1949.

[2] *American Historical Review*, X (January, 1905), 440-441.

3 Edward P. Cheney, "The England of Our Forefathers," *ibid.*, XI (July, 1906), 772.

4 *Ibid.*, XIII (April, 1908), 445.

5 For the reviews by Sidney B. Fay see *ibid.*, XIV (October, 1908), 188-190; XIV (April, 1909), 639-640; XV (October, 1909), 196-197.

6 For example, Harry Elmer Barnes, "History and International Goodwill," *Nation*, CXIV (March 1, 1922), 251-254.

7 For example, Sidney B. Fay, "New Light on the Origins of the World War," *American Historical Review*, XXV (July, 1920), 616-639; XXVI (October, 1920), 37-53; XXVI (January, 1921), 225-254.

8 Sidney B. Fay to H. K. B., August 25, 1948. The review appeared in the *New York Herald Tribune*, "Books," November 11, 1928.

9 *The Constitution Reconsidered*, 159-166.

10 "Neglected Aspects of Political Science," *American Political Science Review*, XLII (April, 1948), 218-219.

11 "Who's to Write the History of the War?" *Saturday Evening Post*, CCXX (October 4, 1947), 172.

12 "Written History as an Act of Faith," *American Historical Review*, XXXIX (January, 1934), 219-231.

13 *Ibid.*, XLI (October, 1935), 74-87; Theodore C. Smith, "The Writing of American History in America, from 1884 to 1934," *ibid.*, XL (April, 1935), 439-449.

14 *Ibid.*, XLII (April, 1937), 460-483.

15 His *American Government and Politics*, first appearing in 1910 and most recently in 1949 posthumously in a tenth edition prepared with the help of his son, contains much historical material, but is not included here since it is primarily a study in government.

16 In some cases the publishers do not have records of the copies sold but of the copies printed. Since, however, the older books are nearly all of them out of print, this approximates the same figure.

17 SALES OF BEARD'S HISTORIES

I. European History

1. *The Industrial Revolution*		12,906
2. *The Office of Justice of the Peace*	Columbia U. edition	377
	English edition	1,000
3. *An Introduction to the English Historians*		5,014
4. *The Development of Modern Europe*, with James H. Robinson		
	Vol. I	78,600
	Vol. II	88,000
5. *Readings in Modern European History*, with James H. Robinson		
	Vol. I	33,000
	Vol. II	42,200
6. *Cross Currents in Europe To-day*		9,000
	Total	270,097

II. American History except Foreign Policy

1. *The Supreme Court and the Constitution*		
	Macmillan editions	2,432
	Facsimile Library edition	500
2. *An Economic Interpretation of the Constitution*		7,908
3. *Contemporary American History, 1877-1913*		13,009

4. *Economic Origins of Jeffersonian Democracy*		3,690
5. *The Economic Basis of Politics*	American edition	9,800
	English edition	657
	German edition	5,000
	Japanese edition	30,000
	Mexican edition	1,200
6. *The Rise of American Civilization,* with Mary R. Beard		
	regular edition	71,199[ab]
	Book-of-the-Month Club edition	62,000
7. *America in Midpassage,* with Mary R. Beard	regular edition	33,863[c]
	Book-of-the-Month Club edition	118,000
	German edition	5,000
8. *The American Spirit,* with Mary R. Beard		11,127[d]
9. *A Basic History of the United States,* with Mary R. Beard		
	regular edition	319,025[abd]
	Book-of-the-Month Club edition	321,000
	Swiss edition in German	9,000[e]
10. *The American Party Battle*		7,256
11. *The Republic*	American edition	183,106[b]
	Brazilian edition	461
	Japanese edition	30,000[d]
	Life edition	4,068,762
12. *The Presidents in American History*		17,000
	Total	5,330,995

III. History of American Foreign Policy

1. *The Idea of National Interest,* with George H. E. Smith		5,009
2. *The Open Door at Home,* with George H. E. Smith		14,647
3. *The Devil Theory of War*		1,000
4. *Giddy Minds and Foreign Quarrels*	regular edition	9,057
	Harper's Magazine edition	107,000
5. *A Foreign Policy for America*		4,250
6. *American Foreign Policy in the Making, 1932-1940*		8,175
7. *President Roosevelt and the Coming of the War, 1941*		20,649
	Total	169,787

Total American History including Foreign Policy 5,500,782

IV. Social Sciences

1. *Politics*		[f]
2. *A Charter for the Social Sciences*	As a member of a committee	8,950
3. *Conclusions and Recommendations*	of the Commission on Social Studies in the Schools.	8,946
4. *The Nature of the Social Sciences*		3,202
5. *The Discussion of Human Affairs*		3,079
	Total	24,177

V. Texts

1. *Elementary World History,* with William C. Bagley		81,784
2. *A First Book in American History,* with William C. Bagley		351,751[a]
3. *The History of the American People,* with William C. Bagley		
	Macmillan edition	437,865[a]
	California State Printing Dept. edition	619,370
4. *The History of the American People for Grammar Grades and Junior High School,* with William C. Bagley		1,753,017

5. *A Manual to Accompany the History of the American People,* with William C. Bagley   13,065

6. *Our Old World Background,* with William C. Bagley   305,834

7. *America Today,* with Roy F. Nichols and William C. Bagley   33,097

8. *America Yesterday,* with Roy F. Nichols and William C. Bagley   34,731

9. *History of the United States,* with Mary R. Beard   360,149

10. *The Making of American Civilization,* with Mary R. Beard   137,444

11. *Schools in the Story of Culture,* with William G. Carr   300,000[g]

12. *History of Europe. Our Own Times,* with James H. Robinson   622,000

13. *Outlines of European History,* with James H. Robinson and James H. Breasted, 2 vols.   406,000

14. *History of Civilization,* Volume II, *Our Own Age,* with James H. Breasted, James H. Robinson, Donnal V. Smith, and Emma P. Smith   101,000

Total 5,557,107

Grand Total 11,352,163

[a] This was printed in Braille and is "available in state schools for the blind and in most libraries."

[b] In 1943-1944 the Library of Congress Division for the Blind provided "talking book" copies for the 26 regional libraries for the blind throughout the United States.

[c] There is a German edition published by Buchergilde, Gutenberg, not included here.

[d] There is a Japanese edition not included here.

[e] There is an Austrian German edition not included here.

[f] No statistics are available.

[g] This reached about 300,000 readers in periodical form in the *National Education Association Journal,* but the additional circulation as a separate item is not available.